POSEY

The Last Indian War

POSEY

The Last Indian War

Dr. Steve Lacy & Pearl Baker
Illustrations by Toni Shumway Lacy

Gibbs Smith, Publisher
TO ENRICH AND INSPIRE HUMANKIND

Salt Lake City | Charleston | Santa Fe | Santa Barbara

First Edition
11 10 09 08 07   5 4 3 2 1

Dr. Steve Lacy
Footprints From The Past Museum Inc.
820 Jefferson
Salt Lake City, Utah 84101
801.359.2264

Published by
Gibbs Smith, Publisher
P.O. Box 667
Layton, Utah 84041

1.800.835.4993 orders
www.gibbs-smith.com

Designed and produced by Kurt Wahlner
Printed and bound in United States of America

Library of Congress Cataloging-in-Publication Data

Lacy, Dr. Steve, 1951–
Posey, The last Indian war / Dr. Steve Lacy & Pearl Baker ;
illustrations by Toni Jean Shumway Lacy. — 1st ed.
p. cm.
ISBN 13: 978-1-4236-0110-4
ISBN 10: 1-4236-0110-6
1. Posey, William, ca. 1863–1923. 2. Paiute Indians—Biography.
3. Paiute Indians—Wars. 4. Ute Indians—Wars. 5. Southern Ute
Indian Tribe of the Southern Ute Reservation, Colorado—History.
I. Baker, Pearl. II. Title.

E99.P2P67 2007
973.91'3092—dc22
[B]   2006021543

DEDICATION

James Wayne Lacy

November 29, 1963 — September 22, 2003

CONTENTS

Chronology of Events

1879

Apr 14   Advance group of settlers sets out for Paragonah to sow crops to be used for the following year's trek to southeastern Utah.

May 1   Advance group of scouts crosses Lees Ferry.

May 13   Scouts cross desert among unfriendly Navajos.

May 31   First camp is made on the San Juan River, just below McElmo Wash.

Aug 2   Ethel Davis is the first white "Mormonee" child born on the San Juan River; her parents are James L. and Elizabeth Davis.

Oct 22   The Cedar City contingent of Mormons start their trek to southeastern Utah.

Nov 6   Apostle Snow writes a letter to LDS President John Taylor, telling him that the trek to southeastern Utah has started.

Nov 27   Settlers reach 40 Mile Spring.

Dec 11   Silas S. Smith and Platte D. Lyman ride to the top of Hole-in-the-Rock, where there are 15 wagons.

Dec 23   Settlers arrive at Grand Flat, near Elk Mountain.

1880

Feb 1   All wagons moved through Hole-in-the-Rock.

Apr 6   Most of the wagons have arrived in Bluff, Utah. Posey meets the settlers.

1881

May 1   Indians pull into Burnt Cabin Spring and kill Dick May, John Thurman, and Byron Smith (his body was never found).

Spring   Pinhook Massacre.

May 21   "Big Dan Howland" kills Isaac Lacy. Hettie Brumley Lacy takes over operation of the LC Ranch, which had been in the area for several years.

1884

July 2   Battle of Soldier Crossing. Rowdy Higgins and Agent Warrington are killed.

1887

June 16   Amasa Barton kills Sore Eyes, Gray Mustache kills Amasa at Barton's Trading Post at Rincon;
Feenie Hyde Barton sends a message with Posey to Bluff, Utah, for help.

1914

Mar 30   Tse-ne-gat kills and robs sheepherder Juan Chacon near Mancos, Colorado.

1915

Feb 23   Havane is killed while escaping from the second floor of the San Juan Co-op in Bluff, Utah.

Mar 1   Joseph Akin, a member of the posse, is killed.

Mar 24   Indians surrender and travel to Salt Lake City.

July   At the Federal Court in Denver, Colorado, Tse-ne-gat is acquitted of murder.

1922

Apr 10   Tse-ne-gat dies of consumption (tuberculosis).

1923

Jan 10   Dutchy's Boy and Sanup's Boy shoot up Disiderio Chacon's sheep camp on Mustang Mesa. (Chacon was a relative of Juan Chacon, who was killed by Tse-ne-gat in 1914.)

March   Posey frees Dutchy's Boy and Sanup's Boy during a lunch break at their trial.

Mar 23   Seventy-two Indians are placed in the stockade in Grayson (Blanding), Utah.

Mar 28   Posey dies of an infected gunshot wound.

Apr 25   Posey's body is found.

FOREWORD

This book has been in the works for the past twenty-five years. I first became acquainted with the subject of William Posey and the last Indian war when my family moved to Grayson, Utah, in the fall of 1959. It wasn't until Albert R. Lyman opened his little museum in downtown Grayson (now Blanding) that I began spending a lot of time visiting with him. That is when my interest in Posey started taking shape; I was between fourth and fifth grades, and Mr. Lyman was writing his book *Indians and Outlaws*. He kept asking me if I was related to Mrs. Isaac Lacy, who owned the LC Cattle Company in Recapture, northeast of Grayson. I answered, "I don't know," little knowing that Mrs. Lacy was one of the first pioneers of San Juan County.

Growing up in San Juan, I was always fascinated with the history of the area, and I must have been a major pain in the butt to Albert R. Lyman because of all the questions I kept asking him. He was very patient with me, and instilled in me a love for local history. He also told me about the involvement of outlaws Butch Cassidy and his brothers, Dan Parker and Arthur Parker, along with Matt Warner, who used to work for Mrs. Lacy and the LC Ranch. All of this became the driving force in my life for the past forty-plus years, resulting in my eighth book, *Last of the Bandit Riders Revisited*, about the lives of Matt Warner and Butch Cassidy.

In 1981 I wrote and directed a short play called *Posey*, which featured my youngest brother, the late James Wayne Lacy, playing the part of General Scott. Soon after that, Pearl Baker and I started to do the research for this book. In 1985 Richard Bingham, from KSL-TV and *Prime Time Access*, and I filmed a small feature titled *Posey Wars*, which was nominated for a number of awards. We interviewed people on both sides of the issues. My father, Claude G. Lacy, helped me get interviews with Clarence Rogers, Lynn Lyman, Alan Black, and Chester and Meyers Cantsee, when he didn't have to go beyond the call of duty.

Pearl Baker passed away in 1992 before we had a chance to publish the book, which is the culmination of thousands of hours of research, more than 3,000 photos, and a lot of love for the subject.

Just recently I learned that the 1915 Indian war in Bluff happened on my family's property there. Polk's camp was on our Cottonwood property; Joe Cordova was wounded there and then Joe Akin was killed moments later on the lower west part of it. Havane was shot, escaped from the second floor of the San Juan Co-op, and made it to our river property, where he died. His captors tied his feet with a rope and dragged him back to town behind a horse.

This book is something that I have worked toward since grade school, visualizing in my mind the whole scene that took place so long ago. I have known a number of the people who actually were involved in these events and some who outlived the others to claim they were part of them. In a small way, I hope this book portrays the feelings of the time and the spirit of the day.

This publication has been put together in the way I would like to read a book full of photos, text, and clippings. Great drawings were made by my sister-in-law Toni Jean Shumway Lacy, and a few of the more than 61,000 historical photos I have collected of Utah and the surrounding area have been used to illustrate the text. Very special thanks go to my best friend, Trevor McCloud Curb, for his support in the final hours. The profits from my part of this book go to setting up a new building for my nonprofit museum called Footprints From The Past.

Just a final note: In this book we will call the Indians by their tribe or their full names, if available. My great-great-grandmother was a full-blooded Kiowa Indian, and so as not to cause any feelings of alienation, the term *Native American* will not be used, as I feel that it causes more problems. It only stands to reason that if you were born in America, you are a native American.

Dr. Steve Lacy
July 2006

Below Old
Swinging Tree,
Bluff, Utah.

INTRODUCTION

Although this is only a small slice of Indian history, it is so different from all the rest that it should be preserved. Everything is unique—the wonderful Canyon Country setting, the difference in Indian social patterns, the forbearance of the pioneers, the firmness in handling the "war," and the final settlement.

Utah's Canyon Country, that red-rock maze of canyons, buttes, arches, and hidden valleys that drains into the San Juan and Grand (later Colorado) Rivers, has a beauty and charm unparalleled in the world. It was always William Posey's desire to lead an army into the fastnesses of that region and defeat the whites.

Posey and most of his followers were Paiutes, and were looked down upon and despised by the Southern Utes. His band and those of Mancos Jim and Polk were called *bronco* Indians, because they would not live on the Weeminuche reservation, where they were loosely assigned. They did not receive rations from the Indian Service, and since the livestock of the white man was depleting the deer ranges, they ate beef. The white man felt the Paiutes had to eat, and often looked the other way.

When final hostilities broke out, the Mormons gathered William Posey's band and held the group for about six weeks in a barbed-wire enclosure, closely guarded, in the town of Grayson (later named Blanding). The U.S. Marshall and the Indian Agent appeared but were told that until Posey was accounted for, these Indians would be held. Water taps, pit toilets, a large hogan, and several tents were provided, and food was furnished until the Indian Service came to their aid.

When William Posey's body was found and officially identified, the Mormons called the Indians into a meeting and warned them that they must obey the white man's law. If they would agree to this, they were promised grants of land *in severalty* (sole ownership) wherever they wished to settle. An Indian Agent was hired to supervise these Indians, to distribute rations and supplies to them, and to help them learn farming methods.

This solution worked; today the descendants of Posey and his band live on the homestead because they respected and believed the dedicated, honest Mormon pioneers. The special flavor of this piece of Indian lore holds a real place of its own in Utah's Indian history.

Both Dr. Lacy and Pearl Baker have agreed that "it has taken over a hundred years, but because the Mormonees never lost sight of their calling and their goals, no matter what Posey did, the descendants of the Hole-in-the Rock migration can proudly say that the Bluff Mission is a success."

Ute Indians
crossing the
San Juan River.

1
POSEY MEETS THE "MORMONEES"

Posey, followed by Scotty and two other Paiutes, rode down through the river floodplain on the banks of the San Juan River in southeastern Utah. A few days before, when they had passed this way on a trip to visit the Utes on Dolores Creek, this part of the country had been silent and empty. Now, there were horses, work oxen, and milk cows everywhere, and in the lower end of the valley, they rode past a cluster of wagons and camps. This was all surprising enough, but the camps were empty; not a person stirred in any one of them (Hurst, "Posey").

Looking around warily, the youths did not stop, but rode their tired horses at a jog trot past the camp toward a grove of cottonwoods along the river. Breaking out of the ring of high rabbitbrush, squawbush, and greasewood, they came upon the people gathered for what the Indians took to be a "sing" on the riverbank under a huge cottonwood tree. At least the people were singing, standing in a crowd, facing three or four men who looked out over them toward the Indians as they rode up.

The last strains of the hymn rolled out, a man said a short prayer, and the people dispersed, all the women and children and most of the men going back toward the camps. The four men remaining there, who had been leading the church services on this first Sunday of the Hole-in-the-Rock mission to Bluff, came forward, right hands up with palms out in a token of welcome, saying, "How."

Posey stopped his leg-weary mount a few feet ahead and said, "Where go?" more to show he knew some English than for any desire for information.

"Go here," Platte Lyman answered. "Live here. Make farms. Plant trees. Pick peaches," and he picked imaginary peaches off imaginary trees, eating them with gusto. "You savvy peaches?"

"Plant melons," Jens Nielson stooped, thumped an imaginary melon, picked it up, lifting it with difficulty. "You savvy melon?" Posey assented that he did. All this was beginning to sound interesting to the always-starved Paiutes.

"You eat biscuits?" Lyman invited, and the four Indians followed him to his camp, where he fed them. Conversation was limited, but by using signs and odd words, the Mormons gathered that the Indians were living at the mouth of Cottonwood Creek and Comb Wash down the river, and would go up on the mountain when the snow was gone. The Indians understood that the "Mormonees" were going to live at Bluff,

RIGHT:
Platte D.
Lyman.

FAR
RIGHT:
Jens Nielson.

making homes and planting gardens and fields, and that they wanted to live in peace with the Indians. Both factions were favorably impressed, but a lot of water would flow down the San Juan in the forty-plus years before they came to a full settlement of their ethnic differences. To understand how and why the Indians and the Mormons beat out a way of life, with the uprising of 1923 the final battle, it is necessary to understand the history of the Utes as well as the unique situation of the "Mormonees." There was good reason for both sides to avoid a massacre, and for forty years they got along as best they might. When the final break came, it was decisive and left both sides, at the least, in a livable agreement.

2

SCOUTING
SAN JUAN COUNTY

The last quarter of the nineteenth century was a tough time for the U.S. Indian Service, not because of the Indians but because of the pressure of white trespass into the reservations. The Ute situation was bad enough, but the Sioux in northwest Montana and the Dakotas put up a real battle for their treaty rights.

These Indians had been granted the Black Hills for a reservation. When gold was discovered and the white prospectors moved in, the Indians were alarmed. There was considerable tension, and an all-out Indian war threatened.

To the south the Utes of Colorado, Utah, and New Mexico were facing some of the same problems of broken treaties, violated reservations, and corrupt agents that had started the Pinhook Battle of 1881, the violent outbreaks of 1915 and 1921, and the 1923 Posey uprising.

San Juan County, as it has finally been established, was one of the last really prime areas of the Intermountain West to be settled. The Mormons had pioneered the western slope of the Wasatch from central Idaho down into Arizona in the first thirty years after their entrance into Utah. But colonizer Brigham Young was far from satisfied with restrictions facing his domain. The western deserts cut off expansion in that direction, and already central Utah was experiencing crowded livestock ranges. If the Mormon Church (The Church of Jesus Christ of Latter-day Saints) sent groups out into the rich valleys and prime ranges of eastern Utah and western Colorado, the southern flock would have to be protected. This Four Corners section—southeastern Utah, southwestern Colorado, northwestern New Mexico, and northeastern Arizona—was ready for settlement, and if the Church didn't do it, someone else would. A canny strategist, Brigham Young had no intention of leaving the back door of these areas open (Apostle Snow letter to President John Taylor, November 6, 1879). He knew this was also well-established Indian territory; therefore, a buffer colony would have to be set up along the San Juan River to protect the settlement of eastern Utah. Brigham had started to set a "call" in motion to move a colony into San Juan when he died in 1877. It took a couple of years for the Church authorities to adjust to his loss and put the plan into action. Had Brigham Young been alive to manage the trek across Hole-in-the-Rock, that disaster might never have become a part of Mormon history.

Nothing was known about the San Juan area, but it did look like a good place to plant a colony, although it would be foolhardy to send people there without first exploring it. In early 1879, the Church authorities chose a group under the leadership of Silas S. Smith to make a reconnaissance trip to study the climate, arable land, range, feasible settlement, Indian attitudes, and other information needed to set in motion a migration of more than a hundred families to that distant location.

Accompanying Silas Smith were Robert Bullock, James B. Dexter, and Nielson B. Dalley; John Butler joined the party near Panguitch. There were twenty-six men, two women, and eight children in several wagons, with 200 cattle and 80 horses in this exploratory group (Miller, Appendix, 142).

They set out from Paragonah on April 14, 1879, with the goal of settling on the San Juan River and planting crops for the use of the larger colony that would follow, probably the next year.

Traveling south they crossed Buckskin Mountain, traversed House Rock Valley, and pulled into Lees Ferry in just a little over two weeks. They crossed their wagons on the ferry beginning May 1, pulled up

RIGHT:
Silas Smith.

FAR RIGHT:
Trading Post at
Montezuma
Creek.

rough, and found bad water at Bitter Spring's Desert, where the caravan went without water for thirty-five miles over the blistering sand. Some of the loose cattle died, and the rest of the stock was in bad condition when the first wagon reached the next springs and unloaded; all the barrels and water containers were filled, and the wagon started back for the rest of the party.

Most of the way had been more or less familiar to the leader, but at Moenkopi they picked up Seth Tanner and an Indian to guide them, and Thales Haskell joined the party for a time. At this Hopi village they found John W. Young building a woolen mill to process Navajo wool; he hired the group for a few days to quarry rock to build the mill, paying them in Indian corn.

Men were assigned to go ahead of the wagons to scout the way through the untracked wilderness; Kumen Jones was helped by Robert Bullock, George Hobbs, James B. Decker, and John C. Duncan. Because the loose cattle were in bad shape with sore and bleeding hoofs, they were left at the Hopi villages under the care of James L. Davis and Wilford Woodruff. The rest of the party set out through a desert on May 13, 1879, among unfriendly Navajos, who became more amenable to the passage of the party as it dug out waterholes and built roads, leaving these for the Indians. Kumen Jones mentioned many years later that the need for water was so constant and urgent that whenever a damp place was found in a wash, shovels and picks were applied, and usually a small spring could be uncovered and a waterhole used and left.

The first camp on the San Juan was made just below McElmo Wash on May 31. After crossing the river,

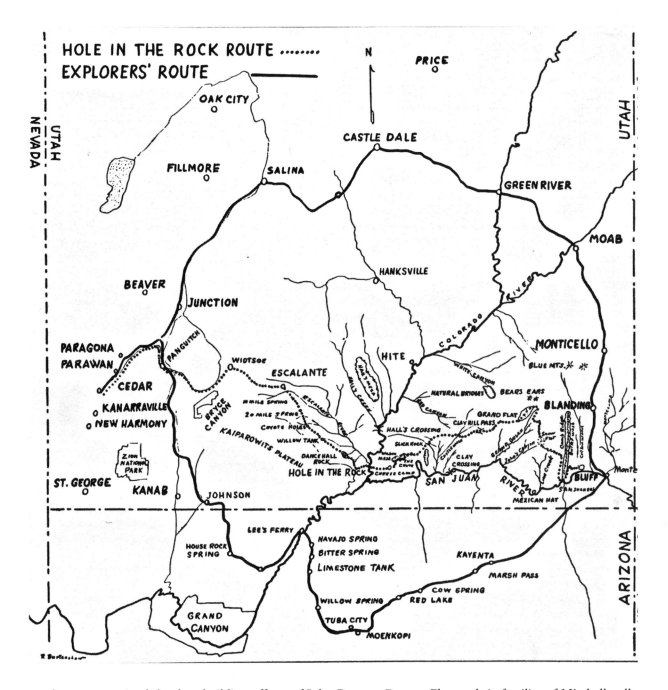

HOLE IN THE ROCK ROUTE ·······
EXPLORERS' ROUTE

N

NEVADA | UTAH

UTAH

PRICE
○

OAK CITY
○

CASTLE DALE
○

GREEN RIVER

FILLMORE
○   SALINA

MOAB

HANKSVILLE

BEAVER

JUNCTION

MONTICELLO
○

PARAGONA
PARAWAN   PANGUITCH

HITE

WIDTSOE   ESCALANTE

BLUE MTS.

CEDAR   BRYCE
CANYON   NATURAL BRIDGES   BEARS EARS

KANARRAVILLE   BLANDING
NEW HARMONY   10 MILE SPRING   GRAND FLAT
                 20 MILE SPRING   CLAY HILL PASS
          KAIPAROWITS PLATEAU COYOTE HOLES
                              WILLOW TANK   HALL'S CROSSING

ZION   DANCEHALL   SLICK ROCK
NATIONAL   ROCK   CLAY
PARK   THE CAVE   CROSSING
                              CHEESE CAMP   BLUFF
ST. GEORGE   KANAB   HOLE IN THE ROCK   Monte
○   SAN JUAN   RIVER

JOHNSON   MEXICAN HAT

LEE'S FERRY

HOUSE ROCK   NAVAJO SPRING
SPRING   BITTER SPRING   KAYENTA
                          LIMESTONE TANK   MARSH PASS

                                                 COW SPRING
                          WILLOW SPRING   RED LAKE
GRAND
CANYON   TUBA CITY
              MOENKOPI

ARIZONA

the men examined the dam-building efforts of John Brewer, George Clay, and six families of Mitchells, all non-Mormons. Down the San Juan River at the mouth of Montezuma Creek, Peter Shirts (Shurtz) had built a cabin. He hunted, trapped, and did a little farming, and was a former Mormon, known to several members of the exploring party.

The men scattered out, exploring the country from above McElmo to the Blue Mountains, and the Decker boys, Niels Dalley, and James Adams built cabins just above the area where Bluff was eventually situated.

The explorers noted the difficulty of building dams in the San Juan River because of the fluctuation of floodwaters and the sandy nature of the riverbed. Only one small field of corn was planted near McElmo, but it was never irrigated and soon died.

On August 2, 1879, a baby girl, Ethel, was born to James L. and Elizabeth Davis. She was the first white child born in the Mormon colony on the San Juan River.

In June, James Decker, Hamilton Wallace, Parley Butt, and Nielson B. Dalley returned to Moenkopi to retrieve the cattle. They had a few adventures but made it back to the settlement on July 17, the same day that Silas S. Smith, his son Stephen, George Urie, and Delbert McGregor returned from a trip to Alamosa, Colorado, for supplies.

In mid-August they began preparations for the return trip. Harvey Duncan and the Harriman and Davis families decided to remain; John Gower and George Urie returned via Moenkopi and Lees Ferry to pick up the broken wagon they had left on the way out. The rest of the party drove their wagons up Recapture Wash to the Blue Mountains, along the mountains to what is now Monticello, down into Dry Valley where they joined the Old Spanish Trail, across the Green River through Castle Valley, down Salina Canyon, arriving at Paragonah in mid-September.

Silas S. Smith reported that the southern route was too far, and that there was not enough water for both people and livestock of the larger colonizing party. The Indians were also somewhat of a threat. They had

Above: Lake Pagahrit, in the southern wilds of Utah.

Right: One of many thousands of Indian ruins located in San Juan County.

grudgingly let the small party pass, but they would undoubtedly look with disfavor on a big colonizing group invading their lands. The northern route was feasible, but it was a good 450 miles, and the San Juan was about 200 miles straight through.

The Grand River (now the Colorado River) had been scouted by Charles Hall, Andrew Schow, and Reuben Collect. Hall had come to Utah from Maine, where he had been a boat builder. He did a lot of exploring from his home in Escalante, and declared he could make a boat to cross the Grand, and that a route straight through to the San Juan was feasible.

Collect and Schow spent most of the spring and early summer choosing a route to the Grand, and finally took a boat of sorts to the river, letting it down over the cliffs by open ropes [tied only on one end]. They explored the south side of the river, deciding that after a difficult passage up out of the gorge into Cottonwood Valley, there would be several miles of pretty fair going; and though there would be road building to do, it was possible to go across that way. It was expected that the whole trip could be made in six weeks. After all, that was less than five miles a day, and even through difficult terrain, they should be able to do better than that.

They didn't know that because of the character of the upended slickrock landscape, a great many days would pass with no progress at all. It was getting into the fall of the year, but both men figured that the party should be well established on the San Juan before the dead of winter. Actually, it took six weeks just to reach the river gorge, which included getting down to the river, crossing it, and covering more than half the distance on the other side.

Margaret Nielson inferred from the Decker writing that "The Cedar city contingent of the San Juan Mission called by John Taylor President of the Mormon church, to locate in Southern Utah to curry favor and win the friendship of the Indians, mostly Navajos, started the trek Oct. 22, 1879, . . . into Bear Valley and spent two days in this beautiful valley getting our drinking water from Holyoak Springs. Jens Nielson, Danish man . . . proceeded to organize his flock and lay down some simple regulations." The caravan moved on to Escalante, then south to 10 Mile Gulch, to 20 Mile Gulch and worked out the road to 50 Mile Point.

The main camp was made at 40 Mile Springs when the advance company arrived there November 27, four weeks after starting a trip that was to have taken six weeks. Snow had fallen, and winter was definitely upon the wagons. Feed for the large herd of loose stock was hard to come by; the Robbs drove a herd of 500

Sun Bonnet Rock, Bluff, Utah, 1921.

cattle with the group. Accounts mention the loose horses because their dust made life miserable for the travelers, but no mention was made of a large number of cattle.

Silas S. Smith, president of the expedition, and Platte D. Lyman rode horseback to the top of Hole-in-the-Rock on December 11. There were fifteen wagons at the top of the Hole, and in the ensuing week or so, the number was increased to eighty-three, with about 250 persons. Smith decided to return to Salt Lake City and raise money for supplies and blasting powder to make the road down through the narrow defile to the river, and Platte Lyman was left in charge of the expedition. Smith was gone more than three months, and didn't catch up with the colony until mid-May, when it had reached Bluff and had spent a month trying to get water out of the San Juan irrigation.

Leaders of the expedition were sobered by the hard road-building from 40 Mile to the river, and faced the final steep narrow gut through the canyon walls down toward the river with alarm. They decided it would be a good idea to send out an exploring party to make sure the wagons could be taken across the broken country east of the river, and George W. Sevy, Lemuel H. Redd, Jr., George Morrell, and George Hobbs were chosen to make a reconnaissance across the river through to Bluff and scout out a road.

Hobbs left an interesting account of this trek, of which he dictated a report to Andrew Jensen, Assistant Church Historian of the Mormon Church, in October 1917. They had a meager eight-days' rations packed on a small mule, and two saddle horses on which they took turns riding an hour at a time. After crossing the river they made a trail out, and were followed by fourteen desert bighorn sheep, which Hobbs termed *llamas*. The next morning, they seemed to have reached the end of the trail as there was no way to continue. A bighorn came near the camp and Hobbs tried to rope it. It dodged his loop, but he followed it down off the rocky ridge, returning later to tell his discouraged companions that he had found a way to the bottom of the wash.

They stumbled onto an old cliff dwellers' trail, which occasionally surfaced from place to place. Though it was barely passable, they followed the trail anyway, heading as close to due east as possible. They finally came to Grand Gulch, which cut them off sharply. Scouting up the canyon, they found the cliff dwellers' trail again, and continued on, staying overnight at Cow Tank and camping the following night at Dripping Springs. On December 23, they arrived at Grand Flat near Elk Mountain. It snowed about eight inches that night, and the next morning the men were concerned because they had no idea where they were. Hobbs was the only one who had ever been to Montezuma Creek, and he couldn't find a landmark that looked familiar. They ate the last of their food on Christmas Day.

Mrs. Allen, one of the early pioneers of Bluff.

Mrs. Allen

Hobbs left the downhearted hungry scouts in the cold camp and climbed a hill. Seeing another mound that looked higher, he ascended it and saw the Blue Mountains, his first familiar landmark. He called the men up to him, and they started on, more heartened but still without food.

After surmounting Comb Wash, they found Butler Gulch with its deep perpendicular cliffs and camped in a cliff dweller's cave. Snow fell again that night, and the next morning they found the tracks of a band of Navajos. The scouts were sure their animals would be gone, but they found the mule and the two horses in a little side canyon. They went up along Butler Wash until they could see the trail on the far east side, and found a place where they could slide their animals into the canyon on the west side. Hobbs hoped one of the horses would break a leg so that they could immediately salvage the meat and make jerky out of it.

Nearing the place where Bluff City was subsequently located, they came upon a calf, which Hobbs was much in favor of killing for food. The rest of them voted him down, saying that they must be near help. Soon they discovered a camp inhabited by Brother Harris and his sons George and Dan, who had come from Colorado after the exploring expedition, having left the San Juan the summer before.

After eating supper that night and breakfast the next morning, the four men went on up the San Juan to the settlement of H. H. Harriman, James Davis, and Harvey Duncan and families. They found these people were short of supplies, eating their seed wheat, which they had ground in a coffee mill.

As the four crossed Montezuma Creek on their way to Montezuma Fort, they met two men well equipped for the wilderness, with good horses and obviously well-loaded packs. Hobbs knew them and introduced them to his companions as Ernest Mitchell and James Merritt (or Merrick; see Kelly, "Chief Hoskanini," 223). These men said they were looking for a cattle ranch because they didn't want anyone to know they actually were looking for gold and silver. The four scouts noticed Lake Pagahrit from a distance and held it out as tempting bait to the two ranchers, intending to join them for part of the way back to the river, but the two men declined and went on their way.

The four scouts were desperately in need of supplies for their return to the Grand River and the main party. The families on the San Juan could survive for about sixty days, but they surely had nothing to share with the scouting party. Finally, Peter Shirts came along and they talked him out of a 48-pound sack of flour

A different view of Lake Pagahrit.

for $20. Harvey Duncan joined the party to return to the Grand, bringing his own supplies. Lemuel Redd bought two mules from James Davis, which gave them each a riding animal.

At Montezuma Wash, they again found Mitchell and Merritt, this time camped in a cabin, and tried to persuade them to go along to Lake Pagahrit. The fellows talked long and loudly, but the two men would not be persuaded. Finally, Mr. Merritt dropped back and told Hobbs that the preceding summer he had crossed Navajoland from Fort Wingate to Lees Ferry, and found three crude smelters where the Indians had been smelting ore that was 90 percent silver. He planned to find the mines, and would share with Hobbs if he went along with them. Hobbs declined, and the two parties separated at the mouth of Comb Wash.

The scouts tried to find an easier way for the wagons on their way back to the river, but in that land of bare rock cut into canyons and buttes, there was just no easy way. When at last they came to the camp on the bank of the Grand River—they had been gone for twenty-four days instead of the week or ten days they had planned—the men waiting at the camp were greatly relieved to see them. After a good supper and a night's rest they crossed the river and climbed to Hole-in-the-Rock, which was slow going, to report that it was just barely possible to get through the terrible broken country east of the river.

3

THE CROSSING

Getting down to the Grand River on the west side was the big problem. The ledges were high, stretching for miles in both directions. The only break was a narrow crack that had to be widened enough for a wagon to pass, and the top carved back until the pitch was not quite perpendicular. The crack was widened by drilling and shooting slices of rock off, which were then used to build up the road bed. After the crack was widened, the last part of the road was carried down one side with pegs driven into the rock on which logs were set, and the road was built with rocks and dirt to let the wagons down the last segment of the sloping ledge.

When the road was declared ready, the first team and wagon approached. According to existing records, six men claimed to have driven the first wagon down the fearsome track. However, a folktale has become a part of this saga: It seems that the teams looked down that incredible chute and refused to enter it until Joe Barton offered to take the first wagon down. He brought his wheel team and hooked it to Hyrum Perkins' wagon. All of the teams of horses had balked after looking down the forty feet of almost-perpendicular road that the company called the Chute. Barton drove his team of horses down, calm and sure, all feeling their way with their big, careful hoofs—for they were totally blind and had been so for more than a year. An epidemic of pinkeye had ravaged the horses of southern Utah the previous two years, and many saddle horses had been destroyed. But this team, entirely dependent on Joe Barton, had been carefully tended and remained useful. So perfect was their confidence in their master that he talked them safely down the dangerous passage while several men holding ropes attached to the wagon held it back to keep it from running over the team.

After the first wagon made it through, subsequent wagons were rough-locked, with logs tied under the hind wheels, the brakes set, and either oxen teams or men with long ropes holding back as much as possible to get them down the first pitch. The first few pushed all the loose dirt and rocks off, leaving the roadbed almost bare rock and slick as glass. The crack was so narrow that anything on the side of the wagon, such as water barrels or chicken coops, was crushed. Women and children walked down after the wagons, holding hands to keep from falling on the steep slippery surface.

The second group of immigrants moved up from Fifty Mile Spring, and by February 1, 1880, all the wagons were down the Hole-in-the-Rock and ferried across the river.

Confronting Hole-in-the-Rock

Many years later, Raymond Smith Jones recorded the story of his grandfather, Joseph Stanford Smith, who had been most active in helping wagons descend.

When all the wagons at the top were down, with some of them even ferried across the river, he looked around for his own outfit, but they were nowhere to be seen. He climbed back through the Chute and found his wife and children huddled in quilts in the cold of late afternoon at the top of the trail. His wagon was standing behind a rock, out of sight.

He was furious that he had helped everyone all day, and yet no one had come forward to see that his wagon was also taken down. Settling his children in a mound of quilts, he told them to stay there and pray and they would be safe; he then prepared to make the descent. He checked his wagon and harness, chained the wheels, wished he had another horse to help his horse Nig hold back the wagon, and then he and his wife, Arabella, went over and looked down the chute.

"If we had a few men to hold back on the ropes, I think we could make it," he said.

"We've got to make it," his wife answered. "I'll hold back on the lines. We can make it."

The first hard pitch pulled Arabella off her feet as she hung desperately to the lines. Then she fell, and the sand stirred up by the wagon and the horse blinded her. She was snapped to her feet and flung against the cliff when the wagon went over a big rock. A jagged rock cut her leg, but still Arabella hung on.

The wagon stopped with the team wedged under the tongue. Stanford looked back, saw Arabella on her feet and got down to extricate the team. The horse was still down, battered and bruised. But he shakily got up in a few minutes, and Stanford started climbing back for the children.

He gathered up the baby and quilts in one arm, held his little boy by the hand, had his daughter catch tight hold of his overall pocket, and they slipped and skidded down the dangerous chute to the wagon. When one man came to help him down, Stanford told him curtly that his wife was all the help he needed.

Hole-in-the-Rock, photographed in the early 1940s, doesn't look like a team of horses and a herd of cattle could make it through, let alone a wagon.

"Head 'em up! Move 'em out!"

It is odd, but no one told of how the cattle herd was taken to Bluff. Even George W. Decker, who made the entire trek with the cattle herd as a young lad of fifteen, doesn't speak of the experience as anything special. These people were stockmen, and the fact that a herd of more than a thousand head of stock cattle accompanied the wagon train didn't impress them enough to comment. Decker did say that he crossed the river more than twenty times when the herd was brought over at Hole-in-the-Rock. He recorded his memories on Wednesday, March 1, 1944:

"Got to Lake (Pagahrit) March 1st, after night. Had to spend the rest of the night telling men what I thot [*sic*] of the chances of getting through to San Juan. I told them I had been clear thru to San Juan Valley where they were to go and we, Dick Butts, Monroe Red [*sic*] & I had dropped about 100 cows and 125 loose horses over Cottonwood Wash where it was supposed by us they were to take their wagons . . . made up my mind to leave the camp on March 3rd for Parawan. . . . Tried to cross the Grand [Colorado] River at the ford where we had forded 1800 head of cattle & horses & had no trouble all thru December to the last of February."

It is probable that the herd was brought to the crossing shortly after the second group of wagons, and crossed in February. It was then driven straight through to the Bluff vicinity, moving right along so as not to use up all the feed. After passing Lake Pagahrit, the herd was undoubtedly taken over the Indian trail that the scouts had discovered, but since cattle can go where wagons cannot, no particular trail work was necessary. Decker states that the herd was delivered to Bluff weeks ahead of the main company.

Box-ed In?

George W. Decker clears up another fuzzy historical happening with his story of the Tom Box family. He greatly admired Tom Box, who had left Texas with his wife, two sons and their wives, two daughters and their husbands, and 800 head of loose stock, in an attempt to find new cattle range. Their camp was in a cart that Decker found incredible; it was built on incredibly large proportions. The two wheels were cross-sawed chunks of trees with tires eighteen inches wide. The box was twenty feet long, with the axle near the center. It was pulled by twelve head of oxen, but Tom Box had ropes and chains galore, and seemed to be able to handle almost any emergency.

With 800 head of loose cattle, it was plain the Box herd would eat out all the feed for the Mormon herd, and since he was not a Mormon and had only a passing interest in the Bluff "call," he decided to leave the caravan near Escalante and make for Colorado by the shortest route.

This was down the Sevier River to Salina, up to Salina Canyon, across to Castle Valley in Emery Country, and on to Colorado on the Old Spanish Trail. Box wintered his herd in Emery County, which gave rise to the report that the cattle for Hole-in-the-Rock migration had been the first cattle to enter Castle Valley. They were and they weren't; they did come from the herds of the immigrants, but they were not really a part of the Mormon herd.

The next fifty miles covered country so broken, ledged, and canyon-slashed that building a road through it was all but impossible. This time of blizzard (during which one baby was born), intense cold, incredible labor, and hardship fused the company together as no other experience could have done. They moved as a unit, building road ahead of them, repairing it while using it, bringing up the wagons of men less energetic or efficient, or with teams weaker and poorer. When they pulled into Bluff on April 6, 1880, after the terrible lift up San Juan Hill over Comb Reef, they were still a unit.

After leaving Lake Pagahrit, which the group reached the last of February, the road was much better except for impassable places, and the feed for the work stock, both horses and oxen, was more plentiful.

This 1940 photo shows most of the people who were left from the Hole-in-the-Rock journey of 1880. Standing: Parley R. Butt (left), Leona W. Nielson, Margaret N. Adams, Mary Jane P. Wilson, Cordelia Perkins, Jennie D. Wood, Caroline N. Redd, Sarah Perkins, and Charles E. Walton Jr.; seated: Kumen Jones.

In spite of George W. Decker's doubts about a wagon road from Lake Pagahrit, the company toiled on. Blizzards slowed them but didn't halt the forward push. In fact, had it not been winter with snow on the bare rocks to furnish water for the camps and stock, the trek could never have been made. But the cold and storms were one more disadvantage to deal with; a baby boy was born to the Larsen family on Gray Mesa during a blizzard.

Finally, the wagons reached Comb Wash, and it was decided to travel down the wash to the mouth and go around the high, impassable Comb Reef. When they got to the mouth of the wash, they found that the San Juan River had cut a narrow gash through the reef, with no room for a road around Comb Reef.

Natural Bridges, 1921. The area was typical of the kind of crossings that the Hole-in-the-Rock pioneers had to endure.

San Juan Hill was one of their most impressive road projects, through which they cut a narrow dugway so steep that teams could not keep their hooves pulling the wagons up. According to Charlie Redd in Dr. David Miller's book *Hole in the Rock*,

"Aside from the Hole-in-the Rock itself, this was the steepest crossing of the journey. Here again seven span of horses were used, so that when some of the horses were on their knees, fighting to get up to find a foothold, the still-erect horses could plunge upward against the steep grade. On the worst slopes the men were forced to beat their jaded animals into giving all they had. After several pulls, rests and pulls, many of the horses took to spasms and near-convulsions, so exhausted were they. By the time most of the outfits were up, the worst stretches could easily be identified by the dried blood and matted hair from the forelegs of the struggling teams. My father (Lemuel H. Redd, Jr.) was a strong man, and reluctant to display emotion; but when ever in latter years the full pathos of San Juan Hill was recalled either by himself or by someone else, the memory of such bitter struggles was too much for him, and he wept."

San Juan River at Rincon, near Barton's Trading Post.

The first three days of April were spent in this grueling task. Once on the summit, the road continued northward along the top of Comb Ridge for a couple of miles, and then drifted off to the east, following a little wash onto the bench that separated Comb from Butler Wash. The pioneers built another set of dugways into and out of that deep, difficult gorge, dropped back, and camped at last on the banks of the San Juan River. In Miller's *Hole in the Rock*, Charlie Redd recalls:

"As they rested in exhaustion from the last intensive strain . . . for the first time they began to see themselves for what they were: weary, worn out, galled, both teams and men. For so long they had walked and slept and eaten and lived on the sloping ground that the thought of level bottom-land was extremely sweet. Yet one woman spoke for the whole group when, recalling this last phase of the journey, she said later, 'I was so tired and more sore that I had no desire to be any place except where I was.'

[Author's Note: Someone pointed out to this woman that the head wagons were already over Butler Wash and onto dirt road. Even then it made no difference; when they began to sing "The Latter-Day Work Rolls On," she had to join in to keep from crying.]

By April 6, most of the outfits had pulled onto the flat river bottom just east of Cottonwood Wash, and although the intended destination, Montezuma, was only another eighteen miles farther up stream, the company simply lost its push. All at once all energy seemed to leave them completely. The travel-worn expedition was just too tired to go on. Here were a few acres of what appeared to be good farmland; here they would stop—at least most of them. Here they would build their homes. At the suggestion of William Hutching they called the new location Bluff City, because of the big red bluffs all around the valley. They began such

important tasks as laying out lots, building houses, and digging a canal to bring water to the parched soil. With "Gawd's help," they would now be able to complete the mission to which they had been called.

The next day was Sunday, and some of the boys of the company were sent with rakes to clean

A B O V E :
The Navajo Twins, Bluff, Utah, 1910.
L E F T :
Early home, part of Fort Bluff, Utah, 1890s.

off a space under the biggest cottonwood tree on the riverbank so that they could hold church services. There under the welcome shade of the first tiny leaves of spring on the old monarch, they gathered to give their thanks and dedicate themselves to the future; and there is where Posey and the other Indians found them. The saga of San Juan had begun.

Jordon Bean,
who lived to tell
about Pinhook.

4
PINHOOK BATTLE

In May 1880, Joseph Burkholder, Malloy Wilson, and Isadore Wilson of Moab camped at what is now the Garner place in the La Sal Mountains. They were hunting range horses, and the next morning when they came into camp, a small Indian boy was waiting to tell them that Indians who were "heap mad" were camped on Bald Mesa. The fellows rode to the Indian camp and, after a powwow, promised to return to Moab after camping on the mountain one more night; they were not bothered further by the Indians (Tanner, 115).

This band of Indians had participated in the Meeker Massacre, and was spoiling for a fight. They moved over into Colorado, where they spent the next year getting into one mess of trouble after another.

An article titled "New Indian War," which ran in the *Dolores (CO) News* on November 13, 1880, talked about the Utes, Paiutes, and Navajos:

> Newspaper comments on his actions has but little weight with the average Ute. It neither breaks his heart nor shuts off his wind. . . . Explosive bullets have more influence with savages than folios of vigorous editorials. We cannot appeal to an Indian's sense of justice or cause him to feel the pangs of remorse. Let us substitute Winchester rifles for brains and note the results.

The next year, May 1, 1881, the same Indians pulled into what is now called Burnt Cabin Spring, where they killed John Thurman and burned down the cabin before killing Dick May. A man named Byron Smith was with Thurman and May, but his body was never found. Thurman's body was found half a mile from the cabin; it was believed he had gone for a horse, as he had a hackamore in his hand. Billy May, Dick's brother, took the word back to Colorado, and it was decided to gather a force of men to repossess the stolen horses and teach the Indians a lesson.

It took a couple of days to gather a force together, but about sixty men under the leadership of Captain W. H. Dawson of Disappointment Valley set out on the campaign. His second-in-command was Billy May. The group split, with May taking his men (from Durango, Mancos, Rico, and Dolores) and going ahead to cut off the Indians who were escaping from the La Sals, and Dawson following the tracks of the big herd of horses the Indians had gathered from the settlers as well as the haul they had taken from May.

Near Cahone, some of the men found the body of Dave Willis, a rancher who had been hunting horses and had apparently been shot by the Indians. They buried the body and then followed the tracks on to Monticello, where they found that the Indians had killed a prospector who had been living in a cabin near Piute Springs.

These bands of Indians were well aware that things were pretty well stirred up, as they rode past Bluff several miles north of the town. In the sand hills four miles north of town, Hanes Joe Nielson was herding the horses of the Mormons (Lyman, *Indians and Outlaws*, 39). The Indians added these horses to their entourage, shooting at Joe to keep him from interfering. He raced into town, and after a hurried conference, five men rode after the Indians.

Overtaking the horses grazing in the little valley, the men laid out in the cold the rest of the night. At

These Ute Indians were involved in the Pinhook Battle.

dawn they started sorting out their horses, which were the very life of the settlement. At this point, the Indians came rushing down into the valley, but the Mormons didn't falter.

After Platte D. Lyman went to the Ute camp on May 6, 1881, he wrote the following in his diary, page 39:

"They seemed very friendly but a few of them were very mad when another stolen horse was taken away from them. As they moved off another stolen horse was taken from them. We traveled with them for several miles and as we returned found that they had been shooting down our cows and destroying the calves. . . . They had about 40 horses branded B. some of them fine large horses of good stock. They also had plenty of greenbacks to which they attached very little value. It is evident they have raided somebody's ranch as in addition to the horses and paper money, they have harness lines and blind bridles and halters."

Suddenly, a commanding voice was heard from a figure on the hilltop: "These are Mormons, they are our friends. Give them their horses and let them go in peace." None of the white men recognized the figure, but they decided later that it must have been one of the local Indians.

After the Mormons got their horses back, the Indians added Polk, Posey, Mancos Jim, and some of their followers to the forty or so of their own, which added up to a considerable band of warriors. They dropped over into Indian Creek, and then came out of Dry Valley, heading for the La Sals, where they had left their main camp. They took the goats and horses of the new recruits, as well as some saddle horses from Spud Hudson's cow outfit near Monticello.

Finding his horses missing, Hudson gathered a posse of about twenty-five men and followed the Indians; later, they joined the Dawson posse. This sped up the Indian migration, but they didn't stop to make

Site of the 1881 Pinhook Battle; photo by Rusty Salmon.

a stand. The Indians were traveling as fast as possible, leaving behind many played-out ponies and goats.

Dawson's posse cut across Lisbon Valley toward the head of Pack Creek, with Billy May a day behind him. At Mule Shoe, both the Indians and the posse were only a mile or so apart when they stopped to water their stock before climbing into the mountains. By now, the Indians were aware that they were in grave danger, and the herd was beginning to slow them down.

A stand was made at Squaw Springs, where an Indian squaw was killed. The Indians dropped back and camped on a bench under Boren Mesa. Here, the posse took possession of the goat herd while the Indians dispersed in the thick timber, crossing through into Mason Draw and down to Pinhook, where the main fight took place. The posse killed seven Indians from the overlook on Bald Mesa while the Indians were getting into position at Pinhook (Tanner, 121).

Trying to get down to the battleground, Billy May got stuck on a ledge and had to return along the rim to find another way down to the scene of action; he didn't get there until the second day of the battle.

According to an article in *Echo* by A. M. Rogers, Billy Dawson and thirty-six men overtook the Indians on Upper Pack Creek, capturing nine squaws and 1,800 horses, including some of the Ute horses as well as the ones that had been stolen in Colorado and at Monticello. Dawson left a squad to guard the horses, but the squaws tricked the guards, stampeded the horses, and set out for Moab.

Meanwhile, Dawson had gone on with twenty-four men, and at Squaw Springs one Indian was killed in a brief skirmish. The Indians fell back, followed by the posse, but as the posse was getting close, Dawson sent four men ahead to scout. These men discovered the Indians beyond a wash, deployed on a little hill covered with oak and boulders. Dawson then called for volunteers, and twenty men stepped forward. Dawson chose fifteen and told them to go ahead, and if they ran into trouble, to drop back to the main force.

This lead detail crossed about 150 yards of brushy ground until they were near the wash, when the Indians opened fire on them. Dave Willis, Jordon Bean, Hag Eskridge, and Jim Hall were either wounded or killed, and the rest, looking back at the 150 yards of open flat, decided to dive into the wash. Only Dawson, Jenkins, and Baumgartner were still mounted and they managed to make a dash for it and got out of the wash. The remaining eight men were pinned down.

The Indians drew close to the banks of the gully. Concealed in the brush, the Indians picked off the white men one by one. Then Dawson sent Tim Jenkins, an old Indian fighter, to order the men back out of the wash. Jenkins rode down and tried to get them to make a dash for it before the Indians could get into position to pick them off. But the men didn't dare make a move, so Jenkins returned to the main body of the posse. The Indians then threw a murderous cross fire into the wash, killing the advance guard. Jordon Bean was the only one not killed; he was shot in the head but managed to hide until reinforcements from Moab came the next day and found him.

The *Dolores (CO) News* reported that this battle took an entire day. A detachment of white men was sent out the following day to search for those who were killed or wounded. They encountered the Indians again and, having the advantage as to number and position, killed an estimated eighteen of them. By Sunday, four days after the battle, the Indians had disappeared, and the posse, augmented by several ranchers among others, found the bodies of their men in the wash and buried them there.

Trevor McCloud Curb plays Hard Tarter, a victim of the Pinhook Massacre.

The victims of the Pinhook Massacre were "Hard" (Harden) Tarter, John Galloway, Wiley Tartar, Hiram Melvin, Jimmy Heaton, and George Taylor of Rico; Tom Click of Delores; Dave Willis of Mancos; and Alfred and Isadore Wilson of Moab. Jordon Bean, Jim Hall, and Harg Eskridge were severely wounded.

In an unpublished story titled "Jordon Bean" from May 14, 1941, Bean told how he and Hard Tarter were ahead of everyone:

"It was every man for himself. . . . [W]e soon found some big rock, lay down there and were shooting at some Indians above us on the mountainside. We were doing fine until one Injun seemed to be a pretty shot for he got me in the left temple. I had my head thrown back so far—the hill was steep—the bullet didn't go in very far but grazed my skull and knocked me.

"[Carroll] told us we were everyone under arrest for attacking and disturbing the Indians. Bill Dawson drew his rifle out of the scabbard and told Carroll he just didn't have 'niggers' enough to arrest his men. Every man pulled their guns. Grigsby and his men, too, never faltered.

"Carroll said, 'Tut, tut. I don't want to fight.'

"Dawson said, 'We have just come from a fight and we can fight some more.'

"Then Carroll said, 'If any of your men will show us the Indian trail, we will overtake them.'

"Dick Curtis and Gus Hefferman [of Rico, Colorado] stepped out and said, 'We will show you the trail.' The group started back the next morning."

The Wilson boys had been camped at their cow camp, and hearing the gunfire, they came to investigate. Their bodies were found riddled with bullets, and it was assumed they had wandered into the field of battle and were cut down by the Indians.

Mancos Jim, a true leader of his people.

Four companies of the Ninth U.S. Cavalry came and followed the Indians back to their reservation, and the men from Colorado returned to their homes. It was the consensus of the newspapers and general public that the whole thing had been inconclusive, badly managed, and solved nothing of the Indian troubles in southern Colorado.

A number of years later on June 16, 1886, Mancos Jim stated the following in an interview with the *Idea*, a Durango newspaper:

Dave Willis never took shelter but stood out in bold relief and fought till he fell dead. The other boys tried to protect themselves by getting into a shallow arroyo or washout, but they were surrounded and when the Indians charged from one side, hanging onto the ponies, yelling and shooting, the white boys would [rise up] to fire, The Indians in ambush in another direction [would] shoot them down.

The white boys were extravagant with their ammunition, which they exhausted about dusk after fighting all day, and the Indians then rode around the washout in a circle, shooting into the living and lifeless bodies till there was no sign of life in the bloody pit.

Since no one could identify the Indians, nothing was ever done to punish them, but stories that they, themselves, told in later years identified William Posey, Polk, and Mancos Jim as participants in the affair. Polk always boasted that he, personally, had killed three of the men. William Posey made no secret of his involvement, for it was here that he met his future wife for the first time. When the Utes were scrambling for cover during the battle, Posey helped a lovely young girl named Toorah up the rocky, tree-covered side hill, and lost his heart completely.

Lacy's Undoing

The real intent of the Pinhook Battle was to fight Indians. The LC Cattle Company ran their cattle on the same range where the Indians grazed their sheep and horses, and Isaac W. Lacy, who owned the LC, didn't want the Indians upset by getting involved in Pinhook. Lacy also ran a saloon and gambling hall, and had hired "Big Dan Howland," a gunfighter from Tombstone, Arizona, to work there. About 3 p.m. on Thursday, May 13, 1881, Howland confronted Lacy at the LC's slaughterhouse near Fort Lewis, Colorado, and demanded $10. When Lacy refused, Howland shot him in the chest and Lacy died soon afterwards.

The *Dolores (CO) News* reported the following on May 21, 1881:

Murder Most Foul . . . I. W. Lacy Killed by One Of his Employees. . . . Suspected That "Big Dan" Howland was not the only Man Who Helped do The Deed. . . .

A squad of twenty men started in pursuit of the murderer about twenty minutes after Howland started but failed to capture him. Handbills were out in a short time offering $3,000 reward for the murder, signed by Mrs. Lacy. It is reported that Henry Goodman, who was Lacy's foreman, has started out after him and the chances are that he [Howland] will be captured.

Hettie Brumley, Lacy's wife, had previously been married to J. W. Short and was the mother of the gambler and gunfighter Luke Short; she was also first cousin to outlaws Ike and Port Stockton. After Lacy's death, Hettie brought in her three brothers from Texas to help her find Howland and those who might have assisted him in the shooting. Mrs. Lacy took over running her cattle on the range where the Pinhook and Soldier Crossing Battles took place.

Body of Victim of Famous Indian Fight at Pinhook, at Last Found

GV.T
Feb 19, 1904

A sequel to the famous Pinhook Indian fight, which took place at Pinhook, six miles south of Castleton, in 1881, was disclosed several days ago, when Robt. G. Bryant, while prospecting at the "battle grounds," found the skeleton of one of the white victims of the fight. The body was lying under a rock on a hillside a short distance from the road. A few feet away was found an old saddle.

In the spring of 1881, a number of settlers of the Mancos section organized to fight the Utes, which for some time had been committing depredations against the whites of southwestern Colorado. The Indians were followed to the La Sal mountains where an engagement took place. They were routed and a small bunch of the settlers, ten in number, followed them. The Indians were overtaken at Pinhook. Here took place a disastrous fight which resembles Custer's last battle more than any other incident in history. All of the white men were killed. Why such a small number of men should attack a much greater force of Indians was never satisfactorily explained, but it is presumed that the whites did not know how many of the savages they were opposing.

When the news of the battle reached the few settlers of Moab a company of men left immediately for Pinhook. A search for the Indians proved unavailing, as they had left for the north and were many miles away when the Moab force reached the scene of the battle. The bodies of nine of the victims of the fight were found and buried, but although a vigilant search was made for the remaining man his body was not recovered. The skeleton found by Mr. Bryant several days ago is undoubtedly that of the man for whom the Moab settlers had so unsuccessfully searched. It is stated that his name was Taylor, and that he lived in Rabbit valley, Utah, prior to the campaign against the Indians.

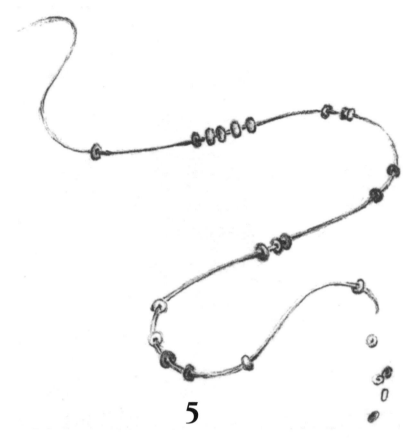

5

WILLIAM POSEY AND TOORAH

When the Pinhook Battle was over and Polk had gathered his family together, he looked with biting disfavor at the amorous glances between William Posey and Polk's sister Toorah.

Polk immediately snatched Toorah into seclusion and declared in no uncertain terms his opinion of the despised Paiute. William Posey, crushed by this savage rebuff, returned to his camp on Blue Mountain, but he didn't forget the lovely Toorah. When he started searching for her, however, Polk had her well out of circulation, even guarded by some of the squaws of the family, or one of Polk's brothers—Hatch, Bishop, or Teegre.

Posey hunted and finally found a teepee at Peter Spring, with saddled horses in the shade of a cedar nearby, where a great and noisy game of "duck-eye" seemed to be going on in the teepee. The game sounded most interesting and he was tempted to drop in and see what was going on. He recognized the voices of the two Rooster boys, Hatch and Bishop's rasping tones, and Polk's grunts. There seemed to be a heated argument over the game, and that promised exciting developments—like a fight. It also meant that the participants would not be out scouting around. Squaws crowded the door, looking in.

Posey concluded that Toorah was not in this camp, but she must be nearby. He tied his two horses to a tree and scouted. Presently he came to tracks leading back into the trees, and he came upon another teepee as the camp dogs ran out to announce him. Inside was Toorah, her hands tied, guarded by two wives of the brothers. One of them looked out to see what the dogs' racket was about just as Posey reached the door, but he was in before she could stop him. He untied Toorah's hands and led her to the door. They ran to the horses and beat a hasty retreat.

The runaways were sure that they would be followed, but as they slipped through the forests and glades of Elk Mountain and camped in hidden secret places at night, they began to feel more secure.

Finally, one day they ran into Polk, meeting him face to face on the narrow trail. They prepared for trouble, but it was soon evident that he was not interested much in them; he had more pressing troubles. In the "duck-eye" game that Posey had so wanted to look in on, the argument had become more and more heated until it broke up in a shooting spree. Hatch was killed, and Polk killed the two Rooster boys. Old Rooster and his friends were hot on Polk's trail, and he and Bishop were hiding out in the canyons. Grasping this opportunity, Polk agreed to accept the situation if Posey would pay him ten head of horses and bring in supplies to him and Bishop. What were ten horses in a world filled with horses! And the flour and bacon Polk demanded could be bought with the jewelry or blankets one horse would bring on the Navajo reservation. Posey felt he had come out of the deal a real winner.

An early photo of Old Polk, his wife, and grandson, lounging beside Akin & Pyle's Store in Mancos River Farm, Colorado. This was the same Akin who was killed in 1915.

He and Toorah settled down to family life, riding openly around the country. They spent their summers on the Blue Mountain at Peavine and their winters camped on the San Juan River at the mouth of Cottonwood Wash. Posey and Toorah had two little boys, Jess (also spelled Jesse) and Anson, about five or six years old in 1889.

During this time, Albert R. Lyman, who was about eight or ten years old at the time, camped with his father, Platte Lyman, near the Peavine camp while they rode for their cattle.

In his unpublished manuscript, "History of San Juan County," Albert R. Lyman wrote the following:

"I was still in my tender years when I made Posey's personal acquaintance; it was at the head of Peavine Canyon on Elk Mountain when his camp was within a stone's throw of ours. No Childish prejudice prevented my standing around his smoky fire to look and listen with his own half-clothed children, imbibing the strange faces of their wild freedom. Neither their ignorance, their superstition nor their filth concealed the real charm of life as they lived it.

"Such extravagant liberties—such novel partnership with the wind and the flowers and the trees! No hands of a clock disturbed their composure and 'thou shalt not' never entered so much as their dreams. I was captivated; I wanted my father to confirm a whispered report that I had a distant Indian ancestor.

"Scotty lived with his brother Posey then, as he has ever since, till the present trouble. How they came to camp in the gray dawn with their 'kill' of deer across their saddles; how they helped us catch wild horses, gave us samples of their salt less dried venison, studying our lives and telling about their own, are matters too lengthy for this story. But Posey's winning young squaw should be mentioned, also his two little boys, his old father, Cheepoots, who herded. And milked the goats; and their genial camp where they prepared their food, their medicines, their buckskin, and where they sang to keep on good terms with the god of fat game and good hunting.

Bluff Co-op, site of many dances upstairs, with outlaws Matt Warner, Tom McCarty, Butch Cassidy and his two brothers, Dan and Arthur Parker shown in this photo.

"Posey traded us a sorrel for a bronco mare, but a few weeks later the pony was replevined by a Navajo from whom it had been stolen.

"Soon after we parted at Peavine, Posey killed his squaw, the mother of his two little boys. I shall not say, as her people declared at the time, that the shooting was intentional, and done in a fit of anger. So far as I know it was but a terrible accident for which Posey paid dearly; not because of the twelve horses her brother Poke required as sort of fine, but because he was a long time in exile, and grief-stricken over the loss. Besides that he was required to marry another of Poke's sisters who, even though the killing was not intentional, has no doubt exacted a substantial installment of the price justice demands."

Posey was close to the Mormons. He visited with them, both on the range and at Bluff, where he hung around the San Juan Co-op nearly every day all winter. He knew them well, and they all knew him better than any of the other Indians. The story of Toorah's death (but never using her name) is a common one in the family histories of the Bluff families, and the consensus is that it was, as Lyman says, a terrible accident. From these sources it appears that it happened probably in 1892, shortly after the family moved down from the mountain to the San Juan for the winter.

Several Indians came by to visit in the forenoon and to look at Posey's new gun. He always carried a good rifle, and at least one handgun, which he kept in excellent condition. However, he didn't leave them loaded around camp. During the discussion about the guns, one of the Indians loaded the forty-five, and William Posey didn't notice it. Indians have an inherent faculty of meddling with things, having their hands on everything, as children do.

In late afternoon Posey aroused from his nap and told Toorah to go run the horses in, a common joke between them. This would always lead to an argument, which they made a great game of. She refused, the argument started, and as a refinement, Posey noticed the 45 pistol, and catching it up, said, "Get horse, or I shoot!"

She refused, and he drew down on her, pulled the trigger and to his horror, the gun discharged, shooting her through the stomach. Posey tried to help her, and then ran to Bluff to get some of the Mormon women to come and help him. Aunt Jody Wood came at once but she knew at a glance that she was beyond saving; there was too much damage to ever heal. She did what she could to make her comfortable and left. Posey stayed with Toorah until she died.

Aunt Jody Wood, a mid-wife who came to help Posey with Toorah, who had been shot accidentally with a handgun.

The next morning after she had died, William Posey went up to the ledge of the canyon and started to heap cedar and pinion trees into a huge pile. When he had a good stack of them, he took Toorah's body, put it on top of the stack of wood, and then set the funeral pyre on fire. He also took her favorite pony and killed it in the wash just below so that she would have it to ride in the Happy Hunting Grounds.

The fire burned all day, and Posey kept adding more wood to make sure she was properly burnt; it was visible for miles. In the early evening, twelve-year-old Lyman and two other boys rode up to see what was going on. Mark Collins interviewed Lynn Lyman, on May 29, 1978:

"[He] and two other boys were herding cows. They would take the town herd of milk cows out to where there was feed of any kind and let them graze all day, and then they would bring them back to the owners at night. These three boys were herding cows out west of Cottonwood. The Indians were camped on the river on what was known as Sand Island. The boys knew the Indians were camped there. Up in the cliffs north of Sand Island there is a cliff or overhang, and a wash that runs next to the cliff. The boys went up to see what this big smoke was; the fire was down in a kind of little canyon or draw.

"Posey wasn't there, he was back at the River; but he saw the boys or saw their horses and he started up there. Two of the boys had stayed on top and Albert went down to see what was going on. The two boys on lookout saw him coming and without giving Albert any warning, took off for town. Albert noticed they were gone so he came up out of the wash and saw Posey coming. Albert was on foot and Posey was on his horse, but Albert started running for town as fast as he could, with Posey chasing him on his horse. Posey was about to catch him when some of the men came from Bluff to rescue him. The other two boys had made it into town and gave a warning. I think it was Albert's father and some other men on their way out and they got there just as Posey caught Albert, I don't know what he would have done to Albert if he had caught him, and I guess Albert didn't want to find out."

When William Posey felt that the cremation was complete, he and Scotty took the two little boys and left for the vastness of the deep canyon country. While the white community did nothing about the murder of his wife, there were rumors seeping out from the Indians that Polk would exact vengeance.

No one knows for sure exactly what happened but Alan Black tells about one of the punishments meted out by Polk. "You killed my sister, now you marry my older ugly sister," a harridan who made camp life miserable for the whole family.

After a few months, William Posey and Polk rode into Bluff together and relations between them ground on about the same as always—fawning servility by Posey and open contempt by Polk. They were often thrown together, but the association was never cordial or on an equal basis.

The Mormons and Paiutes developed a sort of informal truce. The Indians tolerated the Mormonees, accepted their paternalistic attitudes, traded with them, and limited depredations to a heavy, continual but affordable toll of livestock, and with rare exception, contained their warpath activities to threats and bluster that resulted in no loss of life. After a few years, when the orchards and gardens produced fruit and melons, the Indians were willing to let the whites stay and raise these delicacies, with only enough harassment to make things interesting. They considered the Mormons cowards because they did not fight, but there was a good reason for that, which would have been hard to explain to an Indian.

(Author's Note: We have been unable to document Toorah's name, it does not appear in any writing about William Posey, nor does it occur in the other stories about them by other people. She pre-dates any Indian records we have been able to locate. In his novel *The Outlaw of Navajo Mountain*, Albert R. Lyman calls her Toorah, and since he knew her personally, we accept his name for her.)

Albert R. Lyman in his youth, Bluff, Utah.

6

THE MORMON MISSION

The Mormons came into Bluff on a church mission, which added a spiritual goal and religious zeal to the economic advantage of establishing Mormon sovereignty in the Four Corners area. Despite every hazard, they planned to stick it out and complete their mission. They tolerated the Indians because there was the constant threat of being wiped out by an Indian raid; men were often gone for long periods of time out on the range with the livestock, and the small community of Bluff lived always under the threat of a war whoop. Just across the San Juan River were the Navajos, who often came over and traded, and whom the Mormons really feared. But the north side of the river was Paiute country; they camped up and down the river and were always present.

The Mormons did not ask for outside help to control the Paiutes, Utes, and Navajos; they traded with their red neighbors, selling supplies from the store or trading for wool or sheep, limiting their punitive efforts to reclaiming stolen stock, and protecting their possessions as best they could.

Thales Haskell was a friend to the Indians.

Thales Haskell was performing much the same ministrations to the Indians as Jacob Hamblin did farther west in the St. George area. He preached peace to them constantly, and warned them if they did bad things to the white men, they would die. The Bluff settlers said, "When an Indian gets mean enough, he'll die." This seemed to be borne out by the death of several troublesome Indians one spring; and Navajo Frank asked Thales Haskell to write a letter to "Gaud" and promised that he—Navajo Frank—would change his ways if his life could be spared (Lyman, *Indians and Outlaws*, 38).

No crops were raised in 1881 because the ditch out of the San Juan River could not be maintained. The river fluctuated from a trickle to a raging flood that took out both dam and ditch. The Hyde family at

Ute woman
in Bluff, Utah,
late 1890s.

Montezuma built a waterwheel that would pump 23,000 gallons per hour out of the river, and this enterprise was watched with interest by the colony down the river.

That winter President John Taylor sent Edward Dalton of Parowan to re-inspire the settlers with new determination. He baptized them all again in the river, and they rededicated themselves to the difficult task of subduing the wilderness (Hurst, "Posey").

Some of the Hole-in-the-Rock group took their families and went to the mines of Colorado for the winter, where they bought flour and returned in the spring of 1882 to make another stab at fulfilling their mission of establishing a colony in San Juan country. That year the ditch washed out in May, but the settlers moved the dam upriver a couple of miles and got the ditch back in to save the crops. They raised good corn and food crops that year, which was encouraging. Also, a post office was established in October, which made them feel much closer to civilization.

In January 1883, Brigham Young Jr. and Heber J. Grant visited the colony, finding fifty families planning to spend the winter in Bluff. A mining boom along the San Juan had filtered down from the mines of Colorado, contributing to the welfare of the community, as it was the outfitting point. In May 1883, the Kansas and New Mexico Land and Cattle Company, an English company managed by Edmund and Harold Carlisle, moved 7,000 head of cattle onto the range north and west of Bluff, which would be needed soon by the colonists for their own herds. A confrontation loomed, but there simply wasn't the energy or manpower to oust the cattlemen for another year or two.

The year of 1884 was a critical one for the colony. In March, the river rose seven feet above its normal level, ruining much of the ditch and covering crops and farmyards with up to two feet of stinking mud. Cottonwood Wash also flooded, leaving more than a foot of mud and slime on the floors of the houses and in the fields. By May, after another round of floods, the people wrote to President Taylor and asked to be released from their mission to settle the San Juan wilderness. With all the rain, the ranges were lush and the livestock was doing well, but farming along the San Juan seemed to be a lost cause. While waiting to be released, the settlers endured another flood higher than the one in March, which washed several houses away. This flood also took out the Hyde waterwheel at Montezuma Creek.

Bishop Jens Nielson received a letter from Apostle Joseph F. Smith saying that he and Erastus Snow would be coming to make a personal evaluation of the situation, promising that "you have struggled for four years and you shall be blessed if you go away, but those of you who stay will be blessed even more abundantly."

When these two officials came, they instructed the people that they should hold this mission because of its location as a buffer to the Indians. Platte D. Lyman was released as stake president, and Jens Nielson was appointed to lead the colony.

The range situation looked bleak, with the Carlisle outfit and the LC run by Mrs. Isaac Lacy on the northeast, large herds of Navajo sheep moving across the river, and the Nutter and Pittsburgh cattle companies to the north. Only the range north and west of Bluff remained for their small herds. The battle of Soldier Crossing on the fringe of the range alarmed the colonists, who feared that an Indian uprising might be in the making. Since Polk, William Posey, Mancos Jim, and their bands were on one side, and cowboys and soldiers were on the other, there was good reason to be afraid.

Looking north as the children run south; the Bluff Co-op, to the left, was the center of town activities.

Rowdy Higgins, who offered to scout the area with Government Agent Warrington.

7

THE BATTLE OF SOLDIER CROSSING

On July 2, 1884, the Carlisle Kansas and New Mexico Land and Cattle Company, under E. F. Carlisle and representatives from the rest of the major cow outfits in the area, brought their chuck wagons to Montezuma Creek for the beginning of the spring general roundup.

There were 3 chuck wagons, 21 men, and more than 100 head of good saddle horses. Several Indians from the camps of Polk and Mancos Jim rode in and had dinner with the crews. After dinner, four of the cowboys went visiting to the Indian camp, where Fred Taylor discovered a horse stolen from his boss the year before. He took down his rope to catch the horse and one of the Indians rode at him with a drawn knife. Another cowboy shot the Indian and killed him.

The cowboys lit out for the camp, followed by the Indians, and a real battle ensued. Most of the cowboys had only revolvers, and the Indians were well armed with long-range rifles. The Indians surrounded and fired into the camp, killing several horses. Although no cowboys were killed, several were wounded. Two more Utes died before the cowboys managed to break away and retreat toward Colorado and reinforcements. They straggled into Dolores, mounted two on a horse, with the wounded in pretty bad shape.

The Indians burned the wagons, rounded up the horses, and struck off toward Blue Mountain, where they could pick up William Posey and his Paiutes for guides into the Navajo reservation.

The wounded cowboys were taken to the army hospital at Fort Lewis, Colorado, and Captain Perrine organized an expedition of about eighty soldiers and forty cowboys and headed out to retrieve the horses. He told the cowboys not to bother about supplies; he had sixteen pack mules carrying plenty for all of them.

The tracks of the horses were easy enough to follow, and the posse made good time around the base of the Blue Mountains and onto Elk Ridge near the Bears Ears. It was July; rainwater in the rock tanks was scarce, and the cowboys soon rode out of the country that was familiar to them. They spent the second night around a little lake on the ridge and rode out the next morning to the abrupt drop-off into White Canyon. The horse trail led down a steep rocky side hill. A mile or so in advance, they saw two Indians set signal fires, and then mount up and whip over and under toward a column of dust about ten miles away in the open valley of White Canyon.

Getting down to the inner rim of White Canyon, they found that the Indians had camped at a water tank and had used all the water. The goats, which Posey contributed to the campaign, had been there last and had lapped up every drop of water. The Indians took the goats along because they could travel as fast as horses and were instant commissary.

By noon, the pursuers had traveled down the mountain, across the intervening broken ledges, and into the deep gash of White Canyon. It was incredibly hot, the dust was choking, and both the horses and men were suffering from thirst. About dark, they decided to wait until moonrise to see the trail across the rocks

and into the canyon. Moving up the canyon, they ran into a slit of canyon with high unbroken rimrocks in each direction as far as they could see. They waited for daylight to see where the trail went; it left the bottom of the canyon and went up into a narrow crack above a ledge slope. They halted to scout.

Hearing a goat bleat up on top of the ledge, the leaders were afraid of a trap. Captain Perrine didn't believe there was a trap, but his men and horses were in such bad shape, he thought he had better hunt for water. A government scout named Warrington dismounted and told him, "All right, Captain, while you find water, I'll scout around and see what's up there." A cowboy named Rowdy Higgins offered to go with him.

Early prospectors at White Canyon, about the time of the Battle of Soldier Crossing.

They climbed the rough trail up through the little rims and ledges and big rocks, and just as they entered the crack in the caprock, the Utes at the top tumbled a fusillade of rocks down the hill upon the scouts, leaving them badly wounded. Warrington started to run down the hill when another volley sent him down again, and he fell over a big rock. Rowdy crawled behind a rock, but Warrington never moved again, just moaned and muttered.

The Indians were shooting over the top of the ledge and turned their guns on the clustered men. The only hit was one of the horses. The soldiers and cowboys retreated toward a clump of cedars, some of them in such a hurry that they jumped off their horses and left them. Seven head of horses that remained on the side hill were not recovered.

The loose horses and pack mules were in the rear in the care of some of the soldiers; the rest of the horses were sent back to join them while the men tried to figure out a way to make another foray to rescue the wounded men on the side hill. The sun got higher and the heat settled in. About nine o'clock that morning, Warrington was still alive, but he never moved after that; Rowdy died about noon.

Up on the ledge, old Mancos Jim jumped up and down and hollered, "Oh, my Gawd, boys, come and help me!" He was obviously mocking the wounded fellows—he was above them and could hear them better than their companions could. The posse was not entirely out of range, and if they stuck up a hat, it was sure to get a hole in it, but the Indians never exposed themselves.

Finally, it was decided to wait until dark; then, while everyone trained his rifle on the slit in the rock so that no Indians could slip down through it, the men could go up and bring down the bodies.

One of the cowboys, Sam Todd, and three others started up the slope as soon as it was dark. Todd was crawling along a trail on a shale outcropping when he heard horses. He dropped off the trail and lay still, watching the seven horses move up between him and the sky, each horse led by an Indian. He went on toward where Rowdy lay, and found a bunch of Indians gathered around the body, so he backed off and crawled over to where Warrington had fallen. Indians were gathered around him as well, stripping the body. A dog growled, and he beat a hasty retreat before the Indians' attention could be diverted from their grisly business.

The other three cowboys had gone back to their comrades and Todd followed, having decided there was nothing else he could do. No further attempt was made to recover the bodies since a steady firing into the crack in the rock didn't keep the Indians from using the trail freely.

The following article from the *Ute Mountain Country*, June 28, 1884, describes part of the group of Indians who went to fight at Soldier Crossing:

They saw two or three Indians of Narraguinip's band who were shot by the Rico boys in the fight at La Sal. One of them, an old buck, is minus two or three inches of one of his legs, which shortened as it healed. They have very little use for Rico. Oscar Carter, of west Dolores, told them he came from Rico, and every one of his Indian visitors left camp instantly. The Narraguinip band is composed of renegades from Uncompahgre, Paiutes, Navajos, and other tribes, and is not recognized at any agency.

The Bears Ears, San Juan County, 1923.

Captain Perrine gave orders to clear out as soon as possible; if the Indians could use the trail, they could get behind and cut off the only way the white men knew to get back to water. Todd, Sant Bowen, and Joe McGrew offered to follow up the canyon and see if they could find some water; they were all suffering from thirst, and were too few to carry out much of a campaign. Captain Perrine refused the offer. Although the Army didn't know it, William Posey and most of the warriors probably had long gone on up the canyon bench toward Fry Canyon, where they could find water for their animals. Only a picked few had been left at the canyon rim.

The retreating army climbed out onto Elk Mountain and found the lake about eleven o'clock that night. After drinking as much as they could, the men simply collapsed and slept. About daylight, they started waking up, and it was decided to try to get something to eat. Captain Perrine foraged around and found that there were no supplies on the mules, so the company saddled up and rode on to Johnson Creek on the south side of the mountain, where they had seen some cattle tracks on the way down. They ran onto five head of

Marking Graves

The bodies of Agent Warrington and Rowdy Higgins were never recovered. In 1933, Scoutmaster Sylvester Bradford of Grayson (Blanding) asked Lynn Lyman to take his Scouts to the site and mark the graves. Lynn had a stripped-down Chevrolet that would go practically anywhere a pack mule could.

LEFT: Boy Scouts with Scoutmaster Sylvester Bradford.
ABOVE AND BELOW: Gravesites—before (above) and after (below) of Government Agent Warrington and Rowdy Higgins, a member of the posse.

They left Grayson on a summer day with the car loaded with a camp outfit, a small roll of wire fencing, and a sand rock tombstone that the Scoutmaster had procured. On top of the load were Scoutmaster Sylvester Bradford and seven Boy Scouts, including Eagle Scouts Stanley Lyman, Jimmy Harvey, and Mark Lyman; Lynn's brother George; and Jack Taylor, a friend of theirs.

cattle and killed two; the cowboys took one and the soldiers the other. The cowboys started to skin the steer, but by the time they got the hide off, the starving men had cut off the meat in chunks and were roasting it on the fires. The skinners got only what little they could off the backbone—that was all that was left.

In a letter dated March 2, 1925, Sam Todd told Glen Hanks:

From the tracks the goat herd had been watered last, and they had taken it all. (They always took a goat herd with them on the war trail, as they could out travel a horse and they were too busy to hunt.)

We thought we could surely catch them before sundown and kept at a hard gallop. . . . [W]hile we couldn't see them, we thought we were right at them and would catch them in a few minutes. So it kept up all that afternoon.

(Not till total darkness did they get a rest.) We tumbled off, layed [sic] down with the bridle reins in our hands, and lay [sic] there until the moon came up. [We then] took the trail again, a tired thirsty, hungry outfit, [with] our horses.

When full day light came we were at the foot of this wall and the trail led to a narrow break in it, barely wide

LEFT:
Bear Ladder Indian
Ruins near White
Canyon.

RIGHT:
Bluff in its glory
days, early 1900s.

enough for one horse to go into. We halted, of course, to investigate. We knew we were close to them because for the last three miles we had found a number of give-out horses wet with sweat, and some of the last ones were still panting. And while we were talking, we heard a goat bleat just on top, and it was plain to us boys that we were in a trap. The Captain, however, said no, there was no trap and we must climb that mesa, but considering the necessity for water, we would halt and send a detail to hunt for a rain water tank.

Posey took his camp and his goats back on the mountain from Fry Canyon, and the Utes, with some of William Posey's Paiutes for guides, went on to the Navajo reservation with the horses, where they either lost them gambling or traded them for blankets and jewelry. Mancos Jim was back at the agency on ration day with no charges against him; again he could boast around the smoky fire in the teepee during long winter evenings about winning the battle with the white man. The little boy Tse-ne-gat heard these tales and grew up believing that the "Mericats" (Americans) were like horned toads, "Heap big mouth—no can fight."

Although the Bluff Mormons were not involved in this fight at all, it reflected on their relationships with the Paiutes. When nothing was done to punish the Indians, they finally settled down and got along with the white men about as before. The Mormons were soon involved in a threat that was more pressing than Indian troubles: the fight for livestock ranges that were being filled by the big cattle companies.

(Author's Note: The material for this chapter is taken mostly from an unpublished letter from Sam Todd to Glen Hanks in 1925.)

8

THE MISSION PROSPERS

When Apostle Joseph F. Smith and Erastus Snow came to Bluff to release the people from their mission, to their surprise they found that not everyone wanted to be released. Several of the families were beginning to develop small cattle herds, and some of the others were reluctant to give up the mission. Bishop Jens Nielson, who assumed leadership of the colony at this time, stated flatly that he was staying. He had been in the ill-fated handcart company that had been caught by winter storms in its trek to Salt Lake City, and both his feet had been frozen in that awful disaster. He said he would never leave Bluff, that he couldn't make another start; he helped settle six towns in Utah, and the only move he planned was when his body was taken up the hill to the graveyard.

There was no doubt in anyone's mind that agriculture was far too limited to hold a settlement, and the only alternative was livestock, with the Bluff Pool accounting for a meager 2,000 head on the limited ranges west and north of town.

The Carlisle Cattle Company with Edmund Carlisle had become aware that a power struggle loomed, and, because they were English and could not file on land, they had a number of the cowboys file for homesteads to hold the ranges. Also, they fenced canyons and parts of ranges, establishing a real foothold there.

The Bluff colony probably would have been doomed, but the LDS Church sent in Francis Hammond to preside over the San Juan Stake (Peterson, *Look to the Mountains*). He arrived in Bluff just before Christmas and immediately started moving forward. In the first two months of his management of the colony, he started claiming the ranges for Bluff; organized the Bluff Pool, a cooperative stock-raising company; purchased a ranch in Colorado at Mancos to finance a ditch onto White Mesa below Grayson; and assigned riders to keep the LC (owned by Mrs. Isaac Lacy) cattle from straying onto the grazing lands there. Through the Bluff Pool, he asked the Utah Territorial Legislature to tax the stock coming into Utah from Colorado, and sent Lemuel H. Redd, Jr., and Kumen Jones to chase out 5,000 Navajo sheep from the Comb Wash ranges west of town. He wrote letters to friends to come immediately and bring cattle to stock the ranges, and he encouraged the Bluff men to file claims on mountain ranges.

All these were mostly defensive delaying tactics until he could get the ranges stocked with Mormon cattle. For the next couple of years, he was busy entrenching the colony in the livestock business, and he didn't overlook many opportunities.

In 1886 bankers from Durango, with money from rich mines of western Colorado, came into the Mormon economy looking for investments. They knew of the stability of these people, and the past six years had surely proved the Mormons' desire and ability to stay in the country. The Bluff Pool purchased Daniel and McAllister's 6,000 head of sheep and sent George A. Adams to Parowan with $3,000 to buy cattle. Platte Lyman brought in 1,000 head of cattle that winter to add to the Pool.

First school in Bluff, located inside the fort.

In the summer of 1887, when Hammond heard that the LC outfit was bringing in 9,000 head of cattle, he immediately started setting up a ring of obstacles around the range to hold them back. He called on settlers to occupy Indian Creek, Dandy Crossing on the Grand River, and the heads of Butler and Cottonwood Washes; and he suggested to Thanes Haskell that he encourage the Paiutes and Utes to settle close by, dispatched settlers to Monticello, where the Carlisles claimed all the water, and to Recapture, where the LC Ranch was headquartered. In April, Joshua Stevens rode in to report that 1,000 head of cattle were coming in from the north toward Elk Mountain, and he strongly advised that the Bluff Pool beat them to the location.

The settlement at Monticello ran into trouble when the Carlisles ordered the Mormons not to use any of the water from the stream. Hammond and the Carlisles held a meeting about it, but this did not stop the threats. For a few minutes the Carlisle men and the settlers carried guns, and the situation was tense.

Posey was dimly aware that there was considerable activity on the range, but it was beyond his field of interest. He could see that the cattle would eat the range used by game animals, but he liked beef as well, so

RIGHT: Amasa Barton, who was killed June 16, 1887.

FAR RIGHT: Parenthia Hyde Barton, who was known as Feenie.

he was not too much concerned about all the hubbub. Probably he would have preferred the Mormonees to the Americats (cattlemen) in the final analysis, and it looked like the balance was swinging to his friends.

While the Utes and Paiutes were on more or less good terms with the Bluff Colony, the Navajos were always a menace. There was never any real friendship with them. They were supposed to stay on the reservation on the south side of the San Juan River, but they often came over in small groups to trade, though there was no amity in the transactions. In the early days of the colony, the Navajos learned that the settlers didn't work on Sunday; they attended to their church duties and left their livestock practically unattended. The Indians developed the habit of slipping up the river, killing milk cows in the thick brush, and decamping with the meat. This went on for years with no punitive measures except a lack of acceptance of these Indians by their white neighbors.

In 1884 the Navajos killed Amasa Barton at his trading post at the Rincon below Bluff, about ten miles southwest on the San Juan River. Barton had been the blacksmith at Bluff and had the reputation of flying off into maniacal rages—he was not the most popular man in Bluff even though he did serve time as the sheriff of San Juan County.

Parenthia Hyde came into Bluff from Montezuma Creek to teach school, and Amasa paid immediate court to the seventeen-year-old "Feenie." The Hydes had come into the country via Hall's Crossing a couple of years after the Hole-in-the-Rock migration, and bought Peter Shurtz's rock cabin at the mouth of Montezuma Creek. They also found the little cliff-enclosed Rincon below Bluff and built corrals and a barn and other improvements. When Feenie and Barton were married, Hyde moved the family to Monticello and turned the Rincon over to the newlyweds, who brought in a stock of goods to open a trading post to deal mostly with the Navajo Indians.

Barton's rages kept him in trouble with the Indians, but no serious difficulty developed until one day in June, after he had been there a couple or three years, when he caught a twelve-year-old Navajo boy poking a stick through the crack of the logs in the warehouse behind the trading post, twisting it in the pile of wool and pulling out a sizeable hank of wool. A few stabs and he had enough to justify another sale to the store.

William Posey in later years.

Going into one of his rages, Barton beat the boy unmercifully, finally leaving him bleeding on the ground. After a while the boy regained consciousness and crawled to the river, where he was too injured to cross. He was found by a Navajo rider, who took him back to his father's hogan where he died two days later.

Gray Mustache, the boy's father, was an important district chief, but instead of calling together a group of his fighting men to retaliate, he consulted Hosteen Sore Eyes, who was headman of that area. This seer suggested that instead of killing Barton in revenge, they go to him asking for a blood payment, as was the custom of the Indians.

The next morning the two old Indians rode across the river and tied up their horses at the trading post. They were the only customers and went in to smoke a free cigarette in the bull pen, as was the custom. The matter of the dead boy was brought up and Barton knew he was in trouble, probably in deadly peril. He kept his temper under control and let Gray Mustache get his grievance off his mind. When noon came and

A B O V E : In 1981, former San Juan County sheriff Claude Lacy stands at what is left of Barton's Trading Post.

R I G H T : Remains of the ferry rigging at Barton's Trading Post.

Parenthia called him to dinner, Barton took the two Navajos with him, thinking this gesture of friendship might get him out of his dilemma.

Nothing was said about the boy during the meal, Feenie wrote many years later, and afterwards the Navajos thanked her courteously for the food and preceded Barton back into the store adjoining living quarters. But soon angry voices caused her alarm and she concealed a gun under her apron. Going into the store, she slipped it to her husband secretly. Actually, this sealed his fate; otherwise, the two Navajos would probably have overpowered him and tied him up, which was a terrible disgrace according to their customs, but now Barton felt he had the advantage again.

He ordered the two Indians from the building. Earlier, Gray Mustache had brought in his rope to tie up Barton, and when he was ordered from the bull pen, he stopped to pick it up. Barton rushed at Sore Eyes, pushed him to the door, and kicked him outside. Gray Mustache cast his noose over Barton's head and yanked him out the door onto the sand outside, where Sore Eyes sat on him while Gray Mustache took the rope off, but they did not disarm the raging white man.

This commotion brought Parenthia and her mother, who was visiting, into the store. They came to the door as Barton regained his feet, rubbing his neck. He jerked the gun out and started aiming it, Parenthia screamed in protest, and the Indian whirled around. Both Indians were armed with pistols shoved down in their belts, and Gray Mustache started pulling his gun. Barton shot Sores Eyes, and the bullet passed through his body near his heart as he staggered in retreat. Gray Mustache shot Barton in the head. Sore Eyes fell, dead, as Barton raised himself partly upright, and Gray Mustache walked closer and put another bullet in his head.

Parenthia and her mother stood stricken. Because the Bartons had traded with the Utes and the Navajos, Parenthia spoke both languages. Gray Mustache said to her, "I am sorry, Little Sister. He caused all this. You need have no fear. You and your children will not be harmed. Your man was a bad one."

ABOVE: A typical Ute camp in the 1890s.
RIGHT: Kumen Jones.

Picking up Sore Eyes's body, he lashed it across the saddle of the dead man's horse, mounted his own, gathered the bridle reins, and led his companion's burdened animal across the San Juan River into Navajo land.

Barton was still alive, and the women got him into the living quarters and onto a bed. Shortly thereafter, two Paiutes came along, having sat out on the hill and witnessed this drama; one of them was William Posey. Feenie quickly wrote a note that said, "Come quick, someone, please. Amasa has been shot twice in the head. Ma and I are here alone with the children. For the sake of us someone come help us before the Navajos return—Feenie Barton," and gave it to Posey to take to Bluff.

Posey gave the note to one of his followers, who took off in a swirl of dust over the winding trail to Bluff. When he arrived there, only a few old men were in town; all of the younger fellows were out with the cattle. A boy was dispatched to the nearest men and other messages were sent, but it was a couple of days before any number of men had come home to Bluff. Then it was decided that rather than ride pell-mell into who knows what kind of situation, they had better remain in Bluff and protect their own families.

In later years, historians have tried to smooth over this incident, some even claiming that a body of men did go to Parenthia's defense. However, when writing of her experiences later, she states that when Barton died, she and her mother laid out the body and buried it between the Trading Post and the cornfield, from where it was removed later to the Bluff cemetery. Then she and her mother took the two small children in a wagon and drove to Monticello. She later married a man named Dalley.

A short time later, Captain Jon Cooper from Salt Lake City, an old friend of Feenie and her family, was sent into the country with troopers and a pack outfit to investigate the incident. He consoled her as best he could, and then went on to the reservation to talk to Gray Mustache. He reported the affair to his superiors, but since it was deemed that justice had prevailed, nothing was done about reprisals.

A month or two later, when the Hydes found time to go to the trading post, they found everything just

Some believe the Indian with his back to the camera is Posey; this photograph was taken on an archeology dig in San Juan County.

as she had left it, and William Posey was still guarding the place. He neither bothered anything in or around the store, nor did he let anyone else come close. This stood him in good stead when he was taken to Salt Lake City as a prisoner some years later. Parenthia heard he was there—it was a well-publicized event—and came forward and helped him get through his trial; because she was a prominent citizen, he was treated with a great deal of consideration.

A few days after the Rincon incident, a group of angry Navajos rode into Bluff, demanding that the settlement do something in recompense for the murder of one of their chiefs. They were met by Kumen Jones and Jens Nielson, who explained calmly that Uncle Sam's soldiers did their fighting, and if the red men insisted, the Bluff people would call on the soldiers, who would come in force. However, if the Navajos were willing to talk, a beef would be killed and they could all sit down, eat, and discuss their problem. The Navajos opted to eat and the confrontation did not develop. After that, relations with the Indians across the river were fairly peaceable.

Francis Hammond felt that some definite action should be taken with the Indians, so he took his complaints to Fort Lewis, Colorado. While he was there, a cowboy rode in saying there had been a fight between the Indians and cowboys over a horse, and six Indians and three cowboys had been killed in the ensuing skirmish. This turned out later to be just a rumor, but two troops of cavalry were sent to the LC ranch from Fort Lewis, and two more from Fort Douglas, Utah. Because the Barton matter was still so fresh and sensitive, two more troops were brought in from Fort Wingate, New Mexico. This show of force impressed the Navajos and probably helped establish the peace.

The conflict with the Carlisle outfit escalated into a legal battle. The Carlisles were British, and could not legally hold land, so they had some of their cowboys file on claims. Francis Hammond bought some of these claims and contested the others. As the date for hearing the matter approached, Edmund Carlisle ate dinner with Hammond at Jens Nielson's home in the evening, and when Edmund Carlisle failed to show up at the hearing the next day, the selectmen awarded the claims to the Mormons because they were the only group to show up.

In the spring of 1888, a man by the name of Ghaleger brought in a herd of 1,000 Texas longhorns, driving it right through the town of Bluff. The teachers gathered all the students into the schoolhouse and kept them there until the last cow was hazed on through town. The Bluff Pool was firmly enough funded by this time to buy out the herd, and they did so, establishing this wild longhorn stock outfit on the ranges to form the basis of really colorful history of the San Juan Blue Mountain cattle industry.

The settlers were still fighting the San Juan River. As late as 1895, they were still rip-rapping (tearing up and plowing) the riverbanks and trying to grow crops with the dubious supply of water. In 1896, no water flowed in the river during the irrigation season and the following years were even drier with no rain.

By the middle of the 1890s, the whole cattle business changed drastically. In 1896, both the LC and the Carlisle cattle outfits pulled out with about 50,000 head of cattle. The Co-op herd of sheep, bought by the LDS Relief Society in 1888, was sold to private individuals, principally Lemuel H. Redd, Jr., and Hanson Bayles. They soon became the two wealthiest men in the stake, and Redd established an outfit that his son,

Bluff, Utah, looking south, 1890s; photo by Charles Goodman.

Valley of the San Juan, at Bluff, Utah, Nov. 4 - 1895.

Charlie, developed into one of the biggest and wealthiest cattle empires in the west.

When Francis Hammond came to Bluff in 1886 and built a stone house with board floors, it was the pride of his family and the envy of the town. In only five years, there were several substantial brick or stone houses in town, and public buildings were going up—a school, a church, and a large co-op mercantile building. In fact, as a result of intensive stock growing on the fine ranges, Bluff was the richest town per capita west of the Mississippi River by the turn of the century.

The Blue Mountains were a small range; in fact, the Spanish had dubbed them the Abajo Mountains, which name appears on the maps today. They were too low to catch enough snow in the winter or rains in the summer to develop streams big enough, and establishing a town of any size was out of the question without it. Walter Lyman explored the mountains thoroughly and discovered that a deep valley drained a big share of the eastern side of the range, which could be made into a catch basin by a dam at the lower end. A tunnel through one of the ridges on the south side would carry this small stream of water out onto the flat land at the foot of the mountain.

It took several years to get this project finished. When there was enough water to support a town, it was first named Grayson, but the name was changed to Blanding in 1915 when the town was offered a public library on condition that the name of the town be changed to Blanding to honor the donor's mother. The only books donated were a bunch of old textbooks. (Author's Note: In 1980, the author tried to change the name back to Grayson, but to no avail. Albert R. Lyman used to say, "I think it is an abomination," and the author agrees with him.)

By 1905, Platte Lyman and Francis Hammond were both dead, and Jens Nielson followed a year later. Most of the people in the Bluff area had moved to Grayson, which largely replaced Bluff as the center of activity.

But that does not mean that the years between 1885 and 1905 were without incident. William Posey kept the kettle boiling all the time with horse stealing, demanding meals at outlying ranches from terrified ranch women when he could find them alone, and constant efforts to become a "heap big chief" among his people.

FACING: Valley of the San Juan, Bluff, Utah, November 1895; photo by Charles Goodman.

ABOVE: Bluff, Utah, looking west, August 1896; photo by Charles Goodman.

RIGHT: Paiute Indians, Bluff, Utah.

BELOW: Bluff City Oil Exchange, 1908, with Posey at the far right; photo by Charles Goodman.

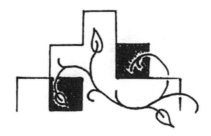

9

WILLIAM POSEY
AND THE MORMONEES

William Posey and the Mormonees never did really understand each other, but they learned to live as neighbors. Had it not been for the big non-Mormon cow outfits, there would have been only minor friction. However, the cowboys and ranchers were at the bottom of most of the really important battles with the Indians, resulting in soldiers and cowboys being killed or defeated by the Indians and making matters difficult for the Mormonees to keep the peace. The fine line often wavered between outright bloodshed and uneasy peace, and the people of Bluff were always aware of their vulnerability to an Indian raid.

William Posey and his half-brother, Scotty, spent the first fifteen or so years of their lives on the Navajo reservation. Old Chee, Posey's father, took his two wives and families into the Navajo Mountain area when the two little boys were pretty small, probably two or three years old, and they lived on the outskirts of the Navajos there until the incarceration of the main tribe at Bosque Redondo took the Navajos out of Arizona. This let the Paiutes move into choice territory when the boys were about ten years old. At that time, William Posey was known as Sowagerie, or Green Hair, since his uncombed sun-bleached hair took a sort of green tinge (Lyman, *Outlaw of Navajo Mountain*).

It was customary for Indians to take the names of white men who came along. A drifting cowpuncher by the name of Posey came into the country for a time, and Posey assumed his name. Scotty got his the same way, and so did Polk and most of the other Indians.

After the Paiutes moved across the San Juan in about 1880 or 1881 and camped down the river from Bluff at Cottonwood or Butler Washes, they were closer to the colony and were more involved with the whites than any of the other Indians of the area, either Utes or Navajos. Other Utes from the Colorado Weeminuches joined the Posey camps, but the political organization was very loose. At no time was William Posey considered a chief or a headman by the other Indians, as were Polk, Mancos Jim, Bridger Jack, and others.

William Posey envied the whites their comfortable houses, but it never entered his mind he could build a log or rock house and enjoy the creature comforts. He sat around the smoky fire in the drafty teepee in the winter, lived in poverty and filth, and seemingly didn't consider improving his conditions. He spent a

The Kiva Snake

Posey was raised in a mixed Indian culture; his roots were Paiute but his childhood had been spent among the Navajos, and he undoubtedly knew and respected some of the legends and beliefs. His attitude toward snakes is a good example.

Likely the Paiutes did not actually revere snakes; in fact, since these were easy prey, they were probably more regarded as a light snack than the errand bearers from the underworld that the Navajos, Hopis, and, to some extent, the Pueblo Indians believed in.

The Hopi Snake Dance is well known, and the story is told about a white woman who lived for many years in a Rio Grande pueblo, teaching the children. One day the girl who did her housekeeping interrupted her school with some excitement, even awe. The teacher hated to be taken from her class, but when the girl made it clear that a rattlesnake had taken up its abode in the wood box, there was nothing to do but go and settle the matter.

The teacher went home, got her Colt .45 six-shooter and dispatched the rattlesnake, but the girl's superstitious awe and fear annoyed her. So did the snake. As a matter of fact, she felt that she had had snakes and Indians right up to here, so when she went to step out the back door and saw a huge king snake curled in the path, she got the gun and let him have it, too.

That did it! She had killed the kiva snake, which the men had brought out for a bit of sun. The public punishment meted out by the Pueblos is to completely ignore the culprit for a period of time. For a couple of months she was absolutely invisible to the Indians; they couldn't hear her, they didn't see her, no request was granted, no gift to them was accepted—she simply didn't exist. Then a new kiva snake was secured, life tipped back in balance again, and gradually, beginning with the children, she once more attained corporeal status.

The Navajos were very superstitious about snakes. In fact, one matron in Bluff sewed up a snake, complete with eyes, to put by her cellar door to keep the Navajos out, and it worked fine. William Posey was influenced by the snake culture, and ran Victor Gallegos, a Mexican, out of camp, threatening to shoot him for killing a snake. Posey maintained that the camp was his, and if the snake was to be dealt with, he had the final say.

ABOVE:
William Posey.

RIGHT:
William Posey
(left) in later years.

great deal of time at the store in Bluff, the San Juan Co-op, managed by Jens Nielson, and he thrust himself into homes from time to time for "biscuits," but his welcome never extended to an overnight stay.

He considered the Mormonees soft because they put such emphasis on ease, and he could never understand why they didn't retaliate when Indians killed their cows for beef, stole their horses, or raided their gardens and orchards. When nothing was done to avenge the Pinhook and Soldier Crossing murders, he despised them as weaklings, never considering that they didn't feel called on to take up another man's quarrel. They felt they had all they could do to abide by the mission and plant a colony in this hostile environment—hostile both in land and people. A vital part of the mission was to bring the Indians out of savagery, since they considered the red man as a descendant of the Lost Tribes of Israel and a brother, however wayward.

A. C. Honaker and Posey on a snowy road to San Juan River, where the store was located. It was the only time that snow had ever been so deep there; photo by Hazel Lyman.

Posey simply couldn't resist trying the patience of the white men as far as possible, and this included the women. He would ride up to an isolated ranch, get off his horse, and look in the windows to see if anyone was home. If he could see the housewife, he would open the door and come in, demanding where the man of the house was. Squaws were almost beneath his notice, and he felt that white squaws were also very inferior livestock. He would demand to be fed and, fearfully, the housewife would comply.

One afternoon he rode up to the Walton ranch and found Jane Walton hoeing in the garden. He got off his horse, came up to her, and demanded biscuits. She told him to wait until she had finished this row, and he broke out in a tirade of abusive epithets, pointing his gun at her. She struck him over the head with the hoe, and he fell like a pole-axed steer, leaving her in terror that she had killed a man. But he came around in a few minutes, got to his feet, and with a blood-curdling yell ran for his horse. The family dog joined the fray and brought the seat of William Posey's pants back to Jane.

It was years before he returned again to the ranch. He came up to the front door cautiously, pushed it open a crack, and stuck his head in, saying,

"Squaw, me no mad."

"Hello, Posey," Jane answered. "I'm not mad either."

"Me heap hungry," he promoted cautiously.

"All right, Posey, as soon as I put this bread into the dipper, I'll fix you something to eat."

And she did. When she finished he went out and chopped wood for a while. He would never have done this for his squaw, but he had noticed that the whites seemed to have a rule that the men did this squaw work.

Posey stole horses continuously, but they were often taken away from him, firmly but not forcibly. When it was brought down to the nitty-gritty, he would give in and return the horse, although he felt constrained to steal it or another from the same fellow as soon as possible to save face.

Hanging around the co-op all the time, he probably knew more of what was going on than anyone gave him credit for, and he grew cocky. He boasted that he was "all same Jes' Chris'—bullets no hit me."

In 1903, William Posey stole a brown mare from Albert R. Lyman, and when Lyman found Posey's boy riding it, he didn't mention the mare when he went to ask Posey to help him with a herd of cattle he was moving off the mountain until the bluebell became less poisonous. A few days later, while Posey and Lyman worked together with the cattle, Lyman mentioned the mare. Posey sulked, figuring that it would be held against him in the settling up. When he got his check in full, he insolently vamoosed with the mare and sold her to a Navajo.

WEDNESDAY FEBRUARY 24 1915

San Juan Co-op. Store at Bluff.

When the new owner showed up in Bluff with her, she was immediately reclaimed by Lyman and the Navajos came back on Posey for her value. This made him angry, and he immediately stole another horse from Lyman and brought it into town, offering it openly for sale. It was also reclaimed, and several men and boys gathered at the San Juan Co-op, wondering what to do with Posey. There would have to be a stopping place, but an Indian war was not really what was needed. He was a leader of sorts, with several Paiutes and drifters hanging out at his camp at the mouth of Butler Wash.

While they were discussing what to do, and had almost decided to let him get away with it, he was invading a garden, cursing the woman who was alone at the time, and threatening to kill Albert R. Lyman and various others until the victim of his rage was scared out of her wits and her children terrified.

Deputy Sheriff Arthur S. Wood was asked to take some action. He sent word to William Posey to come in and talk things over, but Posey refused in great contempt. That did it! The men at the store swore out a warrant for his arrest and a posse rode out to his camp to serve it. Two men were on horseback, ten men were afoot, only two of them had guns.

They came to the door of the wickiup, and Wood read the complaint. Posey spat with contempt, "Yes, me no go!" Before Posey had an inkling of what was going to happen, the men strode in, grabbed him and his fighting squaw, and fell out of the side of the teepee with Posey in the middle underneath. Mary Posey grabbed a rifle, and one of the posse wrenched it away from her, but not before she had fired a shot, which added to the general uproar of dogs, kids, and squaws at top voice, bringing all the Indians on the run. They were stunned at the condition of their leader, long hair flying in disorder and big hat forgotten, as he was handcuffed and started down the trail to town. When the noisy group approached the San Juan Co-op, a bunch of Navajos who had come in to trade, gathered around while a Navajo named Jim Joe laid it out to Posey what a poor specimen he was to threaten his good friends as he had done.

After waiting three days for the prosecuting attorney to come down from Monticello, Albert R. Lyman was appointed to present the case, Frank H. Redd to act as defense attorney, and Justice Peter Allen to hear the case in the schoolhouse. The town was full of sullen Paiutes awaiting the decision of the court. When told

William Posey
in the 1920s.

that Posey was bound over to appear in District Court and would have to go to jail at Monticello until his trial, they stamped back to their camps with a yell, where squaws and papooses ran from place to place; twenty minutes later they had all disappeared—packs, horses, dogs, and all—into the wilderness of White Canyon.

William Posey had talked with Scotty, and that afternoon, he asked to be taken down to the San Juan River to go swimming, as he needed a bath. The guards couldn't deny that, although it had never bothered him before. Jimmy Decker was left on the bank with Posey's clothes while the old coyote waded out into the stream beyond where they told him he could go, dived, and, to the concern of Decker, didn't come up. Finally he surfaced down the river and almost across it, and started splashing and stumbling through the sand and mud to the other shore. Decker fired at him several times, but the range was too great for his handgun and he only nicked the old outlaw in the leg. Posey made it into the willows where Scotty waited with horses.

The posse that followed halfheartedly came back, saying that the horse tracks were so mixed with others on the Navajo reservation that they lost his trail. With all the Indians gone, things were about as well settled as anyone could wish, and everyone went home.

After a few months, Posey sent word that he was waiting on Lyman's range to feed that man to the coyotes as soon as he made another trip out to care for his cattle. More than a year passed, and the constant fear of being caught and the waiting wore Posey down. He missed going to the co-op; the life of a desperado lost its glamour. So he sent word in, couched in the most humble and repentant terms, asking permission to return. Getting no answer, he ventured forth. His friends, the Mormonees at Bluff, having enjoyed a season of peace, were willing to give him another chance. Nothing was done either to conclude his trial or to punish him in any way.

This is not to say that all was peace and quiet. Indians still raided the gardens and orchards and, when apprehended, were at least forced to drop their spoils. If guilt was aimed at the wrong person, there was a great hullabaloo and much anger.

A group of Paiutes at the base of the cliff just north of Bluff; the view is northeast. The lone finger standing up behind them reaches a dizzying height.

Soldiercoat, who had come by his name because he constantly wore the coat he had taken from Warrington's body in the White Canyon killing, was arrested in Bluff for some small infraction. His brother Paddy came marching into Hansen Bayles' house, furiously demanding justice. He was not defending Soldiercoat, who might be guilty as far as he knew, but the gun that had been taken from that Indian belonged to him, and that gun was perfectly innocent. He demanded its return or he would burn the haystacks and do all kinds of other damage.

Other Indians became familiar to the Bluff Colony. There was old Broken Arm, who raised her motherless granddaughter by chewing the baby's food in her own toothless gums and then transferring it to the child's mouth. There was one old squaw who lived principally on milk from female dogs that she kept on hand for a constant supply. There was Big-Mouth Mike, ugly and insolent, and Old Frank, stooped and apparently harmless, who was reputed to be the executioner of the unsuccessful medicine men. He killed a young Indian

A typical canyon trail in southern Utah: the Utah Expedition on the road from Grayson to Bluff; photo by Harper, Utah Architectural Expedition.

who had married Polk's daughter, and when Polk threatened to avenge the murder, the medicine men talked him out of it.

There was no understanding why the Indians lived as they did, and there was no way their code, either personal or general, could be accounted for; it was too apt to change while a man was looking at it. The Mormons treated the Indians as savages always, and dealt with them as children. There was no social intermingling, but they did visit back and forth to some extent.

The Indians were constantly puzzled by the Mormonees' methods. Personally, they found the white men possessed of plenty of courage, but they could not understand why they as red men were permitted to kill the range cattle for beef, which they named "slow elk," with no reprisal. They were constantly begging food and stealing small things. During the forty years between the advent of the white men and the final settlement in 1923, only one Mormonee, Amasa Barton, was killed by the Indians, although Indian attacks accounted for more than one white man a year in the Four Corners area.

RIGHT:
Car stuck in the mud near Bluff, 1908.

FAR RIGHT:
First car in Bluff, 1908.

10
THE INDIAN INVASION
—THE HUNTER BILL—

The northern part of San Juan County was beginning to be settled. Three big cow outfits—the LC south and east of Monticello, Carlisle Brothers with the New Mexico Land and Cattle Company at Monticello and north into Indian Creek, and Cunningham and Carpenter with the Pittsburgh Cattle Company at La Sal— were all established and prospering. Several smaller outfits had also settled at La Sal: Rays, Maxwells, McCartys, Niels Olsen, and the Silvey family. Jack Silvey had been involved in the Pinhook Battle in the La Sals in 1881, and had liked the country and returned with his family. All of these people had herds of a few hundred cattle each, which they wintered mostly in Dry Valley, that beautiful grass valley between the La Sal Mountains and the Abajo (Blue) Mountains.

In the early part of November 1894, the U.S. House of Representatives passed a bill ceding San Juan County, Utah, to the Southern Ute Indians in exchange for their proposed reservation of a fifteen-mile-wide, seventy-mile-long strip of land bordering the Colorado–New Mexico line. The eastern portion, near Ignacio and Durango, was a fertile well-watered district that Durango people had long coveted for ranches. Knowing that the Utes were yearning to return to their traditional hunting ground in Utah, a trade was drummed up in Congress to swap the reservation for San Juan County. The Indian agent at Ignacio, David

Ute camp.

F. Day, sure that the bill would pass the U.S. Senate and become a law in a few weeks with President Cleveland's signature, told the Utes to move to San Juan County.

The Indians were overjoyed to return to their "Happy Hunting Grounds" on earth, and were honest in their move to the new location. "Washington City Man" had given it to them. Picking up their camps and thousands of goats and horses, about 800 of them moved into northern San Juan County.

The residents of San Juan County had heard about the bill but paid little attention to it. Washington, D.C., was a long way off and it was fall, the season to get their herds settled for winter. Cattle prices were low, about $10 to $12 a head, and the cattlemen were already facing a desperate situation (Silvey, "When San Juan County . . .").

Newspapers were scarce, mail service was poor, and many of the white settlers didn't know what was

Bluff home inside the fort.

going on until every waterhole was surrounded by a Ute camp. It was too early in the season for snow, and the wild range cattle would not come past these Indian camps to the water holes in Dry Valley, Hart Draw, Hatch Point, and Silvey Pocket.

A small delegation of Utes headed by Bridger Jack, a sub-chief who could speak English fairly well, met at the Silvey ranch for "heap big talk." The ranchers told the Indians that all they owned on earth was there, and cattle would die of thirst if the Indians remained. The territorial governor at Salt Lake City and all the people in Utah were against the Indians remaining here, and they must go or there would be trouble. Bridger Jack replied, "Room for All, Mormonee, cowboy, Indian. All sit down Dry Valley; sit down La Sal, Monticello; sit down, Blupp [Bluff] City; sit down—all good. Washington City man say come sit down. Salt Lake Capitan no good. Washington City Capitan pretty soon slap 'em jaw Salt Lake Capitan. We no go; we fight; we stay."

It was now up to the settlers to act. In addition to the "slow elk" the Indians were eating, cattle were beginning to die on the range from lack of water. It took some time to get together, but soon the ranchers gathered to decide on a course of action. Some of them were in favor of going to the governor of Utah and the people of the state, and getting the true conditions presented to Congress. Others considered this too slow—they would be out of business before they could get anything done. The best thing to do was fight— Indians outnumbered ranchers ten to one, but the whites could clean out one camp of Indians, wipe out every one, and then get to a safe place as soon as possible. This would bring Federal soldiers at once for an investigation, and that is what was needed.

Cooler heads prevailed, however, and J. S. Cunningham, Lester Taylor, Mons Peterson, and Jack Silvey left for Salt Lake City about the middle of the month to meet with Governor West, who had been appointed by President Cleveland for the Territory of Utah. He had been a Confederate officer in the Civil War and was a down-to-earth leader. He asked many questions of the delegates.

"Mr. Cunningham, what is your occupation?"

"I am general manager of the Pittsburgh Cattle Company, with about 12,000 head of cattle ranging on the La Sal mountains and in Dry Valley," was his reply.

Charlie Redd with Ute Indians, Bluff, Utah.

Lester Taylor told he lived in Moab, and ran his cattle on the mountain and in Dry Valley, and Silvey said he lived at La Sal and ran his cattle with others.

"How many ranchers and small cattle owners are there in San Juan County?" was next asked.

"At Monticello, Bluff City and La Sal, perhaps about fifty families in all."

"How long have they resided there?"

"Some families have been there since 1880–82," was the answer.

"Who are the largest cattle owners?"

"The Carlisle Cattle Company with 20,000 head, the LC Cattle Company owned by Mrs. Isaac Lacy with 10,000 head and the Pittsburgh Cattle Company," was told by Silvey.

"And a majority of the Southern Utes refuse to go back to their reservation?" was asked by Territorial Governor West. The delegation agreed that this was so.

"Gentlemen," West replied, "I have learned from your replies that San Juan County is not all just cattle country but is settled by homesteaders with families who intend to develop the country. I doubt I could justify protecting the big cattle outfits, but settlers must and shall be protected at all costs. I will wire Washington and will call a mass meeting tonight here in Salt Lake City so people may know the facts." (Silvey, "Early History . . . .")

Thousands attended the mass meeting and Salt Lake City was aflame with sentiment that the Indians must go back to their reservation. Colonel Tatlock and Lieutenant West, the governor's son, stated that the state militia had a thousand well-drilled soldiers who could be called up to protect the citizens of San Juan County. Two hundred Springfield rifles and ten thousand rounds of ammunition were sent to the law enforcement officers at Moab.

Ute Indian, Bluff, Utah.

Ranchers in San Juan County were not exactly sitting on their hands. A meeting was called with Neils Olson as chairman, and most of the men still thought that direct action would bring the situation to a head. It was decided that each man act as a committee of one to get all the help available and meet again at the Hatch ranch in ten days, prepared for war. Letters should be written to all parts of the country, warning people to stay off the roads, and that all people in isolated districts move to a place of safety, as there was liable to be trouble with the Indians.

"Boys," said ex-Confederate George Washington Johnson, "I rebelled once and will rebel again. I am with you to the finish."

Territorial Governor West, aware that real trouble was brewing, was keeping the wires hot to Washington, D.C. Sentiment in the eastern states was that southern Utah was a desert country inhabited by large cattle owners and cowboys, a few Mormons, and plenty of outlaws, a country of so little actual value that it might be best just to let the Utes have it.

Telegrams to agent David Day at Ignacio met with little sympathy. He refused to agree to a meeting with West until one of the letters sent out by the ranchers threatening war with the Indians fell into his hands. At last he seemed to realize that the situation was dangerous and wired Governor West: "Hold back your long-haired Aremenians [*sic*] until I can get my squaws and papooses out of your Gawd-forsaken country. Will meet you at Monticello December 2nd."

Territorial Governor West, Colonel Tatlock, and Lieutenant West arrived in Monticello on that date, early in the evening. David Day and Colonel Lawton did not reach there until late at night as their buckboard broke down just inside the Utah line and they had to ride the horse team in without saddles.

Colonel Lawton, who had been one of the main leaders in the capture of Geronimo, the renegade Apache outlaw of Arizona, was experienced in Indian affairs, and acted as chairman of the meeting held at the old log schoolhouse the next day. The Indians had been asked to send out messengers, the Salt Lake Capitans and Washington Capitans would be at the meeting, and all Indian chiefs and sub-chiefs were asked to come in. Cattlemen, homesteaders, and cowboys were also well represented.

The Indians were given the first voice in the meeting. Judge C. L. Christensen was selected as interpreter for the Indians. His nickname was Lingo, because he could speak four different languages fluently—English, Spanish, Navajo, and Ute.

Mariana, head chief under Ignacio, spoke first, and at great length in a fiery and impassioned speech on behalf of the Southern Utes. In substance, he said:

"Washington City man tell us to come here sit down. We sit down. All over this country it is ours. Now you say get out and go back to reservation. What's the matter now? We stay. Our fathers, and grandfathers and our great-great grandfathers have hunted here for many, many snows. We love this country; it's the Happy Hunting Ground for us on earth. We feel the Great Spirit wants us to stay. Washington City man say all right, so we stay."

Sub-chiefs spoke along the same line. Then it was the turn of Agent Day, who temporized by saying that Washington had investigated and found that many homesteaders lived in San Juan County. They had their all invested here, where many thousands of cattle ranged and wintered in good shape, as a rule; that instead of being a desert as was thought by many, this was rich and resourceful country; and that its inhabitants must be protected.

Ute Indian camp on a cold February day, 1890s.

A few of the settlers now gave their views, pointing out that they had suffered much hardship to make homes for their families and could not now leave these homes. But they wanted to live in peace. Territorial Governor West then spoke, saying:

"As Governor of this territory I feel that I must protect as far as possible, the interests of its people. I find that the majority of the settlers here are bona fide home seekers, have built up homes with untold sacrifices. I feel that the Indians, although right in a way, have encroached. They must go, and I will use all my power as Territorial Governor of this district of the United States, to see this accomplished."

Mariana again spoke, also some of the sub-chiefs, saying they would not go back to the reservation. Colonel Lawton then rose, representing the Indian Service. He said that Lawton and the Indians had talked for two hours and hadn't made any headway. He went on plainly that the Indians must go back to the reservation, at once, or he would bring in soldiers and see that they did.

There was no answer to this from the Indians, only sullen silence. Colonel Lawton was a man of action, and following the meeting he called a conference with Governor West, Colonel Tatlock, Lieutenant West, and Agent Day. They decided to send for federal soldiers. Dispatches were sent to the commander of Fort Chiv, near Denver, to get three troops of cavalry in readiness to be shipped to Thompson, Utah, to quell Indian trouble. These were signed by Colonel Lawton. Orders were sent to Salt Lake City to get the territorial militia prepared to travel. T. B. Carpenter and Jack Silvey took these dispatches on horseback to Thompson, 105 miles away, to the nearest telegraph station. They made the trip in eleven hours.

Three hours later further dispatches were readied, and Frank Silvey and Lieutenant West volunteered

Jesse James and his wife moving camp.

to take them. West was an inexperienced rider, but thought he should make the trip. Silvey relinquished his finest saddle mount, a gentle easy-gaited horse with great stamina, to the young soldier to give him every advantage. Jack Taylor offered Silvey a fine-looking black horse, and Frank asked if he was gentle.

Jack answered, "Yes, fairly, but a little hard to mount—better cheek him."

Frank was a fine rider, and knew that he should grasp the cheek of the bridle headstall in his left hand to keep the horse from whirling away from him; if the horse jumped or reared, he could then pull it toward and under him as he mounted. The horse was rearing and dancing, and as Frank jerked him sharply left in swinging up, the rifle butt hit the pony in the tender flank and he came down bucking. Frank wasn't worried about riding him, but the ground was covered with ice and snow, and there was a high probability that one or more of the six legs involved in the melee might be snapped if both of them slipped and fell. However, he was catty (nervous), and they took off like a rocket at about nine o'clock in the evening.

Crossing Dry Valley, Silvey, Taylor, and West saw many Indian campfires, but they kept on, loping and trotting, until they came upon a freighter camp at Hatch Wash. They drank some coffee, ate some hardtack, and let their horses rest a bit; then they rode on to Kane Springs, where they watered the horses sparingly and climbed over the hill into Moab Valley. Here Lieutenant West began to lag, and finally near Moab, he pulled up and said he could go no farther, giving the dispatches to Silvey to carry on. They pulled into the Old O. W. Warner ranch, and Silvey changed his saddle to his own horse and went on to Thompson Springs, arriving there fourteen hours after leaving Monticello.

At Monticello, "Lingo" Christensen stayed up all night, going from one Indian campfire to another of the Indians camped near town, and pleading with them to return to the reservation. The Indians refused to budge, saying, "We will fight first. We can whip the cowboys. Mormonee good friends, they won't fight us."

Christensen pointed out that while there were not many cowboys, true, and the Mormons did not want to fight if it could be prevented, Washington's soldiers were as the sands of the great river—countless. It

Ute Indians preparing to move camp.

would be useless to fight against them. Unless the Indians returned to the reservation, it would mean death for many of them.

The powwow went on all night, and finally at sunrise, the Indians started to agree reluctantly to "mebbeso go pretty quick," and things looked brighter.

That night the people of Monticello gave an entertainment, supper, and dance in honor of the illustrious visitors—Territorial Governor Caleb West, with Frank Silvey, Jack Silvey, and Lingo Christensen—and in celebration of the bloodless victory over the Ute invitation into San Juan County. School children gave a fine program; grown-ups gave recitations and sang old-time songs; Territorial Governor Caleb West thanked them, complimenting their training of the talented young people in so isolated a district.

"I shall always remember," he said, "your hospitality here at Monticello, and will think of you pioneer settlers here. You certainly deserve peace and prosperity for all time." He danced every set, and everybody had a great time.

The next morning the visitors departed, and the Indians, with a few exceptions, began to move their camps farther east. By the middle of March, few remained in the valley, but there were many camped along the eastern part of the county, and few had actually gone back to the reservation. A petition to Governor

West asked for action on the matter. He notified Washington, and soon the Ute Indian police from Colorado rounded up the balance. By April 1, few remained with the exception of the renegades, which numbered about seventy. Small bands under Posey, Mancos Jim, and Bridger Jack stayed, as they had never considered themselves as belonging to the reservation and had not been included in the Dry Valley migration. They had always lived west of Grayson, and there they remained, with the warning that they must behave themselves.

Immediately Andrew J. Hunter, Representative-at-large from Illinois and a member of the House of Representatives Committee on Indian Affairs, introduced House Resolution #6792 into the House. It suggested that all treaties made with the Indians to remove them to Utah be disapproved, and that they be allotted in severalty (individual homesteads as opposed to a large allotment like a reservation) where they elected on the former Southern Ute reservation, with those not so allotted to be settled on the west forty miles of the reservation in common (*Congressional Record* 36, 4230)."

This bill was introduced in the Senate on June 18, 1894, where it came under attack by senators who felt that the Colorado delegation was trying to move the Indians onto the unproductive land of the western portion in the hope of opening the eastern part to white settlement. The bill was amended to allow the Indians to take allotments anywhere within the boundaries of the 1879 reservation, which satisfied the Capote and Muache bands, who did not want to leave the eastern portion of the reservation.

In its final form, the Hunter Bill gave the Southern Utes the right to choose land in allotment anywhere on the old reservation or land in common on the western forty miles. It passed the Senate on January 28, 1895, and was sent back to the House. By February 11, both Houses had agreed to the bill as amended, and President Grover Cleveland signed it into law. Congress and the president had finally settled the Ute question, but implementation was another matter.

Meredith H. Kidd was appointed to go to the Ute Reservation to consult with the Indians and get their signatures of acceptance. He was joined in an office in Durango by Thomas P. Smith, Assistant Commissioner of Indian Affairs, and later by agent David F. Day. They were to carry out provisions of the treaty of June 15, 1888, approved February 20, 1895, and get consent from the majority of all the adult male Indians now located on the reservation.

In a letter of report to D. W. Browning, the Commissioner of Indians Affairs, Kidd says,

Chief Ignacio expressed a willingness to meet me in council at the south end of Ute Mountain, the western part of the reservation, but positively refused to attend any council at the Agency. Thereupon I arranged to meet the Mohauches [sic] and Capotes at the agency on the 8th inst. . . . and the Weeminuches at the south end of Ute Mountain on the 15th inst. . . . Many of them expressed a strong desire to locate on the reservation, build houses and commence farming. This was notable among the leaders of those from Blue Mountain in Utah. . . . Ignacio, the chief exclaimed, "Bueno, good, good." . . . Mancos Jim and Red Rock, Chiefs of the Blue Mountain band insisted I should point out where they could have their farms, as they were anxious to commence building their homes.

Kidd missed the Indian humor of this. Instead of showing cooperation, they were actually asking, "Where, in this arid, rocky wasteland could a man establish a home and make a living?" Browning answered,

This band has not drawn rations or clothing, and are very destitute. Their poverty has evidently convinced them that they must commence farming and support themselves. This band has been sometimes designated as Pi-Utes [sic]; they are not Pi-Utes but are Pah-Utes—which signifies runaway or renegade Utes. They are in fact a part of the

Two young Utes getting ready to move camp, 1920s.

Southern Utes, of Colorado, and are entitled to be enrolled, rationed and clothed and enjoy all the rights of Southern Utes in the reservation, and under the treaties. At least, this is my conclusion from the facts I have been able to gather. These Indians should be cared for and attached to some tribe, and I am not able to learn that they have any rights with any other tribe. In common humanity, they ought to receive the aid of the Government, unless there are facts and conditions of which I am ignorant, they ought to be incorporated into the Southern Ute tribe and treated as part of the Weeminuche band, and this the Weeminuches are anxious shall be done. All the men present, to the number of twenty, and whose names did not appear on the census rolls, signed the acceptance of the provisions of the act of Congress.

Among the Muaches, Buckskin Charlie and Washington were opposed to accepting the allotments. Agent David Day opined that from the checks Buckskin Charlie had been cashing at the trading post, he was paid to oppose the allotment of ground by men who were then using the reservation as grazing ground and the meadows for hay. However, he finally came around.

The commission made 371 allotments, which were approved by the Department of Indian Affairs on

June 12, 1896, and the commissioner of the general Land Office was ordered to issue the patents to title at that time.

David F. Day was very unpopular in southern Colorado at this time. He had been editor of several newspapers and could take an overall look at situations. He always seemed to take the part of the Indians; his encouragement for them to move into Utah had finally crowded the resolution of the reservation and settlement proceedings. He commented that Kidd was difficult to get along with, and was inclined to treat the Indians unfairly. He urged the Utes to choose the best land, which was wanted by the white people of southern Colorado, waiting for the matter to be settled.

After the allotments, the remaining land of the old reservation was thrown open for white settlement. A great land rush was expected, but when President William McKinley proclaimed the land available on May 4, 1899, only a few people from Durango filed claims; the Indians had all the best parcels, and only marginal farming land was left at best.

The main agency was left at Ignacio, but sub-agencies were established at Los Pinos on the Pine River and Arboles on the Piedra River near the New Mexico–Colorado boundary; a Weeminuche agency was established at Pacific Springs. This was moved later to Towaoc, which means "good place to live."

Medicine man Buckskin Charlie (right) and his brother.

PIUTE REBEL CAPTIVE IN DENVER

Tse-Ne-Gat, alias Everett Hatch.

FEAR OF WHITES MADE REDS FIGHT, SAYS PIUTE

11
TSE-NE-GAT

In April 1914, four Indians walked into Claude C. Covey's office at Navajo Springs, Colorado, a few weeks after the killing of Juan Chacon. They were Harry Tom, cousin of Antonio Buck, who was a grandson of the Muache Chief; Buckskin Charlie; Little Tom, also going by the names of Walter Lopez and Na-car-petz; and John Miller, known also as Ma-car-atz.

John Miller, who was the spokesman, said, "We find dead man near Cowboy Springs, head cut off. This bad thing. That is what we think. Sheepherder Juan Chacon, close by Ute Toe." The Ute was in reference to the toe of sleeping Ute Mountain.

Covey asked, "When did you find this body?"

"Six weeks gone, maybeso seven Tse-ne-gat killum," answered John Miller.

Covey continued, "How do you know Tse-ne-gat killed him?"

"We seeum, from top of hill, hear three shots quick; boom, boom, boom. Pretty soon come Tse-ne-gat on bay horse, dragging dead man by lariat. When he see us he throw body in Arroyo, ride fast, heap scared," John Miller answered.

Covey went on to ask, "But why did you wait so long to report to me? Why didn't you tell me as soon as you witnessed the killing?"

"We heap scared," Miller answered.

Harry Tom went on with the story, "Tse-ne-gat was riding toward the arroyo when we saw him. When he reached the arroyo his horse reared up and he got off. Then he saw us. I didn't see whether he had a rifle or a scabbard because he was so far away. I also saw a sorrel horse and a roan horse, but they were thin and poor. When Tse-ne-gat saw us he rode fast, in a direction away from the agency. None of us got off our horses, but we rode up to the arroyo and saw the body of the Mexican. It did not have any head."

RIGHT:
Buckskin Charlie on his favorite horse.

SCHOOLHOUSE at Bluff, which is a typical western settlement of about twenty-five families, who are menaced by the Piutes.

A prayer book with the name *Nievecitas* was found on the body; Chacon's wife said it was his. It contained a note for him to hurry home.

The next morning, Miller rode out with District Attorney George W. Lane and Coroner George M. Zufall from the county seat at Cortez, Colorado, and the Indians who had helped bury the body. They went about six miles north of the New Mexico line and six miles east of the Utah line, where they threw off the brush from a shallow grave in a gully and dug up the body. They found the body intact with its head. Chacon had been shot through the back and chest.

On May 16, 1914, a telegram was sent to the Commissioner of Indian Affairs at Washington, D.C.:

THE SCENE OF THE KILLING WAS SIX MILES NORTH OF NEW MEXICO BOUNDARY AND SIX MILES EAST OF THE UTAH LINE. UPON EXAMINING THE BODY, THE AGENT, THE CORONER AND DISTRICT ATTORNEY HAD FOUND THREE PAY CHECKS TOTALING $105.00, DATED MARCH 20, MADE OUT TO JUAN CHACON AND SIGNED BY DUNCAN & WESCH. ALSO ON THE BODY WAS A NOTE FOR $50.00 GIVEN BY "SOME MEXICAN," AT COYOTE, NEW MEXICO. CHACON'S NAME WAS ON THE BACK OF THE PRAYER BOOK.

THE MARSHAL WAS TOLD THAT SHORTLY AFTER THE KILLING TSE-NE-GAT HAD APPEARED AT CORTEZ "WITH HIS POCKETS FULL OF MONEY."

At this point, Covey turned the case over to the county coroner and went back to the agency to gather all the Indians involved and get their testimony. He personally thought that since the crime had been committed on the reservation, the case should be tried in federal court, but there was some sentiment that it might be a state matter.

He brought in Ca-vis-itz's son John Fields, together with Henry Goodman and Sa-wow-we-rats' son, Alphonso Bush, and Mark Kooken. Ca-vis-itz's son stated:

I, Ca-vis-itz' of lawful age, being duly sworn depose and say that on or about March 30, 1914, I was going to my home from the agency and met on the road Polk's son; that Polk's son asked me if I had met a Mexican; that I told him the Mexican was not far ahead. He said, "I am going to kill the Mexican." That I asked him why he wanted to kill the Mexican and he said the Mexican had a lot of money.

We, the undersigned, of lawful age, being duly sworn, depose and say: that we are Indians residing on the Navajo Springs reservation; that on or about the 30th of March, 1914, we were hunting cattle together on the plain below Ute Mountain; that a little after noon as we were coming back we came to a little point of a hill and heard three gun shots in rapid succession; that we then rode in the direction of the sound as rapidly as we could; that as we came up over the hill we saw a man pulling something; that when the man saw us coming he appeared to push the object he had been pulling over in a little arroyo; that he then jumped on his horse and rode rapidly toward the Agency, leading another horse; that we were close enough to recognize the man and his horse; that he was a Ute Indian, the son of Polk, known to us as Tse-ne-gat; that we then went over to where this Indian had been and saw in this little arroyo the body of a Mexican; that the body was lying face up and the man was dead; that we went home without touching the body; that the next day in company with John Fields, Henry Goodman and Sa-wow-we-rats' son we went back and buried the body where we had found it; that we did not examine the pockets or clothing but there appeared to be a watch on the body. That was the reason we did not report the matter at the time, the Superintendent was away and we did not know what to do and that besides we were afraid of this Indian and his father, as they were known as bad men, the father, Polk, having killed a number of Indians, including two of Rooster's sons and that we now fear that he will try to kill us for having told this; that Polk the father of the Indian who killed this Mexican was with his son this trip to the agency and that they went home together; that we believe that Polk knows that the Mexican was murdered; that Polk and his son have said that they would kill Indians or white men who tried to arrest them; and that they are now wandering from place to place and the last report we had was that they had gone to the Blue Mountains in Utah; that we are very anxious that these men both be arrested at once for this murder as we fear that they will murder Indians or white people; that when we buried the body of the Mexican we found that he had been shot three times, in the right arm, right and left breast; that we found three empty shells near the scene of the shooting and that these shells are now in the possession of John Miller.

There were no signatures on this document, but the three who had come in to report the murder were John Miller, Little Tom, and Harry Tom. Some of the details seem to be cleaned up from the original report they made.

There was a great deal of scurrying around by those in authority. The murder had been committed on reservation lands; therefore, only the U.S. federal agents had command; county and state officials were reluctant to handle the hot potato. Tse-ne-gat was living with his family at the mouth of Cottonwood Wash, below Bluff on the San Juan River in Utah, and Utah officers would not move without an indictment.

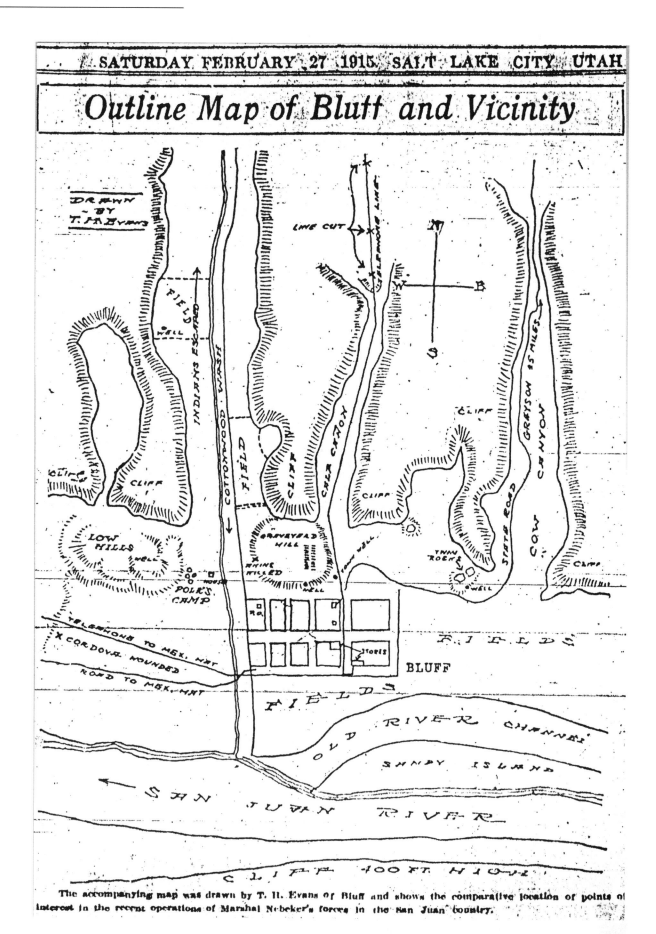

SATURDAY FEBRUARY 27 1915 SALT LAKE CITY UTAH

Outline Map of Bluff and Vicinity

The accompanying map was drawn by T. H. Evans of Bluff and shows the comparative location of points of interest in the recent operations of Marshal Nebeker's forces in the San Juan country.

TSE-NA-GAT, outlaw Piute, as he appeared when E. J. Milne, probation officer of the juvenile court, was in Bluff last summer. Mr. Milne is seen standing beside Hatch.

TSE-NA-GAT (Everett Hatch), the Indian who is being sought by the posse in southern Utah and who, with his father, Old Polk, is leading the defiant Piutes in rebellion against the federal government. The picture was taken at Grayson, Utah, at the home of L. H. Redd.

FAR LEFT:
Tse-ne-gat
and E. J. Milne.

LEFT:
Tse-ne-gat.

The Department of Indian Affairs hoped that Hatch (Tse-ne-gat) would ride into the Navajo Springs agency, where he could be arrested by the Indian police, who had no jurisdiction off the reservation. In fact, during the summer, Tse-ne-gat and his father, Polk, did start for the agency, but they met an Indian policeman and his interpreter, and the interpreter told them that the case was strong against Hatch, and he had better go back to Utah and stay there.

In July, the matter was stirred again, but it was September before the Utah authorities acted (Jones to First Assistant Secretary to the Attorney General of the United States).

U.S. Deputy Marshal David Thomas went to Bluff to arrest Tse-ne-gat. He found his man in Hyde's store on September 24 with a number of white men present. He explained to Tse-ne-gat what he wanted, and stated that he was not to use force to arrest him. The Indian refused to give himself up, saying he was afraid he would be killed and not get a fair trial in white man's court. Several of the white men urged Thomas to go ahead and arrest the Indian, but Thomas declined and returned to Salt Lake City, reporting that it would take force to make the arrest.

BELOW LEFT:
Tse-ne-gat,
also known as
Everett Hatch.

BELOW:
Jess Posey (right),
wrongly identified
as Old Polk, his
uncle.

EVERETT HATCH (Tse-Ne-Gat), son of Old Polk who was responsible for the Piute uprising by refusing to submit to arrest to federal authorities to stand trial on the charge that he murdered a Mexican sheepherder; below, Brig. Gen. Hugh L. Scott, chief of staff, U. S. A., who effected the capture of the leaders of the renegades.

Y, FRIDAY MORNING, FEBRUARY 26, 1915.

THREE GENERATIONS OF THE FAMILY of the chief of the renegade Piutes. At the right is Old Polk as he posed for Mrs. H. P. Dalley, nine years ago. At the left is Tse-Na-Gat (Everett Hatch), his son, taken by Mrs. Orem Lewis, several years ago. In the center is the child of a daughter of Old Polk, a photograph also taken by Mrs. Lewis.

Louisa Wetherill heard about this at Kayenta, Arizona, and with her husband, John, made a trip to Bluff to see Tse-ne-gat and tried to get him to surrender before the affair got out of hand. Called Lula by her friends and Asthon Sosi ("Slim Woman") by the Navajos, she had a strong influence on all Indians of the Four Corners area, both Navajo and Ute. Tse-ne-gat had already made one trip to Kayenta asking her what to do, and she had tried to get him to give himself up, but he refused to do so. During the last of September, she and her husband spent three days in the Indian camps, talking to the Indians, but Tse-ne-gat was out on the range with the goats and refused to come in to see her. Polk persisted that he would kill anyone who tried to arrest his son, and Asthon Sosi and the women cried together for three days before she gave up and went home (Covey to Commissioner of Indian Affairs).

Someone in the U.S. Marshal's office or on the state attorney's staff in Salt Lake City realized that they had no authorization to take a federal prisoner without indictment.

Covey then gathered his witnesses and made a trip to Denver, where an indictment for murder was brought against "Tse-ne-gat, otherwise called Pa-Woo-Tach, otherwise called Everett Hatch." This was brought in on October 14, and was finally tried in the U.S. District Court at Denver as case #2850. The indictment left no excuse for the U.S. marshals in Utah, and Aquila Nebeker took the matter under his peculiar ideas of control (Nebeker to Attorney General, December 7, 1914).

Reports and rumors were going out to the newspapers and back to Washington, D.C., to the Department of the Interior, Indian Affairs, and the Attorney General, but officialdom had other matters to worry about. The world was on the brink of the First World War, and Mexico was in civil strife; the far-out wilds of Utah and Colorado could hardly be considered by American statesmen of primary interest.

However, the situation was of more than local importance, hinging as it did on the overall uneasy situation of the Ute Indians of the Four Corners area, with the always potentially warlike Navajos directly to the south of them. Polk, William Posey, Mancos Jim, and a number of others again refused to settle on the reservation, and took up abode in the Blue (Abajo) Mountains and the San Juan River. This area was extremely remote from any military establishment.

Harry B. Tedrow, U.S. attorney at Denver, stated in a report how remote it was to get to Tse-Ne-Gat: "It is 479 miles from Denver to Dolores, Colorado, where the 14-mile stage line to Cortez begins. From Cortez to Bluff is 70 overland. From Bluff to Mexican Hat is 25 miles overland. Kayenta, Arizona, where the Wetherills live, is approximately 75 miles from Bluff" (Tedrow to Attorney General).

U.S. Marshal Aquila Nebeker commented: "These Indians are located in a particularly inaccessible region, remote from railroads and routes of regular travel, habitations of white men of any considerable number and what white men are in that section, as a matter of self-preservation, are unwilling to render such assistance that we may find necessary. The country is traversed by "box" canyons leading into the Colorado River and sparsely provided with subsistence for man or beast." (Nebeker to Attorney General, March 1, 1915).

Nebeker believed in stating his reports in the proper language and he became so involved in sheer wordage (with an occasional glaring misuse of a word) that his material is tough to understand. Not the simple sentence maker, Nebeker; he favored the long, involved, tenuous paragraph, winding off into the sunset.

In his December letter he pointed out that Polk would probably have to be arrested also, as the old Indian was muttering threats to kill his first victim, who would be the one to take Tse-ne-gat prisoner. Also, Nebeker had no means of identifying the person wanted and no assurance that "I can obtain the necessary assistance in making the arrest. I desire to know of you if you can furnish sufficient number of your Indian Police, possibly five, to deliver to me both father and son at some convenient place, say, Bluff or preferably Grayson." He never did say for what crime Polk was to be arrested.

There the matter bogged down while the winter ground its slow way, with near starvation by both the Indians and their livestock during the heavy storms, deep snow, and blizzards. In February the weather broke slightly, and the thawing conditions replaced the snow with gummy mud.

Nebeker left Salt Lake City on February 1, 1915, for the Four Corners area to set in motion a police action against Tse-ne-gat. He spent some time in Monticello, Grayson, and Cortez. The Indians in camp below Bluff were aware that he was prowling, and they were determined to resist whatever he advanced. He insisted that the posse was too small, and recruited several of his old buddies in Cortez and Dolores (Warren to U.S. Attorney General, February 19, 1915).

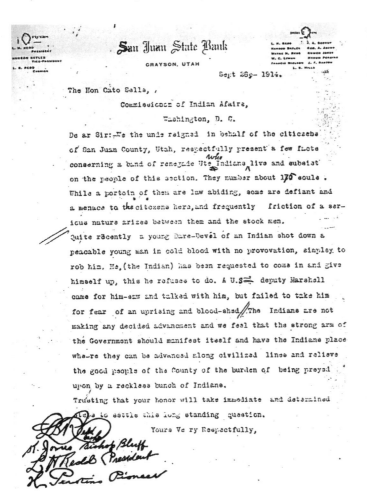

Nebeker Knows Range Well and Reds Know Him

AQUILA NEBEKER.

FAR LEFT: Communication from the San Juan State Bank.

LEFT: Aquila Nebeker.

According to one newspaper account, Nebeker declared that either he would get the Indian alive or dead or he would not return. In selecting the posse, he chose men he knew from his cowpunching days in the area, men noted for their courage and marksmanship. He knowingly expected many of his men never to return, although he did not intend to storm the Indian stronghold but to approach cautiously and pick off the Indians one by one until, through thirst and hunger, they would all be driven to surrender.

Another newspaper report tagged the posse as booze fighters, gamblers, and bootleggers. It also stated that before leaving Dolores they had talked as if they were going rabbit hunting.

When Agent Jenkins, who had replaced Covey, heard that Nebeker had left Dolores for Grayson, he became alarmed and wired Special Indian Agent for Scattered Bands, David B. Creel, in Salt Lake City that he wanted to meet with him about the affair and try to take Tse-ne-gat without a battle. Creel agreed to meet him in Bluff as soon as he could get there.

DEPARTMENT OF THE INTERIOR
UNITED STATES INDIAN SERVICE
Navaho Springs, Colo. March 1, 1915

The Honorable,
Commissioner of Indian Affairs,
Washington, D.C.

Sir:

Referring to the trouble at Bluff, Utah, resulting from an attempt of the U. S. Marshall for Utah to arrest Everett Hatch and Billy Hatch (alias "Polk"), Indians of this reservation, I have the honor to submit the following report: On Feb. 19, 1915, your Office sent me this telegram:

WASHINGTON, D.C., FEB 19, 1915, JENKINS, SUPT. NEWS ITEM LOCAL PAPER INDICATES TROUBLE BY REASON ATTEMPT TO ARREST EVERRETT HATCH. MAIL FULL REPORT AND KEEP OFFICE ADVISED. (SIGNED) MERITT, ASS'T COM'R.

Although I had no information as to the proceedings of the U.S. Marshal and had not even seen newspaper reports of the last attempt to serve the warrants, in his possession, (this Agency is remote from railroads and gets mail only tri-weekly), I mailed you the report called for with such information as could be had at the time.

Not having been consulted regarding the Hatch case and the matter having been turned over to the Marshall by my predecessor I had refrained from interfering in the arrest further than to advise the Indians, as the subject came up, that it was their duty to assist in the peaceable surrender of Hatch, as well as of all members of their tribe for whom warrants have been issued.

Later in the day I received your second telegram, as follows:

WASHINGTON, D.C., FEB. 19, 1915, JENKINS, SUPT. CREEL WIRES FROM SALT LAKE SITUATION HATCH MATTER IS GRAVE. ENDEAVORING TO AVOID BLOODSHED IN CONNECTION RADICAL ACTION UNTIL CREEL AND YOU CAN GET IN TOUCH WITH POSSE AND CONFER WITH INDIANS. PROCEED AT ONCE TO SEAT OF TROUBLE AND ACT WITH CREEL IN ENDEAVORING TO BRING ABOUT PEACEABLE SURRENDER OF HATCH. KEEP OFFICE ADVISED. (SIGNED) SELLS, COMMISSIONER.

I immediately wired Creel, sending you copy of Telegram, as follows:

NAVAHO SPRINGS, COL., FEB. 19, 1915.—INDIAN OFFICE, WASHINGTON, D.C.—YOUR TWO TELEGRAMS REGARDING EVERETT HATCH RECEIVED. HAVE MAILED REPORTS REQUESTED ALSO WIRED CREEL AT SALT LAKE AS FOLLOWS: NAVAHO SPRINGS, COLO., FEB. 19, 1915.—CREEL, SPECIAL AGENT, SALT LAKE CITY, UTAH.—WHERE CAN I SEE YOU TO CONFER REGARDING HATCH MATTER? WIRE FULL PARTICULARS. ROADS ALMOST IMPASSABLE AND STILL RAINING HERE. SUGGEST EFFORTS OF MARSHALL TO ARREST HATCH BE POSTPONED TILL WEATHER CLEARS. CONFIDENT I CAN GET HATCH TO COME TO THIS AGENCY PEACEABLY IF NOT AUTHORITIES. (SIGNED) JENKINS, SUPT.

Also wired Creel and your Office of My starting out as Follows:

NAVAHO SPRINGS, COLO., FEB. 20, 1915.—CREEL SPECIAL AGENT, THOMPSON STATION, UTAH—OWING TO UNCERTAIN TRAIN SERVICE NORTH OF HERE AM GOING TO BLUFF OVERLAND. EXPECT TO GET THROUGH BY MONDAY NIGHT. WILL SEE YOU THERE. (SIGNED) JENKINS, SUPT.

NAVAHO SPRINGS, COLO., FEB. 20, 1915.—INDIAN OFFICE, WASHINGTON, D. C.—AM STARTING FOR BLUFF IN MORNING OVERLAND, EXPECT TO REACH THERE MONDAY NIGHT, HAVE NOTIFIED CREEL. WILL WIRE YOU CONSERVATIVE VIEW OF SITUATION SOON AS POSSIBLE. (SIGNED) JENKINS, SUPT.

As stated in my telegram, weather conditions were unusually bad and roads almost impassable, but I made a start with an interpreter early the next morning (in a snow storm) breaking the buggy and crippling a horse on the way, but managed to reach Bluff at 4 p.m. the 22d.

When I arrived at Bluff I found that the "eggs had been scrambled." The excitement among citizens was intense and the Marshal's posse, a poorly organized band of ranchers and cowboys, apparently filled with a determination to "get" every Indian in the country.

I held a conference of the citizens with the Marshal and some of the leaders of his posse and insisted that such Indians as had been friendly and not disposed to harbor Polk and Hatch should be treated with friendly consideration, and I immediately went to the friendly camps to quiet the Indians and urge them to return to the reservation.

Telegrams were sent your Office from time to time in order to keep you posted as to developments. I wired you on the 22d, as follows:

BLUFF, UTAH, FEB. 22, 1915.—COMMISSIONER OF INDIAN AFFAIRS, WASHINGTON, D.C.—MARSHAL'S POSSE OF 22 MEN ATTEMPTED TO ARREST HATCH AT INDIAN CAMP ONE MILE WEST OF HERE SUNDAY MORNING. POSSE SURROUNDED CAMP; INDIANS OPEN FIRE KILLING ONE POSSE MAN. WHITES RETURNED FIRE KILLING ONE INDIAN. BATTLE LASTED TWO HOURS. INDIANS LOCATED IN ROCKS KEPT UP FIRING ON MEMBERS OF POSSE DURING DAY. NO FURTHER FATALITIES. WILL HAVE CONFERENCE WITH MARSHAL NEBEKER TONIGHT AND WIRE FURTHER PARTICULARS. ABOUT 70 POSSE MEN HERE; SITUATION RATHER TENSE.

On the 23d I wired you as follows:

BLUFF, UTAH, FEB. 23, 1915.—COMMISSIONER OF INDIAN AFFAIRS, WASHINGTON, D.C.—SITUATION HERE STILL SERIOUS. CITIZENS MUCH ALARMED AND WANT GOVERNMENT TO TAKE DECISIVE ACTION. CONFERRED WITH MARSHAL NEBEKER. HE VERY PROPERLY INSISTS THAT WARRANTS BE SERVED. INDIANS HIDING IN HILLS. AM ENDEAVORING TO GET IN TOUCH WITH FRIENDLY ELEMENT OF INDIANS AND HAVE THEM ASSIST IN EFFECTING PEACEABLE ARREST OF HATCH.

On the 24th I wired you as follows:

BLUFF, UTAH, FEB. 24, 1915.—COMMISSIONER OF INDIAN AFFAIRS, WASHINGTON, D.C.—SITUATION HERE UNCHANGED. HATCH, POLK AND POSEY, WANTED BY MARSHAL, ESCAPED TO

HILLS AND STILL HIDING. NO IMMEDIATE PROSPECTS OF APPREHENDING THEM. ONE OF INDIAN PRISONERS HELD BY POSSE ATTEMPTED ESCAPE LAST NIGHT AND WAS SHOT BY A GUARD; PROBABLY FATALLY WOUNDED. THIS DEPLORABLE INCIDENT ADDS TO EXCITEMENT. WILL WIRE FURTHER DEVELOPMENTS.

The Indian shot by a guard, referred to, died two days later. His name was Havane [also Ha-van] and he was said to be a son-in-law of Polk.

On the 26th I wired you as follows:

BLUFF, UTAH, FEB. 26 1915.—COMMISSIONER INDIAN AFFAIRS, WASHINGTON, D.C.— SITUATION STILL CRITICAL. RENEGADE BAND OF ABOUT 40 UTES UNDER POLK AND POSEY WITH ABOUT 20 PIUTES HAVE ENTRENCHED THEMSELVES IN CANYONS TEN TO TWENTY MILES SOUTH-WEST OF HERE. ABOUT THREE-FOURTHS OF CAMP WOMEN AND CHILDREN. MARSHAL'S POSSE WILL UNDERTAKE THEIR PEACEABLE SURRENDER, WHICH IS VERY DOUBTFUL. I VISITED FRIENDLY CAMP OF UTES EIGHT MILES NORTHEAST OF HERE YESTERDAY AND GOT CONSENT OF ABOUT 60 TO REMOVE AT ONCE TO RESERVATION. THEY ARE MUCH EXCITED AND ANXIOUS THAT POLK AND POSEY BE CAP-TURED. WILL START FROM THE AGENCY TOMORROW WITH INDIANS MENTIONED AND RETURN HERE AS SOON AS PRACTICABLE TO INDUCE BALANCE OF UTES TO RETURN TO RESERVATION. CREEL ARRIVED WEDNESDAY NIGHT AND WORKING WITH ME.

On the morning of the 27th, the situation being unchanged, I joined with U. S. Marshal Nebeker, U.S. Attorney Cook and Special Agent Creel in a telegram to the Attorney General and to your office advising for the safety of the citizens, the enforcement of law without additional bloodshed and for the ultimate peaceable and permanent return of the Indians to their reservation, that a troop of U.S. Cavalry be stationed at Bluff until such time as order has been fully restored.

I trust prompt action will be taken in respect to this matter as the situation warrants it from every viewpoint, not the least of which is the best interests of the Indians.

It can be of no benefit to any of us to find fault with policies and acts leading up to events above outlined, but it will be of great benefit to all concerned if we can and will profit by the lessons.

In the first place these Indians should never have been permitted to live in the wild country entirely without super-vision, as has been the case the past 35 years. To assume that an agent residing 90 miles away by wagon roads or trails—inaccessible much of the time—could exercise any restraint or supervision over them would be assuming beyond reason. The consequence has been that the so-called "freedom" of these wandering bands has not only made most of them lawless, or at least ignorant of the law and discipline, but has also had a bad effect on all other Indians belonging to the reservation. They complain that they are not allowed the same unrestrained privileges and the result has been to their detriment as well as adding to the difficulties in handling them.

As stated in my telegram of the 26th, I succeeded in getting a band of about 60 of the Bluff contingent started back to the reservation. They are in charge of one of the Indian police and appear very glad of protection and refuge. They are in destitute circumstances, the weather and roads are bad and it will probably be another week before they reach here. There are two other small camps in the vicinity of Bluff and 50 others live in the vicinity of McElmo canyon and Montezuma Creek, 20 to 30 miles west of here. I will visit all these camps as soon as possible and undertake to have every Indian remove to the reservation.

The stationing of troops at Bluff would greatly aid this movement.

As to the Polk and Posey band, as stated they are hiding in the canyons somewhere southwest of Bluff. No definite information could be obtained as to their exact location and as that section is one of the roughest portions of the country it is doubtful if they can be dislodged. It is possible after the excitement dies out and the Marshal's posse gives up the hunt I can get in touch with Polk and induce him to come in with his son and Posey and surrender peaceably to the officers of the court.

Polk has about twelve to fifteen male adults in his band, and it is said a number of Piutes have joined him, which may be true or not. Polk's camp consists of about 40 persons, three-fourths of which are women and children, and I am confident the majority of them would be glad of the chance to return to the reservation. The great difficulty is to allay the excitement among whites as well as Indians so that the Indians can be reached. This may take weeks, but I believe such a method better than to attack the Indians in their stronghold, which might mean the killing of women and children as well as Indians who were not the original offenders, besides members of the posse.

This affair at Bluff ought to convince the Office, it would seem, that no further delays should be tolerated in looking to the interests of these Indians and this reservation. The boarding school should be completed so that the children can be acquiring much needed education and supervision. The irrigation work projected should be rushed as promised

San Juan Co-op was the informal headquarters for the war; here they are hauling supplies for oil drilling.

yearly since 1893. Requests for purchases made by me the past two months for various needed improvements should be allowed without delay. And there should be no let-up in supplying funds for the employment of all able-bodied Indians on road improvements, water development; etc.

In this connection I wish to urge the establishment of a farm station with farmer in charge at Mariano Springs, 12 miles west of the present agency. This is where the majority of the Indians who are now moving to the reservation will locate. It is a vary [sic] fertile section with good water and abundant grass for stock. Numerous good little farms could be opened and there is water to irrigate two or three hundred acres, which might be further developed. The farmer would require a small cottage, stable, root-cellar, machinery shed, corral for branding, etc., but I consider the investment absolutely necessary under the circumstances and one that would be of great benefit to the Indians of that section.

The telephone line should also be extended from the Agency to Mariano Springs and from there to the trading store or Navajo farm station just southwest of this reservation on the Navajo reserve near Aneth 15 miles farther southwest. Our Indians trade there a great deal and having telephone communications would help very much in preserving order and keeping in touch with them. All the work of building the line, supplying and getting poles, etc., could be performed by our Indians.

I trust you will authorize the establishment of this farm station and the extension of the telephone line without delay and I will at once ascertain the cost of same.

The removal of the Indians from Bluff, many of whom are old and helpless and most of them destitute, will require more or less outlay for provisions while en route and until they can get established here and the able-bodied members earning money to purchase supplies. I trust my requests for expenditures for such purposes, as made, will promptly be authorized.

Unless otherwise directed I will proceed to Bluff, McElmo, Montezuma Creek, and other points where Indians belonging here are said to be camping and induce them to remove to the reservation. This work will probably require a large part of my time during the coming two months, going back and forth, and if all are finally established on the reservation before summer ends I will feel that I have accomplished a work of great benefit to these people and settle a problem that has perplexed the Indian Department for many years.

Trusting this report and suggestions offered meet with your approval.

Very respectfully,

J. E. Jenkins
Superintendent.

On February 17, 1915, Charles Burke reported in the *Rocky Mountain News:*

Today the posse started out forty strong on seventy-five mile ride to the desert citadel. It will join with another posse organized in Utah, and plans to reach the San Juan River tomorrow morning.

The main posse was formed in Colorado because the men in the neighborhood of Bluff hesitated to take part in the attempt. They feared the vengeance of the Indians, which would be exercised on their livestock and homes after the officers left.

In Burke's next article—"McElmo Cañon by Indian Courier to Cortez"—he reported:

[T]he posse was accompanied by two wagons carrying food and ammunition. Each man carried 500 cartridges. A. N. Gingles, deputy sheriff of Montezuma County, was in charge of the Colorado contingent. . . . A few ranchers, many of them squaw men, are unwilling to make enemies of the roving Paiutes, and no help is expected of them. The leaders plan, under cover of night, to surround the stronghold. They are prepared for violent resistance. . . . [Burke quoted Marshal Nebeker:] "Everything is serene. To announce our plans would defeat the ends of justice." The marshal, has established censorship and refused to discuss the situation. "This is taken to mean, that he has made up his mind to waste little time in parleying with the Indians."

Two nights before, on Saturday the 20th, Nebeker had taken his force of twenty-two men from Grayson, arriving at Bluff in the middle of the night. He waited until almost morning, and then rode down to the camp. At Old Polk's camp there were eighteen males, including teenage boys and Mexican youth Bruno Lagura (also spelled Segara), and around two dozen squaws and children. Jess (Posey's son) and Havane were overnight guests there with Old Polk, his wife Etta, Tse-ne-gat and Chatta and the couple's as yet un-named infant son. Polk's other family—Orwin, 45 years old; Steve, 39; and Rosa, 25—rounded out the group.

The night before the battle the weather was cloudy and calm, with off and on rain and snow. There was from six inches to a foot of snow on the ground. The thermometer read 38 degrees. The posse hid in the rim rocks surrounding Polk's camp.

They waited all night without a fire, and as dawn arrived, it began to snow, making it difficult to shoot accurately.

Outlook magazine quoted R. E. Pool of Cortez, Colorado: "Nebeker made the mistake of gathering a posse of men composed chiefly of the rougher element of cowpunchers. These proceeded to tank up in anticipation of the coming fun with the Indians."

It is not clear who opened fire, but the Indians did several things at once. The men forted up among the rocks, ledges, and brush, while the women and children scattered like quail toward the horse herd and river. The first volley began when Chicken Jack Brother was trying to rescue a squaw (who had been wounded in both legs) and her child near the San Juan River bank as some of the Indians were trying to escape across the river. Reportedly, she was drowned in the crossing. (Author's Note: In the records of 1915, Indian Agent A. H. Symons paid $25 to buy back a Ute Indian slave girl from the Navajos. This was the one they thought had drowned at the 1915 battle at the river crossing near Bluff but who was actually kidnapped by the Navajos.)

Because A. N. Gingles was supposed to know the country around the camp, Nebeker put him in command.

The testimony of Mr. Gingles at the inquest March 1, 1915, is presented below, concerning the body of Joseph Akin held by Justice of the Peace F. H. Karnell:

"I split the posse there and sent part of them west and part of them to the north. When the boys coming north reached a distance of about 175 yards of the Indians' camp there was Polk and his Boy in front of the wickiup dancing, whooping and yelling and they opened fire on the posse. Some of our men went farther north and some went around the hill and in the draw around the Indians' wickiup. Polk and his boy and another Indian ran about straight north and got behind a sandbank in Cottonwood Wash. Mr. Stavely and I were in Cottonwood Wash where we could not see the Indians and we went around on this side of the wash by the knoll about north of east of the location of the Indians. There were three Indians behind this sandbank and they were shooting constantly at Mr. Stavely and I.

"Mr. Akin came across the wash and joined us. He laid down behind this bank and stuck his head over. I pointed the Indians out to him and he made an attempt to reach his gun and raised his head and just as he raised his head there was a bullet came from Polk and killed him, entering over his left eye and lodging back of his right ear."

It was said that Joe Akin was getting ready to shoot Posey, who came riding on his pony when Joe was shot and killed. Posey with his 30.06 rifle, dashed up to take a hand in the fun. He saw two horsemen coming, so put a white rag on a stick, and as he approached them, waved it. The two posse members decided he was neutral, a peaceful Indian, and rode off the bank into the wash. Posey jumped off his crow bait pony and drilled J. R. Cordova through the arm, through the body below the heart, and through the other arm, wounding him gravely.

JOSE CORDOVA   DR. JOHN STANLEY

BUCK WHO CAUSED IT ALL SHOOTS DOWN COLORADOAN

TSE-NA-GAT, known as Everett Hatch, who, according to reports, shot and killed Joe Atkins of Dolores, Colo., yesterday when the posse attempted to storm the Indians' position.

This took an awful lot of fight out of the posse; they left their horses and scattered into the countryside. The Indians dashed for cover in tall greasewoods or sand washes. They could have picked the posse off one by one, but this seemed to be a sort of exciting game of Hide and Seek to the Indians; they did a lot of shooting, but mostly to stir the white men up, not to kill them and put an end to the fun.

Posey put great stock in his high-powered rifle, and climbed up on a point that he considered out of range for the posse [this Cottonwood property is now owned by the Claude and Thelma Lacy family]. He turned around, patted his rear and made other derisive gestures at the posse gathered in the wash below. Finally one of them, armed with a 30.06 also, shot a spurt of snow and dirt right between Posey's legs and put an end to the horseplay. Posey hunted cover.

Indians and white men were crawling around the rocks at the top of the cliffs, with the white men cut off from their horses, which were taken back to Bluff about noon. Some of the posse didn't make it back to Bluff until toward morning, having spent the whole day and night out in the rain and snow without food or shelter.

Meanwhile the peaceful Indians, the noncombatants, cowered in terror that they would be wiped out either by the bronco Indians or the crazy posse.

The next morning the Indians gathered south of the San Juan River with what supplies they could carry as they left the camps. The posse had burnt Polk's camp. Probably they were aiming for Navajo Mountain, but they felt at home anywhere in that maze of canyons and mesas south and west of the Mormonee settlements. William Posey was sure they would be followed and he could make a name for himself by wiping out the pursuit.

The *Montezuma Journal* of Cortez, Colorado, printed a letter from posse man John Stavely after the attack:

> Arrived at top of Cow canyon 5:30 this a.m., arrived at Indian Camp at daylight. Polk and son opened fire as soon as they sighted us, but no one hurt until a young buck was dropped when crossing an arroyo to a better position.
>
> Akins was struck in the head and instantly killed in the act of firing at Polk and his son. In

returning the fire into wigwam one papoose was killed and another wounded. In the confusion that followed, a squaw fell from her horse in crossing the San Juan to get out of range and was drowned.

One member of the posse is dead, four unheard from. Three Indians dead, two wounded. Five Indians and one Mexican captured.

Later: The boys that were cut from town sent horses in with notes that they were o.k.

Special Indian Agent Lorenzo D. Creel and Assistant District Attorney David S. Cook were on their way from Salt Lake City to meet with Nebeker and Jenkins at Bluff. Attorney Cook reported to the Attorney General on February 23:

Arrived tonight 100 miles interior (Monticello) from railway and now 50 miles from Bluff, Utah, scene of Indian hostilities. Had as detailed a conversation with Marshal Nebeker tonight as country party line with many connected phones and common excitement of communities through which line passes would permit.

Since the engagement with the Indians on Sunday morning by a part of the Marshal's posse, snow has melted so that tracking of Indians in the narrow precipitous and rocky defiles of the most inaccessible part of mountains west practically impossible by whites. Needless to say that such an expedition under most favorable circumstances would be attended by every possible hazard.

Marshal's scouting parties were attended today by two Indian police from Shiprock reservation. Found these men invaluable because of cultivated and natural ability of Indians for tracking. Marshall believes services of four to six additional of such would render invaluable service to his expedition. . . .

Posey's family, with Indian agent Elfa Bacca.

Posey's second wife, Mary, in Bluff, Utah, 1916.

William Posey's camp contained Mary Posey, 45; Jess, 25; Nancy, 22; Ella, 18; Effa, 15; Ned, 6; Lily, 5; John, 4; Peter, 4; Ora, 4; Phoebe, 3, and Ruby, 1; with the family of Negro John Taylor and his Ute wife Kitty Cloud, together with others numbering about forty in the main group escaping into the wilds (Parkhill, 1962, 70).

> *Creel, Special Agent, cooperating in wire to Indian Department. . . . Am frank to say, however, that such a campaign to succeed against these Indians in the country they now occupy, which in itself has been sufficient protection for many years, would require weeks of not only dangerous but questionable effort and would leave small contiguous communities exposed to savage attacks while their male population were engaged as posses at distant points.*

Lorenzo D. Creel, special agent for scattered bands of Indians, was on his way from Salt Lake City also, and he reported to the Commissioner of Indian Affairs later that he made all haste possible because of the gravity of the situation.

THE WEATHER

The Salt Lake Tribune.

VOL. XC, NO. 131.   SALT LAKE CITY, MONDAY MORNING, FEBRUARY 22, 1915.   14 PAGES—FIVE CENTS

POSSE AND INDIANS IN BATTLE; ONE WHITE, TWO PIUTES KILLED

SCENES OF THE INDIAN FIGHTING in southeastern Utah and men who figure in the situation. Top, left to right—Bluff, Utah, looking to the southwest across the San Juan river. Head of Cow canyon, northeast of Bluff, and through which runs the only wagon route from Grayson to Bluff. The Indians under "Old Polk" are intrenched in this canyon. Bottom, left to right—"Old Posey," outlaw Piute chief who is aiding "Old Polk" in his fight against Marshal Nebeker; "Scotty," one of "Old Polk's" tribe, and, beside him, Frank Adams, of Bluff; L. D. Creel of Salt Lake, U. S. Indian agent, who is on his way to the scene of hostilities.

BLUFF AT MERCY OF HOSTILE REDSKINS

J. D. Akin of Dolores, Colorado, Falls at First Fire; Jose Cardova, Wounded While on Guard; Reinforcements Under "Old Posey" Reach "Old Polk" and Make an Attack From Rear.

FEDERAL TROOPS MAY BE CALLED

Massacre Is Feared; Outlaws Cut Telephone Wires; Federal Forces Between Two Fires; Relief Bands Are Started From Various Points to Aid of Deputies.

AMERICAN STEAMER STRIKES MINE OFF THE GERMAN COAST

Captain and Crew Saved; Evelyn, Loaded With Cotton for Bremen, Victim of the Disaster

SINKING OF BRITISH TRANSPORT REPORTED

WASHINGTON, Feb. 21.—Secretary Bryan announced the receipt of a telegram tonight from the American consul at Bremen reporting "the loss" of the American steamer Evelyn. The cause was not stated. The crew was saved.

BRITISH TRANSPORT SENT DOWN

BERLIN, Feb. 21, by wireless to Sayville—The report of the sinking of a British transport with troops and the accompanying steamer, reached Berlin too late for comment by the morning papers.

SUBMARINE SINKS STEAMER

LONDON, Feb. 21, 6:40 p. m.—The small Irish coasting steamer Downshire was sunk last night by a German submarine off Gulf of Man, an island in the Irish sea.

EVELYN FIRST AMERICAN SHIP TO STRIKE MINE

GERMAN AIRMEN RAID THE BRITISH COAST

Bombs Dropped at Colchester and Braintree; No Damage Done.

AUSTRIANS FIRE ON ITALIAN FISHERMEN

Riot in Rome Over Neutrality Question; Mobs Dispersed by Police.

PROPOSES, MURDERS, COMMITS SUICIDE

T. W. R. Nelson of Rupert, Idaho, Kills Woman and Takes Own Life.

DEATH OF SOME BIG MEASURES CERTAIN

Press of Business Before U. S. Senate; Mystery About Shipping Bill.

MAN BADLY INJURED IN MINE EXPLOSION

In Creel's report to the Bureau of Indian Affairs, he said the following:

I reached Thompson, (the railway point for Southeastern Utah), at 2 a.m. on the 21st in an awful snow storm which grew steadily worse, I caught about an hour's sleep while waiting for daylight. No team could be procured. A heavily loaded stage was my only way to get to Moab over roads nearly hub-deep in mud and snow. While telephoning for a relay team to meet the stage, the awful news of the battle at Bluff reached me over the wire. I immediately sent telegrams to the Office and the U.S. Attorney and proceeded to Moab as fast as the condition of the road would permit. I reached there at night, went to the telephone exchange and remained up with the manager nearly all night sending and receiving such reports as came over the wire. The line is a cheap one, built to accommodate ranchers and business men; therefore it is only by relaying from point to point that messages could be gotten through. The country was panic

L E F T :
Moab, Utah, in the mid-1920s.

R I G H T :
Indian camp goats, 1915.

stricken and as soon as a message would start, down would go every receiver on the line and stay down until it was ended. This rendered it exceedingly difficult to get any message at all.

I waited in Moab until overtaken by Assistant U.S. Attorney David S. Cook, when we proceeded on our way to Bluff together. We traveled alternately from stage to stage by wagon, sled to wagon through mud often hub deep and snow from three to four feet deep. We got but little sleep until we reached Bluff on the night of the 24th.

I found the population still in the wildest excitement. School had been closed and all business suspended. My first efforts were in restoring harmony among the white elements and quieting the fears of the citizens.

Against advice from people in Bluff, Agent Jenkins and I started out with a wagon and team to contact the non-combatant Indians. The first half mile from town convinced me that the Indians were in an awful state of terror and every other mile on the trail confirmed my belief. About ten miles out of the town we found an old Indian acting as lookout who stood his ground and talked with us. In a short time the men came out of the rocks a mile or two away, and finally we talked to them and shook hands all around. Mr. Jenkins had Jim Allen, Interpreter and Carumbet, Indian policeman, with us. Through these we explained fairly who and what we were. Jenkins stated that the reservation was the only safe place for them, that he could give them plenty of food for their families. All except Mancos Jim agreed to start for the reservation the next day, and when it came right down to it, he went along, too. Mr. Jenkins then returned to the reservation and I remained at Bluff to gather up and care for the Indians' property, their sheep and goats—also to care for the sick which were left behind in their flight.

According to General Hugh L. Scott, in his publication *Some Memories of a Soldier*, five young men from the peaceful Indians came into Bluff and gave themselves up. These were Havane, Jack Ute, Jack Rabbit, Noland May, and Joe Hammond. At this time, a Mexican named Bruno Lagura was living with Old Polk's band. John Taylor, a Negro veteran of the Civil and Indian Wars, was living with Posey's family group. He had "married into the family," taking Kitty Cloud as his thirteenth wife. They were held in the hall above the general store; on what charge was never revealed. Considerable criticism has leaked down that the guard put guns to their heads and threatened them. There seems to have been a good bit of alcohol involved in the whole posse activity. Havane, Polk's son-in-law, became frightened, tried to jump out of the window, and was shot by one of the guards. He lived a day or two, but this tagged [meant] out and out murder by public opinion at Bluff; the rest of the captives were taken to Salt Lake City to be held for trial.

During the night of February 23rd, Havane attempted to escape and was fatally wounded as he jumped from the second floor of the San Juan Co-op.

ABOVE:
Sheriff J. T. Pehrson (left), Bruno Segara, Jackrabbit, Havane, Joe Hammond, Jackrabbit Soldier, Norey, Frank Adams, Henry Ince.

RIGHT:
Back row: Willard Butt (left), Gene Powell, Jens Nielson, Joe Hammond, Jackrabbit, Polk, Henry Ince; front row: Havane (left), Bruno Segara, Jackrabbit Soldier, Norey; photo from the Creel Collection.

ABOVE LEFT:
Havane, in earlier times.
LEFT:
"X" marks the window on the San Juan Co-op from which Havane jumped and was shot.
RIGHT:
Joe Hammond (left), Jackrabbit Soldier, and Bruno Segara.

ABOVE: Gathering up Havane (a staged photo for the newspapers; no one is dead here), Sheriff J. T. Pehrson, on his horse (left); Deputy U.S. Marshall S. H. Gleed Jr. (standing); unidentified man (standing); Frank Adams, on his horse; Henry Ince (standing); and Sheriff Grover Brittain, on his horse, of Dolores, Colorado, considered the best Indian fighter in southern Colorado.

ABOVE: Jackrabbit (left), Norey, Joe Hammond, Jackrabbit Soldier, and Bruno Segara.

Indian Mortally Wounded In Attempting to Escape

(Special to The News.)

Bluff, Feb. 24.—Hovane, who is also known as Joven, one of the five Indians and a Mexican, captured after the fight Sunday morning was shot and mortally wounded last night as he attempted to escape. Four shots were fired and one took effect, passing through his abdomen and perforating his intestines. He was given immediate medical care, but there is little hope of his recovery.

The captives have been kept in the upstairs portion of the San Juan Co-op, which stands in the heart of the town. This large brick building afforded the best place for the keeping of the prisoners and they have been confined there under heavy guard. The Indians have been pleasant but appeared to anticipate something. They are all well known in Bluff every one of them having worked in this place for various people.

Hovane is a large, young Indian and a good worker. He has been about Bluff all his life.

Last night Hovane obtained permission to go outside for a moment. When he was brought back he exclaimed that he was sick. Slipping his handcuffs, he made a break for the door. Instantly four shots rang out in rapid succession. One took effect and Hovane fell to the floor. The Indians fearing that they would also be killed shrieked and the citizens of the town were greatly excited, believing that a general attack was about to be made upon the town.

The attempt to escape is believed to have been planned during the day and Hovane was to receive assistance from either Old Polk's or Old Posey's band, once he had escaped from his guards. As a result the town was strongly patrolled last night.

SAYS PIUTES ARE STILL IN AN UGLY MOOD

SHERIFF J. T. PEHRSON and renegades captured at Bluff. Left to right—Sheriff Pehrson, Norey, Joe Hammond, Jackrabbit, Jackrabbit-Soldier and Bruno Segara.

Ute Uprising 1915 Bluff Utah.

The Indian Rights Association under the direction of M. K. Sniffen published "The Meaning of the Ute 'WAR'" from General Scott's publication. This was very pro-Indian, even to the cost of stretching the truth. In reference to Havane being shot, the Sniffen report stated the following:

They were shackled hand and foot and armed guards placed in charge of them. After the posseman was killed, his friends were eager to "shoot anything that looked like an Indian," and it was not strange to learn that one of the prisoners who "attempted to escape" by jumping from the second-story window was shot.

The prisoners were securely ironed and incapable of doing serious harm to the armed guards, who were fully prepared for any emergency. It is claimed by one of the prisoners, after his release that the guard indulged in the "gentle" pastime of holding guns to their heads and against their bodies, at the same time threatening to shoot.

In view of these circumstances it would seem that the shooting of the prisoner was deliberate act of vengeance, since he readily could have been restrained by physical force.

Laura B. Holderly of the Indian Service visited in Salt Lake with the Indians. They were all confined in one cell in the county jail. Ute Jack, one of the Indians, told Holderly, "White men kill my brother, shoot my little girl. No fresh air or exercise here."

The people at Bluff had reason to be alarmed. While they were aware

Both of these buildings were the scenes of many activities that took place during the 1915 War: Lemuel H. Redd home (above) and the hotel in Bluff (below), 1915.

that the Indians were not blaming them for the attack, it could still set off a general uprising. Aquila Nebeker was making all kinds of warlike sounds, insisting that a troop of U.S. Cavalry be sent in. The posse was apparently filled with a determination to get every Indian in the country.

BLUFF RESIDENTS FEAR NIGHT ATTACK BY PIUTES

People Feel That Posse Under Marshal is in Need of Assistance—Nebeker Wires Department for Twenty Navaho Police to Help Track Renegade Piutes—"My Men Will Take Care of the Fighting." Adds Marshal—Anxiety Felt for Safety of John Tanner, a Cattleman, Supposed to be West of Butler Wash—It is Feared Renegade Utes Will Join Polk and His Band—Situation More Serious.

(Special to The News.)

Bluff, Feb. 24.—A party left here, early this morning to look for John Tanner, a cattleman from this place, who is supposed to be somewhere west of Butler wash. Great anxiety is felt for his safety as he is in the country infested by Old Posey's band. This country takes in a rocky part of this county between Butler wash and Comb wash. Beyond Comb wash the country is more open across the oil field to the Cedar mesa, where it again becomes broken and eroded with many steep canyons, including John's canyon, the Slickhorn, White Horse canyon and others. Large numbers of cattle range from Comb wash west.

Several men went out this morning to fix the telephone line running over Butler wash, Comb wash and the oil fields to Goodrich, at the south end of the oil field. This line is 22 miles long. It was cut some time last night. This is to the west of Bluff.

The situation here is growing more serious and it is feared that a band of renegade Utes from the reservation in Colorado will join Polk and his band, as word comes from there that the Indians believe that the posse has killed 25 squaws and papooses.

PEOPLE FEAR NIGHT ATTACK

There is a strong feeling here that the posse is badly in need of further assistance and that the troops should be called out at once. It will take three days after the troops are called to reach Bluff and in the meantime the citizens are fearful that the Indians will secure reinforcements and make a night attack. Marshal Nebeker has wired the district attorney at Salt Lake and also the United States attorney general at Washington, D. C., stating that he must have at once 20 Navaho Indian police to help track the outlaws.

"My men will take care of the fighting," says the marshal.

J. N. Gingles and a party has just left for White Mesa, near Monticello to meet and escort U. S. Indian Agent L. D. Creel and D. S. Cook, assistant United States district attorney, into Bluff.

General
Hugh L. Scott.

At the office of the Commissioner of Indian Affairs in Washington D.C., with meager reports alarming and getting worse, Land (Secretary of the Interior) and Cato Sells (Commissioner of Indians Affairs) met with General Hugh L. Scott at Fort Myer, Virginia, and asked him to go out to Utah and take care of the situation. Scott had handled a matter on the Navajo reservation with great success only the year before.

He had served on the border of Mexico and was viewed with favor by all the Indians. However, Scott doubted the wisdom of the principal assistant of the Secretary of War for sending him to the sagebrush and snow of Utah at a time when the situation with Germany and England was so tense and Mexico was in an uproar of civil strife.

THE SALT LAKE TRIBUNE, TUESDAY MORNING, FEBRUARY 23, 1915.

SCENES INCIDENT TO THE WAR WITH THE PIUTE INDIANS. (1)—Tse-Na-Gat (Everett Hatch), taken by Mrs. Oren Lewis of Salt Lake, formerly Miss Edith Redd of Bluff. (2)—Band of Piute Indians, "Old Polk," the chieftain, on the extreme right, and his son, Tse-Ne-Gat, at the extreme left. The white man is Jense Nielsen, a resident of Bluff. (3)—The home of L. H. Redd at Bluff and a representative dwelling of the little village. (4)—Members of the Colorado posse now fighting the Indians. Left to right—Jose Cordova, who was wounded. Henry Ince and Sterle Thomas, deputy sheriff and interpreter. (5)—Grover Brittain, sheriff of Dolores county, considered the best Indian fighter in southern Colorado. (6)—Chuck and supply wagons being used by the posse.

RENEGADE INDIANS WAR WITH POSSE

ATTEMPT TO ARREST RED MAN CHARGED WITH MURDER PRE-CIPITATES FIGHT.

One White Man Killed and Another Wounded When Posse Runs Into Ambush, While Five Indians Are Shot Down.

Salt Lake City.—The attempt of a posse headed by United States Marshal Aquila Nebeker to arrest Tse-Na-Gat, a Piute Indian charged with murder, has precipitated a small sized war in southern Utah, which has resulted in the death of at least five of the red men, while one of the posse, J. O. Aiken of Dolores, Colo, has been killed and Jose Cordova, of Cortez, Colo, was seriously wounded. The list of casualties will undoubtedly be greater before the posse has succeeded in capturing the Indian.

The hostilities began Sunday, near Bluff, Utah, when the posse and the Indians engaged in a battle, and has since been continued intermittently.

The posse ran into an ambuscade, and it was then that Aiken and Cordova fell. The Indians were strongly intrenched and the white men were unable to dislodge them.

The scene of the fighting was in Cottonwood gulch, a short distance from the thriving settlement of Bluff. The gulch is a very narrow one, with almost perpendicular sides, and is very easy for the Indians to guard against a superior force.

Tse-Na-Gat killed a Mexican some time ago, but the officers have been unable to apprehend him. They have always believed there would be trouble should an attempt be made to place him under arrest, and this is the reason given for the large force of men who are being sent out after him. His people have taken up his defense, and as a result many more lives may be lost before the present trouble is ended.

A number of the Indians have been captured, and one of them, Havane, was killed while trying to escape from his captors. Havane slipped his shackles and leaped from his bed in the room in which the prisoners were confined, expecting to escape from the window. He had just passed through the window when one of the men on guard fired and the Indian was mortally wounded.

Scouts sent out by Marshal Nebeker Tuesday afternoon to try to locate the Piutes, reported that they had traced them to a point about six miles southwest of town, near Butlers canyon, but lost the trail there. These Indians, believed to be the band headed by Old Posey, evidently left hurriedly Their camp fires were still warm and the bank of the San Juan river was freshly torn up, showing that the Indians had crossed a considerable number of goats and horses. Old Polk's band is believed to be hiding in the rocks close to Bluff

Marshal Nebeker says he is determined that the entire party of hostile Indians, whose strength is estimated at from fifty to 150, shall surrender, now that they have defied the officers, and that all will be prosecuted to the limit.

Thirty-four of the Grayson and Monticello volunteers have joined Marshal Nebeker's posse All maintain that the law and dignity of the states of Utah and Colorado must be upheld

Lake Tribune.

Y, THURSDAY MORNING, MARCH 25, 1915

GENERAL HUGH L. SCOTT and party as they appeared en route to Salt Lake. Left to right, A. B. Apperson, general superintendent D. & R. G.; Indian Agent L. D. Creel, General Scott, U. S. Marshal Aquila Nebeker, Posey's son, Old Posey, Lieutenant Colonel R. E. L. Michie, Tse-Na-Gat (Hatch), Old Polk. Below are General Scott and Colonel Michie as they appeared at Mexican Hat.

ONE WHITE MAN AND TWO INDIANS KILLED

Forces Under Marshal Nebeker Surround Indian Camp Near Bluff and Sharp Engagement Follows in Which J. C. Akin of Dolores, Colo., a White Man, is Killed, Also An Indian Known As "Jack's Brother" and An Indian Girl—Posse Capture Two Indian Warriors—Joseph E. Cordova, of Cortez is Wounded — Several Indians Are Captured—Battle Still in Progress Last Night.

CONDITIONS BETTER AT BLUFF

The following telegram was received at the office of the First Presidency this morning from L. H. Redd, President of the San Juan stake, who spends his time at Grayson and at Bluff.

Grayson, Utah., Feb. 21.—Fight still on between Indians and posse at Bluff. Four additional Indians captured. Twenty-nine men from Monticello leave Grayson at midnight for Bluff to take part. Conditions a little better. Assistance asked for from Shiprock agency. L. H. REDD.

THE SALT LAKE HERALD-REPUBLICAN

Utah's Greatest Newspaper and Advertising Medium

Herald-Republican Want Ads Are the Real Money Makers.

SALT LAKE CITY, UTAH, TUESDAY, FEBRUARY 23, 1915   PRICE FIVE CENTS

INDIANS LOSE FIVE IN BATTLE AT BLUFF; FIVE WHITE MEN CUT OFF FROM COMRADES

TRAP REDS IN CANYON

Believed Decisive Struggle Will Come When They Try to Leave Cottonwood Wash

POSSE GROWING

Sharpshooters on Either Side Keep Up Constant Battle on Outskirts of Bluff While Indians' Main Body Moves Away

BLUFF, Feb. 22.—Scouts reported tonight that at least five Indians have been killed and possibly more have been wounded in the battle on the outskirts of this town between a posse under command of Aquila Nebeker, United States marshal for Utah, and the Indians under Old Polk and his son Tse-Ne-Gat, otherwise known as Everett Hatch. Intermittent firing has been going on all day, sharpshooters on either side being ready to shoot the instant an opponent shows himself.

The whereabouts of the main body of the Indians is not certain. The majority of the posse are of the belief that the red men are caught in a trap in Cottonwood wash, the mouth of which is not far from the borders of Bluff. In that case, it is said, the Indians will not be able to get out except by fighting their way free, and the crucial struggle of Marshal Nebeker's campaign will take place close to Bluff.

On the other hand it is asserted with apparent reason that the Indians have probably taken up a position down the San Juan canyon, three miles from the town, where the natural facilities for defense will make it a difficult task to dislodge them.

Five members of the original posse of twenty-six which came from Colorado have become detached, and their whereabouts is a subject of great anxiety to their comrades. A rescue party today reached the spot where they had been and found the horses, with a note from them pinned on the saddle, to the effect that they had left. Either these men have been captured by the Indians, or are isolated on the sun rocks about two miles from Bluff.

The five men, Mertus Williams, Frank Wheatland, Roy Moore, Dick Lewis and Roscoe Houston, are well supplied with ammunition but have been without food or water since the battle opened early Sunday.

Further efforts to find the men is expected to be made upon the arrival early tomorrow of reenforcements. The fighting is within a half mile of the town, and the workshops, or huts, of Tse-Ne-Gat and his father Old Polk have been burned by the posse. Marcus Jim, an Ute chief, tried to persuade the Polks to surrender "to save the squaws and children," but was met with refusal.

SITUATION IS STILL CRITICAL

With Old Polk and his son still at large and Indians scattered all around here, another pitched battle, worse than the one fought here yesterday, is expected momentarily. The situation is still critical.

One white man, Joe Akin, is dead and another, Jose Cordova, is shot through the lung. Five Indians and a Mexican who has been living with the Indians in their camp here, are prisoners, handcuffed and shackled, and held under guard.

In spite of reenforcements, the posse is in need of all the help it can get, as these Indians are on the warpath and determined to kill all the whites they can before they give up their own lives or liberty.

A troop of twenty-five Indian police from the Navajo reservation at Shiprock, N. M., is on the way here and expected to arrive some time tonight.

POSSE HAS THE ADVANTAGE

In the main the posse has been on the winning side in the fighting so far, but there is not a man who has not had more than a few minutes' sleep since Friday night. The Indians have employed every trick known to them in their wild methods of warfare. Broken up into small groups after their first attack, they have taken refuge in the rocks around here and the posse men have been forced to be on guard every minute.

Five members of the posse, who were cut off from the main body at the outbreak of the battle yesterday morning, have been fighting for their lives and were surrounded by Indians, these men were without food or drink all day Sunday and today. It is believed they have plenty of ammunition, though not enough for any extended engagement.

MEN SURROUNDED MAKE ESCAPE

A posse sent out to rescue these men late this afternoon went to the point where they had been stationed and found it deserted. But the horses of the five were there and one of the saddles was found, a note stating that the men and pack had left. Where they went is not known, but it is presumed they escaped into cover of darkness last night and fled to the cliffs bluffs of the river. Their horses were brought into camp by the searching party.

Fighting has been going on here at intervals for nearly forty-eight hours. The posse is divided up into separate stations at various points around the little town, and whenever an Indian is seen concentrated fire is opened on the position. Thousands of shots have been exchanged in this manner, the Indians replying viciously.

The Indians are as widely scattered as are the members of the posse, but they seem to be well armed and plentifully supplied with ammunition. Their reply in force to every attack and in some instances upon the firing of the posse guards. Fighting was kept up all night and today, but aside from the main engagement yesterday, there has been no pass fighting. The exchanges have been, as described skirmishes between sharpshooters of the two sides.

INDIANS' DEFENSE UNEXPECTED

No attempt is made to deny that the Indians have proved stronger and more defiantly in their attitude from members of the posse thought they had reason to expect. It was believed that after the first fight, the Polks would be agreed to surrender, but they are fighting just as hard tonight as at the first time and although they are not as numerous as at first, are as dangerous and a constant guard is being kept.

(Continued on Page 3.)

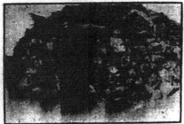

In the center at the top is shown a part of Cottonwood canyon, half a mile northwest of Bluff. In this canyon, it is reported, Tse-Ne-Gat and his father "Old Polk" are trapped. In the lower left hand corner is shown a band of Navajos and Piutes near Bluff, where the battle took place Sunday and yesterday. The picture was taken when the band was assembled for an "Enato" or sacred sing. The Indian at the left is an old Navajo and the Indian at the right is a Piute of types commonly seen at Bluff. Below the Piute is shown Tse-Ne-Gat's brother. In the lower center is shown a family group of Navajo and on the right at the bottom is an Indian hut of the kind inhabited by members of Tse-Ne-Gat's band. The Navajos are for the most part friendly to the whites, and Navajo Indian police were expected to reach Bluff late last night or early this morning to fight on the side of the posse.

DIRIGIBLE DROPS BOMBS IN CALAIS

Five Civilians Killed in Bombardment of French Coast City by Zeppelin.

PARIS, Feb. 22.—The official announcement issued by the French war office tonight tells of the bombardment of Calais by a dirigible airship, which dropped bombs and killed five civilians.

"A Zeppelin bombarded Calais this morning. It dropped ten bombs but which killed five persons belonging to the civil population and caused very unimportant material damage.

"The enemy violently bombarded Reims Sunday night and Monday. The bombardment resulted in considerable damage to the cathedral whose stones represent the full historic value of the last few days.

"In Alsace we have retaken the hamlet of Ammerzwiller on the Dollar heights, which we hold close to the village station yesterday.

"A dispatch says the human names from Calais state that a German dirigible warship dropped a number of bombs over what did straight damage to one of the forts. Bombardment and English railroad lines in the suburbs of the cathedral and train service was interrupted. Two submarines made several dwellings in the suburbs.

"Pcontinued to a mile and a half miles south of St. Omer, which is but twenty miles southwest of Calais."

ALLIES TO UNITE IN REPRISAL MEASURES

LONDON, Feb. 22.—The map of modern warfare, the submarine, the menace of which Germany has declared she will blockade the British isles, daily becomes a factor of more and more importance in the armed war of Europe with regard to its influence on the policies of the nations engaged in connection with the contraband question, as most in neutral states.

Almost coincident with the official reports that Austria proposes to follow the example of her ally by making, as at its purchase slip in the Adriatic, came the announcement by Premier Squith to the British house of commons that she would discussed retaliatory plan at Great Britain, though still speaking was much depends to adopt than had been previously suggested, to that to meet a matter that the consideration of all the allies and that a joint note concerning it might be dispatched from the allies.

The statement was likewise made in the house of commons that the British government might deem it necessary to alter its drastic warship action, up to the present, but not been classed as contraband.

Amsterdam reports that two German submarines are situated on their coast Cuxhaven, but whether they have been lost is not known. Traffic in the North has remained somewhat disorganized and trades and foundations sailors are showing a reluctance to go to sea owing to the menace of both submarines and mines. Beyond from this the Scheldt and England has been temporarily discontinued and not officially confirmed.

The British newspapers print today German views.

IRE OF DUTCH IS FAST RISING

Blockade Protest Unanswered by Germany; Troops Being Assembled on Frontier.

THE HAGUE, Netherlands, Feb. 22.—Ever under order of fearing that two different underwear of fearing may break for the land that a whole class blew in, is aroused by its part uncertainty made by the German warfare attitude of the Netherlands will be its best outcome that three now been affected in at their fate.

In case of their fighting lands, the governmental sense, are to be pointed for the individual causes, while there is seem whether this item is correct.

The clarification is the result of the war and Austria common warning, as it more in the gateway of England. In the western war, Amsterdam a position of its own land, and with the loss of pass of the few yards of commerce. There is lay reports made the naval, clearing the allies emphasizing their gain, and the German newspapers rebuke these commenting on the affair so.

D. & R. G. TRAIN WRECKED

Engineer Killed and Several Persons Injured Near Colorado Springs.

Colorado Springs, Feb. 22.—Engineer Frank Pischenberger of Denver was instantly killed and several others were slightly injured when passenger train No. 4 on the Denver & Rio Grande railroad was derailed this morning near Palmer Lake.

Herald-Republican

DISCUSS NATION'S DEFENSE

Senate Devotes Day to Army Appropriations, While House Continues Debate on Bill Providing for Fortifications.

COMMITTEE INCREASES FUND FOR SUBMARINES

Senator Smoot Favors Making Provision for Fifty Seagoing and Twenty-five Underwater Craft for Coast Defense

AMENDMENT IS REJECTED

WASHINGTON, Feb. 22.—Appropriation for national defense occupied the attention of both houses of Congress today in the general rush to clear up the supply bills for the government before the adjournment. The Senate discussed until late tonight the army appropriation bill, carrying approximately $103,000,000, while the House continued debate on the fortifications bill.

While congress was being made on the three measures, the Senate committee practically completed consideration of the naval appropriation measure and the Senate passed for four minutes to pass without debate the pending bill carrying $164,000,000.

Naval Bill Reported.

At the night session the Senate naval committee submitted its report on the naval bill, carrying a total of $152,363,243.93, an increase over the House bill of $2,112,499.

Increases for submarines and auxiliaries over provisions of the House bill are provided for in the Senate naval committee's amendments, including $5,000,000 for increases constant of $500,000 as authorized in the House bill, provisions for six seagoing submarines instead of two, and sixteen instead of eleven of the smaller type submarines. $500,000 for a production plant, $100,000 for naval reserves, provision for high-power radio station, and $1,850,000 to be applied in continuation of an armor plate factory not to cost to extend $5,000,000, if the estimates of the last board proportionately submitted is to market at a lower price than and provisions also is made for the appropriations of $480,000 for the marine barracks at Norfolk and Mare Island.

Senator Smoot's Proposal.

Senator Smoot would recommend unanimously to speed up fifty seagoing and twenty-five of the smaller craft defense submarines.

"The European war has demonstrated beyond any question," said Senator Smoot in introducing the amendment, "that submarines are invaluable for defense of coast shore and ports. None of the naval defense we may expect. Notwithstanding the progress made by construction in the Senate, there were noticeable under that not all the bills could be passed as we, though we attempted every means to reform the ship yard last night. Several house committees in past very limited in origin no money. I adopt some management of our rivers that in the doing hands of the enemy. So far as the ship bill is apparent, nothing can be let here done by the engaged government."

Loans Reappropriation Postponed.

Consideration postponed a study and completion of two years bill. In saying pending a loan matter of a homestead as provided that there was absence of homesteaders at the organization of the great vote making improved, the adoption of the amended property production and reserves also was adding more a production and a measure of a margin.

State quarrel was the lengthy a result on the fortifications bill the question of any measure.

Representative Mandell of Wisconsin and member of Massachusetts. Smoot is now much more substantive studying preparation.

Superinaturat a Mince of Wisconsin, and Speaker of Massachusetts. Smoot is now much more adequate studying preparation.

IN upper left-hand picture, left to right, are Tse-Na-Gat, Paul S. Randolph, orderly to General Scott; Old Polk; Bob Martin, Navajo Indian interpreter, and Jim Allen, Ute Indian interpreter. Upper right is an Indian pow-wow at Mexican Hat, preceding the surrender. In the lower picture are shown Orderly Randolph holding Helen Spencer, daughter of Indian trader at Mexican Hat, and Chief Bzoshe beside him with three Navajo Indian scouts. At the right, General Hugh L. Scott.

Close to the Abajo (Blue) Mountain, near Monticello, Utah; photo taken on General Scott's trip in 1915.

The San Juan River, just below Mexican Hat, Utah; photo taken on General Scott's trip in 1915.

Aftermath of the 1915 Indian War in Bluff, Utah

ABOVE AND BELOW: Photos of Old Polk's camp, situated by Navajo Twins, Bluff, Utah, 1915.

ABOVE: One of the posse members shows where Joseph Akin was killed near the Lacy property.

BELOW: The posse stayed in this camp near Bluff, Utah, 1915.

Paul S. Randolph (above, top left), orderly to General Scott, sitting next to Chief Bzoshe; three Navajo scouts, with Taiyoonihi (Squeezer) sitting on the front left, also appear below, Mexican Hat, Utah.

When appealed to, Secretary of War Garrison agreed to let Scott go out and settle the Indian revolt in Utah and Colorado, and Scott left on March 8, 1915, for the West. He was held up by storms in Kansas, which upset his schedule, so he took time to stop over in Denver and confer with Colorado U.S. Attorney Harry B. Tedrow. Then Scott changed his destination from Dolores to Thompson, Utah, thinking it might be closer to the scene of action.

Scott had asked before leaving Washington that the old Navajo Bzoshe and his sons meet him at Bluff. Bzoshe was the Indian he had arrested the year before, and Scott felt that the Indian's word would carry weight with the Bronco Indians regarding the treatment they would receive from him.

The first off-railroad stage of General Scott's journey to Bluff was to Moab by car, but the next morning he and his aide, Colonel Michie, and another man, Paul S. Randolph, loaded into the mail buggy with the mail and express for Monticello, Grayson, and Bluff. They rode in this open mail hack until eight o'clock that night, when they arrived at Grayson. The next morning they went on by sleigh in a bitter storm, arriving at Bluff on March 10. The first thing Scott did was insist that Nebeker send the remnants of the posse home.

Aquila Nebeker at Mexican Hat, Utah, 1915.

In a letter to the Attorney General on March 18, 1915, William W. Ray (a government official) wrote:

During the battle on February 22, when Cordova [part of the posse] had been wounded, Dr. John Stavely and Miss Ester Nielson, a trained nurse, cared for him until Nebeker sent for Dr. E. E. Johnson of Cortez, Colorado, who came to Bluff, staying there for a total of twenty-six days, attending to J. R. Cordova and to Havane for the brief period he lived after being shot. Dr. Johnson left his practice and moved to Bluff for this period and was having difficulty collecting his bill, which was $15 per day, plus $2 for his board and room and $10 per day for feeding his team. The bill came to $502, and D. S. Cook, assistant attorney general for Utah, did not think it excessive.

On the ground, General Scott investigated and reported the following:

We reached Bluff on March 10 and learned that the renegades had gone to Navajo Mountain one hundred and twenty-five miles south of Bluff. [Actually, they were far short of this, having stopped on Douglas Mesa.] *We stayed at Bluff and then went on to Mexican Hat. Some friendly Navajos met me at Bluff and went ahead to tell Polk of my coming. Among them was Bzoshe, the old Navajo Chief with whom the government had had so much trouble a year ago and who now is a fast friend. When I asked Bzoshe to go and parley with the Utes, he was very reluctant to do so, saying he was afraid of them. I joshed him about this, and finally he said he would go if I would promise if we were all killed, he could be buried by me.*

Mr. Jenkins, the Indian agent of Navajo Springs, Mr. Creel, Colonel Michie and my orderly [Paul S. Randolph] accompanied me to Mexican Hat. None of us had a gun. The trader's wife was away visiting, and the trader let us stay in his home, while he bunked in the store with the rest of the company.

Ute Indian camp, Bluff, Utah, 1915.

John Wetherill was in the party, while his wife, Louisa, was trying desperately to get some help for the Indians. According to correspondence and telegrams between Mrs. John Wetherill and General Scott, she wired the Indian Department, asking that a return message be sent to her before four o'clock on the 12th, giving Polk his assurance that they would not be hung and what possible sentence they might expect if they surrendered without further fighting. She asked that the wire be sent to her, in care of Peter Paquetee, Fort Defiance, Arizona, via Gallup, New Mexico, and a messenger from Chinley School would deliver it.

Cato Sells wired her that she could advise Polk and his son that they should surrender to General Scott, in whose charge the matter had been placed and who was authorized to promise that they would be taken to a place of safety and given a fair trial and just treatment. Sells then wired Scott about this exchange.

William Posey had long been yearning for a chance to lure the Mericats into the vastness of the San Juan canyons and pick them off, as had happened before. But he wanted a big company of soldiers to make it worth telling about later. This looked like the time.

But Nebeker was dragging his feet, and seemed to be losing his grip. The cavalry and other forces he had bragged about didn't seem to be appearing, which was close to the truth. Nebeker had pretty much reduced his activity to sending out brave-sounding messages to the newspapers instead of slogging around in the cold and mud.

According to a local story circulating at the time, a newspaper correspondent covering the uprising went out with a party of two or three men to repair the telephone line, as he wanted to call in the story of a young Ute woman who had been killed. The men asked if this was true; had someone actually been killed? He admitted that no one had, but if he didn't send in something interesting from time to time, the newspaper would call him in, and he didn't want to go because he was enjoying himself too much.

An example of Nebeker's strategy is surely worth preserving; this was the code he set up to report on so that unauthorized people could not tell what he was saying over the party-line telephone. In a letter to his superiors in Salt Lake City, he said:

Fine is request. Snow means inaction; wind equals Calvary [*sic*] *troop; rain outlawing; hail means detridation* ["detridation" must mean "depredation" in this case]; *fine is subject and hat means secret.*

However, this seems to have been used only once:

Find snow here. Wind to fine such we think most satisfactory means adjustment of the whole situation. Situation involves establishment, two hundred renegade Utes not heretofore subject to Government authority on the Reservation. Above only satisfactory means of accomplishing transaction and terminating system of rain and series of hail to which settlers have always been fine. Sanitary ["salutary" in this context] *effect on sympathizers on Reservation continues. U.S. may avoid further losses in arresting fugitives['] sleet* [secret] *movement* [at] *Hat* [Mexican Hat], *wired Shelton to hold Indians action here. Await your reply.*

(Author's Note: It was said in a number of publications that the 1915 and 1923 Indian wars contained a lot of "yellow journalism," and that they weren't really wars. I beg to differ; the newspapers went with the best information they had at the time, even if it was not accurate. Communications were very limited. With the exception of Monticello, telephones were not installed in other towns (including Bluff and Grayson) in most of the county until the latter part of 1915. The Indians cut the lines during the 1915 and 1923 wars, and Bud Corbin of Midland Telephone had to walk the twenty-two miles to fix them. So before the advent of the telephone, they had to travel to Moab or Cortez to send a message or letter. It was at this point when stories got twisted with facts and hearsay. After looking at the news reports of the day, I don't think most of the newspapers did this on purpose, but maybe there were a couple of them on both sides of the fence with axes to grind. And for those thinking it was not a war—well, people died and lived in fear; all I can say is, the people on both sides sure in hell thought it was a war.)

The Lacy Property, Site of the 1915 War

BELOW:
The Lacy property, looking northeast.

FACING, RIGHT:
Jim Lacy, Dr. Steve Lacy, and Toni Shumway Lacy reenact the early pioneers of the area, 1974; the property is owned by the Lacy family.

FACING, FAR RIGHT:
Claude and Thelma Lacy stand on their property where the 1915 war was fought.

FACING, BELOW:
Looking down from the top of Lacy's Point toward the south; it was a cold snowy day during the 1915 war.

General
Hugh L. Scott.

12

THE SURRENDER

When Polk and William Posey joined forces south of the San Juan River and made their run toward the eminence of Douglas Mesa, perfect for defense, there were a few drawbacks and still some promise of action. Surely the Mericats would follow, and surely the pursuit could be ambushed and wiped out. They had chosen Douglas Mesa in the summer, with the grass for ponies and goats waving high, the shade of pinyons and cedar trees cool, and the many small, clean water tanks full. The trail up was narrow and easy to defend.

This was a different season; snow and rain were slashing over the canyon country as they beat their winter-poor ponies to the top of the mesa, where the miserable animals stood tail to the freezing wind until they fell and died. Some of the Indians then turned back until only a few of the most loyal followers remained with the immediate families of the renegades, to the number of about thirty-five.

They had left without proper clothing, little bedding, less food, and no way to provide shelter. Slogging along through the rain and snow had been bad enough, but the next few days with no place to camp except the snow and mud, no shelter except the brush piles that did little to ward off the cutting winds of daytime, and nothing to shorten the suffering through the long bitter nights, put the whole matter in a different light. Snow was still piled high under every tree, and when it was trampled in the camp, it became ice-crusted slushy mud.

It seemed to the old renegades that the camp was never free of the crying of some child. The squaws were doing the best they could, but still hands and feet were always freezing, and no one was ever dried out from the constant slush and sloppiness. The fun sort of went out of the game.

The situation was as bad as it could get when Bzoshe and his two sons came into camp with a few supplies. The wagon, of course, was not brought to the mesa top, but Bzoshe did bring in a little coffee, bacon, and flour. After cooking and eating at least part of a meal, the Indians were a little more amenable to peace talk. But they still were wary.

At Mexican Hat, Jim Boy, a friendly Paiute, stopped on his way back from a trip to Kayenta for supplies, which looked very meager to feed thirty-five people. General Scott loaded his mule to capacity with blankets and food and sent the message to Polk and Posey that he was waiting at Mexican Hat for them to come in.

Three days later William Posey and four Indians came in to talk to General Scott. Feeling that they would be easier to deal with if fed and rested, Scott sent them word that he was not well and didn't want to talk at length to them that evening. He had a beef killed and gave them flour and coffee from the trading post. This was the first good meal they had had for weeks, and they found it far superior to poor horse meat. He also issued

Old Polk at Mexican Hat, Utah, in 1915, with meat from a beef that General Scott gave him.

more blankets, and they returned to their families, who had followed them from Douglas Mesa and were camped near Mexican Hat, both in Utah.

The next day, March 19, Polk and Tse-ne-gat and about ten others came in to see General Scott, and he asked them to tell him their troubles. Posey came forward as spokesman, "Bad—bad," he started out. "Pony die," and he pointed and then indicated graphically the death of the ponies. "Allatime papoose cry," he rocked the papoose. "Squaw mad," he looked apprehensively over his shoulder as he tiptoes a few steps. "Hand cold." He held them over an imaginary small fire. "Wind make cry," he wiped tears from his cheeks. "Allatime belly heap flat," and he indicated this with proper gestures. "Indians no make war." He folded his arms and stepped back.

General Scott then told them his troubles: He didn't like his Indian friends and wives and children chased all over the mountains by soldiers and cowboys, and he wanted to help them. He didn't push matters but asked them to talk things over and decide what they wanted to do. After a short conference they said they would do anything he wanted them to. He advised them that he wanted Tse-ne-gat, Polk, William Posey, and Jess Posey to go with him to Salt Lake City, and the rest to go back with Agent Jenkins and promise to stay on the reservation.

"Squaws stay camp?" Posey asked.

"Yes," General Scott agreed, "the squaws and children can stay in camp until this is settled."

"Get flour? Get bacon? Get coffee?" Posey said craftily.

"Yes," General Scott laughed, "get food, too."

"Okay," William Posey agreed, and Polk and Tse-ne-gat nodded assent. "We go."

When they had their minds made up, General Scott loaded the four Indians into a wagon, letting the squaws bring up the rear as best they might. The men would have been little use to the families, anyway, as the squaws always did the moving.

It was getting late, and General Scott sent Colonel Michie on ahead to Bluff to make arrangements for his "friends" for the night.

In Bluff, there had been a good deal of amusement about the "armchair experts from Washington" who were going to subdue Posey and Polk. When Colonel Michie asked for a warm room and a hot meal, the men of Bluff were disapproving—didn't he mean a guarded room for prisoners? He insisted that all he

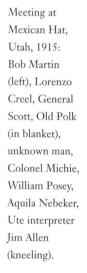

Meeting at Mexican Hat, Utah, 1915: Bob Martin (left), Lorenzo Creel, General Scott, Old Polk (in blanket), unknown man, Colonel Michie, William Posey, Aquila Nebeker, Ute interpreter Jim Allen (kneeling).

needed was a warm room, and this was provided. When the prisoners and Scott arrived, there was a good meal for all of them.

According to General Scott, "These Indians are poor ignorant grown-up children who have had no advantages and no knowledge of our laws and customs. They are victims of mutual misunderstanding between two well meaning races."

Grand Valley Times, Moab, Utah, reported on March 26, 1915, that Old Polk had had a bad cold, so he rode on the mail hack with General Scott and Colonel Michie. William Posey, Jess Posey, and Tse-ne-gat followed on horseback. After staying overnight in Moab, the group went on to Thompson Springs to the railroad, which the Indians viewed with great amazement. After bedding down for the night in the Thompson Hotel, the Indians got up early on Wednesday morning, March 25, 1915, in anticipation of the train ride to Salt Lake City. Apperson, general superintendent of the railroad, sent his royally appointed private car down to transport the prisoners, who were now famous from the nationwide publicity. However, when the train came in, they were wary and waited for Bob Martin, a Navajo interpreter, to board first.

Meetings with Ute leaders in Mexican Hat, Utah, 1915

Helen Spencer with
her parents, 1915.

Grand Junction Daily Sentinel, August 29, 1982

Train Ride to Salt Lake Excited Ute War Leader

By Dr. Steve Lacy

The Utes of western Colorado and eastern Utah had always been warlike people, living by hunting and raiding since they didn't grow much of their own food. As the white man's civilization took root and began spreading through San Juan County and pressure of encroachment built up, the incidents of Indian depredations increased. The Utes felt that anything owned by the white man was fair game.

The murder of a Mexican by a Ute in 1914 triggered the 1915 Indian war. On March 10, 1915, Brig. Gen. Hugh L. Scott, chief of staff of the U.S. army, arrived in Bluff, Utah, to arrest Tse-ne-gat, or Hatch as he is called by the Mormon settlers, for the murder of sheepherder Juan Chacon in 1914.

Unarmed and without the slightest show of strength, he accomplished what had been predicted he could not do—he talked Tse-ne-gat as well as Old Posey, the leader of the band of Indians in the 1915 Indian war; Posey's son, Jess; and Old Polk, Tse-ne-gat's father, into surrendering. Scott told the story this way:

Tse-ne-gat and his father, Old Polk, 1915.

Left, Old Polk, who is held prisoner in Blanding, and Old Posey, leader of the Piute Indian band which is disturbing the San Juan region, and members of which are being trailed into the wilderness by sheriff's posses and citizens under the direction of United States Marshal J. Ray Ward, and for whom federal warrants have been issued. The pictures are from a group of tribesmen and were taken several years ago.

These photos of Old Polk and Tse-ne-gat were taken in 1915 and used in 1923. They identified Tse-ne-gat as William Posey.

"We reached Bluff on March 10 and learned that the Indians had gone to Navajo Mountains, 125 miles southwest of Bluff. We stayed a day in Bluff and then went on to Mexican Hat. Some friendly Navajos met me at Mexican Hat and went ahead of me to tell Poke's band of my comings. Among them was Bzoshe, the old Navajo chief with whom the government had so much trouble with a year ago and who is now our fast friend. I had sent for him to meet me at Bluff. Mr. Jenkins, Indian agent at Navajo Springs, Mr. Creel, Col. Michie and my orderly accompanied me to Mexican Hat. None of us had a gun.

"Jim Boy, a friendly Paiute, was sent out to tell the other Paiutes that I wanted to see them. Some of them came near where I was camped but it wasn't until the third day that anyone dared to come to the camp. Posey and four other Indians then came in. We talked a little through a Navajo interpreter. It was in the evening, and I just asked them how they were. I told them I did not feel very well and did not want to talk to them until the next day. They helped us kill a beef and we gave them a good meal, the first they had in weeks. We also gave them some blankets. Posey and his men didn't have any weapons, but I have reason to suspect that they had hidden them nearby.

"The next day Poke and Hatch and about 25 others came to see me. I asked them to tell me their troubles. I said that I didn't think they would like to have their children chased by soldiers and cowboys all over the mountains and killed and that I wanted to help them. I didn't try to push the matter with them but asked them what they wanted to do. After they had talked among themselves, they said they would do anything I wanted them to do."

The four surrendering Indians were as excited as little kids on Christmas morning when they heard they would be making the trip from Thompson Springs, now known as Thompson, Utah, to Salt Lake City aboard the train.

After they arrived in Moab, Utah, on horseback, they rested at the home of Mrs. Garrity. Scott and his prisoners caused a sensation in Moab, where they remained until the next afternoon. A band of reporters and spectators came to watch the sideshow affair.

The Indians consented to pose for pictures, especially when they were given a few packages of cigarettes and a .50 cent piece. The Indians gazed with amazement at the wagon without horse or mules that had arrived to take them to Thompson. The evening soon set in, and the party bedded down in the Thompson Hotel.

The Momentous Trip to Salt Lake City, 1915

Stopping in Moab

ABOVE:
Thompson Hotel, Thompson, Utah.

RIGHT:
Bob Martin (left), William Posey, Jess Posey, Tse-ne-gat, and Old Polk in Moab, Utah, 1915.

FIFTEEN CENTS
MURAD
TURKISH CIGARETTES
S. ANARGYROS

SALT LAKE CITY, UTAH, SATURDAY, MARCH 6, 1915

SHERIFF PEHRSON OF SAN JUAN BRINGS PRISONERS OF POSSE TO SALT LAKE TO BE HELD FOR FEDERAL JURY

SHERIFF PEHRSON and his captives snapped on their arrival yesterday in Salt Lake; left to right, Sheriff Pehrson, Noland, Joe Hammond, Jack, Jack Rabbit, Soldier, Bruno Seguro (Mexican) and Lucian H. Smyth, deputy United States marshal. The four Indians and the Mexican were captured by the posse following the fight in Cow canyon a week ago Sunday.

Snapshots Taken at Moab During Indian Excitement in San Juan

Above is the sign posted at the postoffice in Moab on February 24, and General Hugh L. Scott; below, reading from left to right: Old Posey, Tse-Na-Gat (Everett Hatch), Posey's Boy and Old Polk. These pictures of General Scott and the Indians were taken in Moab Monday of last week, when the party passed through en route to Salt Lake.

PHOTOGRAPH of Indians taken at county jail yesterday. The men in front are: L. D. Creel, agent in Utah for scattered bands of Indians, Posey and United States Marshal Aquila Nebeker; behind Mr. Creel and Old Posey are Bob Martin, interpreter, Tse-Ne-Gat and Old Polk, father of Tse-Ne-Gat. General Scott is the man with the cap, standing on the top step, and at the extreme right is Posey's boy.

William Posey (left),
Elaine Garrity, Mrs.
Martin, and Polk,
March 24, 1915.

Tse-ne-gat
and Jess Posey

The Momentous Trip to
Salt Lake City, 1915

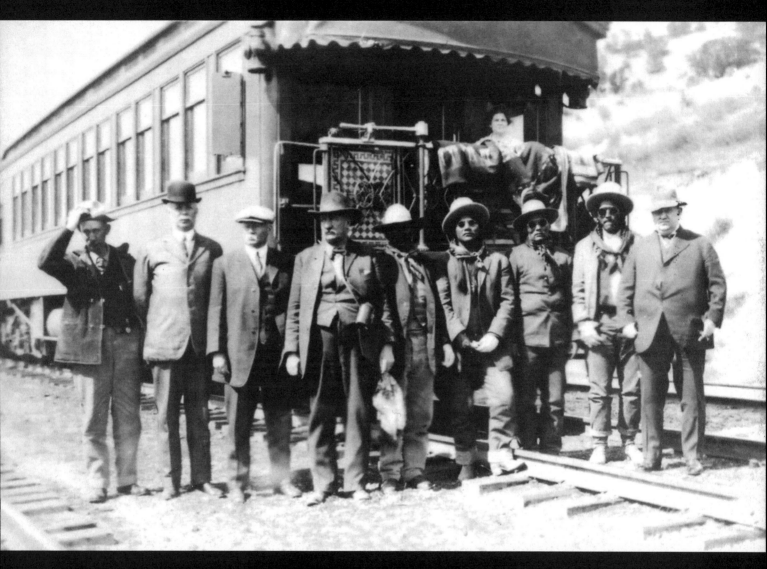

FACING, TOP:

Bob Martin (left), William Posey, Aquila Nebeker, Jess Posey,
Tse-ne-gat, Polk, and Lorenzo Creel.

FACING, FAR LEFT:

General Scott and Lorenzo Creel.

FACING, LEFT:

Reporters scramble for a news story in Moab.

ABOVE:

Lorenzo Creel, guide (left), Colonel Michie, General Scott,
Aquila Nebeker (with camera), Polk, Jess Posey, William Posey,
Tse-ne-gat, A. B. Apperson (superintendent of D&RG Railroad;
Mrs. Martin is standing on the train.

Train Ride to Salt Lake Excited Ute War Leader

(cont'd)

The Indians got up early Wednesday morning March 24, 1915, in anticipation of the train ride, but when it arrived the four Indians were a bit timid about boarding. Bob Martin, a Navajo Interpreter who trained at the military academy in Hampton, Virginia, served as guide and was the first on board. Posey finally mustered up enough courage to get on and the others followed suit. The Indians were standing on the back platform of the train car when it started to pull out and had gone a few hundred feet when Posey's hat blew off and skidded along the cinders by the tracks. Scott had the train stop, back up, and waited while Posey clambered down to retrieve his hat.

A big surprise came to them when they had breakfast on the diner. They had never dreamed that they could eat in comfort and luxury while moving at such speed. They enjoyed the huge steaks, which Martin ordered for them, a treat they had never had before.

After breakfast, they were taken to the smoking compartment, where they had their cigarettes. There another treat greeted them. Their eyes were wide open as a passenger was washing his hands and face. The water taps were a great source of curiosity. They were all excited and eager to try the new device. Somehow they did not think they could get the fun of seeing it work without having to wash. One by one they proceeded to remove their coats and wash. As soon as they got through, they repeated the operation. The lavatory soon was becoming a pool from all of the splashing the Indians were doing. They were then escorted to the private car of A. B. Apperson, general superintendent of the railroad. Apperson presented each with a cigar. Although the Indians had smoked cigarettes for years, this was the first time they had tried cigars.

The Indians puffed the big cigars with great delight as was shown by their broad grins. As soon as they finished them, Posey made it known that they wouldn't be offended if the treat was repeated.

All day long, the Indians smoked cigars, which Apperson supplied. He carried only the finest 25 cent cigars, and during the course of the day, the Indians each smoked about $2 worth of cigars. Apperson commented to Scott that if he entertained Indians again on his private car, he would have a box of the nickel variety on hand.

The Indians sat on lavish chairs at the rear of the veranda of the private car, while Martin pointed out places of interest. The Indians were a little afraid of the tunnels at first, but finally got used to them.

Posey's Boy (Jesse) was a picture of terror when a passing train tooted its whistle. He started to climb over the others to escape this new source of fright.

At 2:40 p.m., the train eased into the station in Salt Lake City to meet a crowd of 5,000 curious people, all anxious to get a look at the Indians.

The Indians were taken to the county jail, where they found four Indian prisoners who had been brought from Bluff a month earlier. After a few days, Tse-ne-gat was taken out and sent to Denver for trial where he was acquitted. The remaining Indians, Joe Hammond, Ute Jack, Noland May, Jack Rabbit Soldier, Old Polk, Jesse Posey son of Wm. Posey and Wm. Posey were told to go back to the reservation after they placed their thumbprints on a paper saying they would be good Indians. They were then released to the custody of agents Creel and Jenkins.

For the next two days, the Indians were given the grand tour of Salt Lake. They were taken on rides in electric cars and automobiles. Lights were explained to them and they were taught about telephones. All the witchcraft of civilization was displayed to their wondering eyes. They were even taken to the movies where ghosts of men and women walked before them with realism of life.

Mrs. Laura B. Holderly, Attorney Cook's secretary, took the Utes in hand and showed them everything she could think of; they were taken to the top of the Walker Bank Building on Main Street and gazed at the small people below. They went to Fort Douglas where they were shown a cannon and machine gun in action. To the new Capitol Building and all the glittering tinsel of the big city, leaving them dazzled with these wonders, and convinced that they were invincible and very much the conquering heroes.

The Indians went back home, but trouble broke out again in 1923, ending that year when Old Wm. Posey led what was to be called "The Last Indian War in America."

The Utes rode
this train through
Castle Gate, Utah.

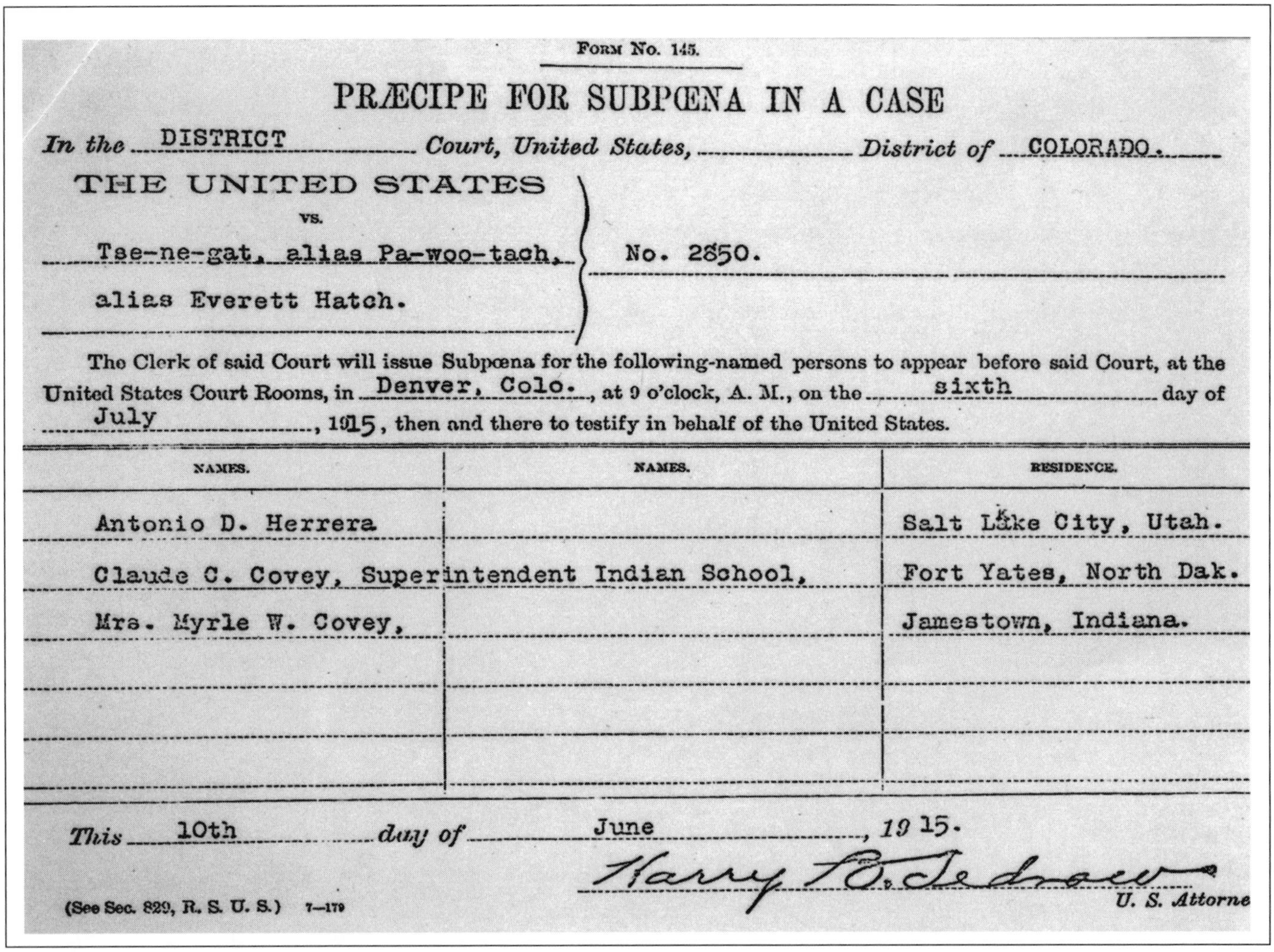

FORM No. 145.

PRÆCIPE FOR SUBPŒNA IN A CASE

In the _____DISTRICT_____ Court, United States, _____ District of _____COLORADO._____

THE UNITED STATES

vs.

Tse-ne-gat, alias Pa-woo-tach,   No. 2850.

alias Everett Hatch.

The Clerk of said Court will issue Subpœna for the following-named persons to appear before said Court, at the United States Court Rooms, in _____Denver, Colo._____, at 9 o'clock, A. M., on the_____ sixth _____day of _____July_____, 1915, then and there to testify in behalf of the United States.

NAMES.	NAMES.	RESIDENCE.
Antonio D. Herrera		Salt Lake City, Utah.
Claude C. Covey, Superintendent Indian School,		Fort Yates, North Dak.
Mrs. Myrle W. Covey,		Jamestown, Indiana.

This _____10th_____ day of _____June_____, 1915.

Harry B. Tedrow

U. S. Attorney

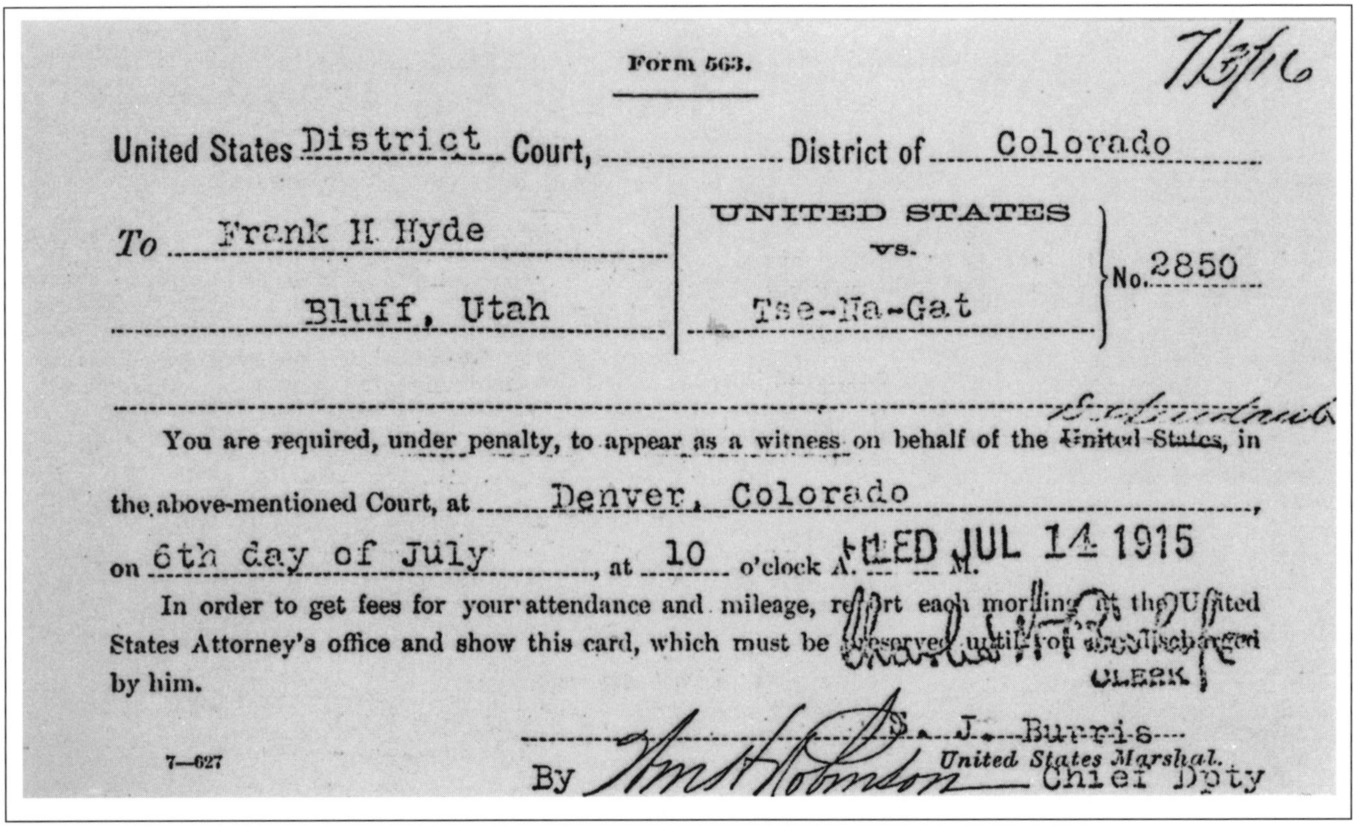

Form 563.

7/13/16

United States _____District_____ Court, _____ District of _____Colorado_____

To _____Frank H. Hyde_____

Bluff, Utah

UNITED STATES

vs.

Tse-Na-Gat   No. 2850

You are required, under penalty, to appear as a witness on behalf of the United States, in the above-mentioned Court, at _____Denver, Colorado_____,

on 6th day of July, at 10 o'clock A. M.   FILED JUL 14 1915

In order to get fees for your attendance and mileage, report each morning at the United States Attorney's office and show this card, which must be preserved until you are discharged by him.

CLERK

_____A. J. Burris_____

United States Marshal.

By _____Wm H Robinson_____   Chief Dpty

7—627

At the end of the affair, the state and army dignitaries hosted a dinner at the Bonneville Club in Salt Lake City for General Scott, where he paid tribute to the courage and honor of the Indian prisoners. The next morning he met with U.S. District Attorney to find out the gravity of the charges against William Posey, Jess Posey, and Polk.

Tse-ne-gat would have to stand trial for the murder of Juan Chacon, but there was some doubt of the legality of holding the other three, as well as the four already in jail. General Scott had given his word that he would see they got a fair trial, and he meant to settle the matter before returning to Washington. He told the district attorney that the Indians had murdered a man and had resisted arrest. General Scott asked if the raiding party had identified themselves as officers, and when the reluctant answer was in the negative, he went on to ask: "Did the posse wear uniforms so that they could be identified as marshals and not a mob?"

"Well, no."

"Then," General Scott pointed out, "where is your case?"

"I guess we haven't got one," the district attorney admitted. While the judges were making up their minds what to do with Polk, William Posey, and Jess Posey, who had been put in the same cell with the Indians who had given themselves up earlier at Bluff, Mrs. Parenthia (Feenie) Dalley came to see Posey and renew her acquaintance with him. She had remarried after leaving the Rincon Trading Post following the killing of her husband, Amasa Barton, and had moved to Salt Lake City, where she had become a person of importance. Remembering Posey's help in her time of need, Feenie made a stand for the Utes to the officials, and in a few days got the charges removed.

On April 10, Polk, Posey, Jess Posey, Jack Ute, Jack Rabbit, Noland May, and Joe Hammond were brought before Assistant District Attorney General Charles Warren and signed a statement of intention by affixing their thumbprints. They agreed that they were lawfully in custody and that they were Indians of the Ute Mountain Indian Reservation, and they agreed to the following:

1. To return immediately to the reservation.
2. To stay there with their families.
3. Not to leave without permission from the Agent.
4. To aid and assist by labor or otherwise in making improvements upon the reservation.
5. To care for stock and property and to be frugal, industrious, and honest.
6. To send their children to school.
7. To desist from the practice of carrying arms, and to be subject to all of the regulations of the reservation.
8. To submit peaceably to all the proper writs and processes of the courts and generally to abide by, support, and assist in the enforcement of the laws and regulations under which we live.

This applied to all the prisoners except Tse-ne-gat (also known as Everett Hatch), who was still under indictment for the killing of Juan Chacon. He was remanded to the custody of the Colorado officials.

The seven Utes and Paiutes were then sent back to Bluff, where they never did go to the reservation but took up life very much where it had been interrupted some two months earlier. However, spring had finally come, and things looked much brighter. William Posey decided that he was invulnerable, and often said, "Me like Jes' Chris—white man's bullets no kill me!" But Jess would reply to this, "He crazy!"

At the federal courthouse in Denver, Tse-ne-gat was told to explain what happened on the day of the murder. Some of his testimony in court is as follows; his voice was almost inaudible because of the

United States __District__ Court

__District of__ Colorado

May ___ Term, 19 15.

THE UNITED STATES
VS.
Tse-ne-gat, alias,
etc.
}

No. 2850.

PRÆCIPE

For Subpœna on the part of the United States for

Witness.

Filed this ___ day of ___ , 19 ___

FILED JUN ___ 915

_____ , Clerk.
CLERK

Issued _____ , 19 ___

7—179

tuberculosis in his lungs, but he still was able to relay his answers through the interpreters:

Avery, who was for the Defense asked, "Did you kill Juan Chacon?"

Tse-ne-gat answered, "No, I could not kill my friend. I had known him for five years."

Avery asked, "Didn't Chacon accept the hospitality of your tepee two nights previous to the killing?"

"Yes, Juan stayed all night with Chatta (Tse-ne-gat's wife) and me and had breakfast with us. He often visited me," Tse-ne-gat replied.

"Did you visit Chacon's sheep camp the night before he was killed?" Avery asked.

Tse-ne-gat said, "Yes, I visited him then. He told me that if I would visit him he would give me some sheep meat. While I was there, Juan's boss, Mister Duncan, wanted to give me a mule in trade for my gray horse, but I did not trade."

Avery questioned, "Did you and Chacon and Sam Ramon gamble during your visit at his camp?"

"No, I said to Juan, 'Let us gamble.' He said, 'No I do not want to gamble. I must take my money home to my wife.' So we did not gamble." Tse-ne-gat answered.

"What happened then?" Avery inquired.

"I left Juan's sheep camp and went to the tepee of A-na-pu-get, also called Old Sam. He accused me of stealing a horse from him, but I convinced him he was wrong and he was my friend and we ate crackers and canned peaches together," said Tse-ne-gat.

Avery explained, "*The Crackers and Peaches testimony*, while not an actual alibi, tended to show, the defendant was too far away to have reached the scene of the crime at the time Chacon was killed."

Tse-ne-gat went on to say, "That night there was to be a Spirit Dance, or Dance to Gawd, near Sam's place, and that's why I changed from boots to moccasins and went to the dance and danced all night. I met John Miller and Little Tom there and they said nothing about the killing of Juan Chacon. Two days later I returned to the agency for the Bear Dance. I remained there and danced for three days."

"What was the color of the horse you were riding?" asked Avery.

Tse-ne-gat's black eyes swept the courtroom and finally he pointed to the gray necktie of a juror.

He spent nearly six hours on the stand; one thing he forcefully said was, "My name not Tse-ne-gat, my name Tse-quit, "Man who never cried."

What's in a Name?

Tse-ne-gat—Pah-woo-tach—Tse-quit—Everett Hatch

Tse-ne-gat got his name quite by accident; when he had just learned how to walk, he stumbled into a campfire and began to cry after burning his hip. Old Polk showed no compassion and kept calling him crybaby. His mother, Etta, smeared deer fat on his burn and gave him the fruit of the yucca plant to suck on. His father thereafter called him Tse-ne-gat, "One who cries."

Tse-ne-gat was listed on the rolls of the Indian agency in four different ways, including Pah-woo-tach (meaning "No Paiutes") and Everett Hatch; the name he had chosen for himself was Tse-quit (meaning "Man who never cries").

The name Tse-ne-gat is spelled three different ways, Tse-ne-gat, Tse-na-gat, and Tse-Nat-Gat and they are all correct. Since he couldn't read or write, he didn't know how to spell it and relied on other people to write it down. All three names are used in this book.

Billy Sunday

As Tse-ne-gat's trial was going on, his wife Chatta gave birth to a boy, and she made a cradleboard of yellow buckskin with lots of fancy beadwork on it. (Author's Note: Had Chatta had a girl, the cradleboard would have been made of white buckskin.)

While Tse-ne-gat was in Denver, he was taken to see famed evangelist Billy Sunday. He was so impressed with him that afterwards he planned to name his son Billy Sunday because he said, "No smoke, no cuss, and no drink fire water." When he got home after the trial, his wife, Chatta, objected to the name, and on the official rolls of the tribe he was listed as Everett Hatch Jr.

The Attorney General, July 15, 1915
Washington, D.C.

Sir:

United States v. Everett Hatch, the Ute Indian.

On May 6, 1915, upon my return from a visit to the reservation, I wrote you, among other things, about Mr. Jenkins. On May 19 you advised me that you had called the attention of the Secretary of the Interior personally to some of the matters in my letter of May 6. I find that the Commissioner of Indian affairs sent to Mr. Jenkins, under date of May 29, a letter, a copy of which I enclose you herewith; that Mr. Jenkins received this letter, a copy of which I also enclose you.

One of the three Indians who came upon Hatch as he was dragging the Mexican's body to the arroyo is Harry Tom. The other day shortly before Harry Tom was to go upon the witness stand here in Denver, and while he and other Indians were waiting in my outer office for consultation, Harry Tom was called for by Agent Jenkins and taken away. As it subsequently developed, he was taken to the office of Mr. Avery, one of the attorneys for the defense. I did not know what took place in Mr. Avery's office, but before Harry Tom went upon the stand, he told me that prior to coming to Denver he had been offered money by Antonio Buck, the Indian interpreter acting for the defense, if he would change his story, but that he proposed to adhere to the truth, as he had always given it. Just before he was sworn an ostentatious display was made before the jury by opposing counsel in calling loudly for Mr. Jenkins to come in and sit down, and also in requesting the judge to expressly caution this witness as to the pains and penalties of perjury. The court thereupon allowed the opposing counsel to interrogate Harry Tom as to his acquaintance with the sanctity of the oath, etc., and among the questions propounded at this time as I recall it was this: "Did not Agent Jenkins tell you that you would be put in jail unless you told the truth?" In spite of this plain attempt at intimidation, following what had preceded, Harry Tom upon direct examination told his story exactly as he had always told it, and in substance the same as testified by the other two witnesses, Little Tom and John Miller, who with him had come upon Hatch at the time of the murder, and who had preceded him on the stand. Under cross examination of Harry Tom it then developed and he admitted, that at the Navajo Springs Agency in May, after my visit there and during the visit of Avery, he said that the story originally told by these three Indians and adhered to at that time was untrue; that when he was taken from my office by Jenkins under the circumstances narrated, he had again said that that story was untrue. When opposing counsel inquired of him why on direct examination he had returned to his original story he said that he was in court now and proposed to tell the truth; that the different story was told Mr. Avery because he was not then in court, and among other things, he had been offered money by Antonio Buck. On repeated cross examination the money episode was rather discredited, and the poor Indian became confused and it is perhaps doubtful what he was trying to say. In closed [sic] find a transcript of the cross-examination of Tom. Allowance must be made for the great difficulties of interpreting the questions and particularly those of cross-examination. The interpreter was not a very good one. From the cross-examination enclosed some idea may be reached as to whether third degree methods were used upon Harry Tom, and whether Mr. Jenkins was a party to it. Mr. Jenkins admitted on the stand that he knew about this supposed change of story on June 5, when he wrote to the Commissioner that he had "given the prosecuting officers all the information in my possession regarding the case." The explanation made for this untruth to the Commissioner was that the information he possessed on this point was confidential. Whether he was actually a party to the attempt to corrupt this witness at Navajo Springs does not yet appear, but it was plainly elicited in evidence that he was a party to the affair that occurred in the attorney's office. The admission by Harry Tom that he had told a different story at another time was the hardest blow the prosecution received.

On June 6, 1915, the day following the letter to the Commissioner, Mr. Jenkins went out to the scene of the crime, accompanied by the post trader, Frank Noland. They testified a rifle was then fired from the point the three Indians said they heard the shots, and another from the scene of the murder, and that sounds could not be heard over the distance.

The foregoing seemed to me to be the limit of activity against the Government on the part of a Government official, but I was to discover that I did not know where the limit was, for, to my amazement, Mr. Jenkins not only testified about the firing of the guns and the change of story of Harry Tom, but qualified himself and testified that the reputation for truth and veracity of our principal Indian witnesses, upon whose statements the Indian Service presented the case originally to the Department of Justice for prosecution, was bad, and that the character of the band of Indians to which they belonged [Mariano's band] was bad and that band hostile to the band of renegades to which Hatch and his father, Old Polk, belonged. Mr. Jenkins said his predecessor, Mr. Covey, and others had told him of the bad character of these Indians. Fortunately, I had Mr. Covey at hand, and Mr. Covey being put upon the stand did not corroborate Mr. Jenkins on this point.

Frank Hyde Trading Post in early Bluff, Utah.

Fortunately, also, I had three old time white residents of the region who testified to the splendid character of these Indians and that no such feud has existed, and who tell me privately that these Indian witnesses for the Government are men of good character and entirely credible. [Author's Note: During the trial, three residents of Bluff appeared as character witnesses: Frank H. Hyde, Frank H. Karnell, and James B. Douglas.]

To have the Indian agent on the stand for the defense at all was bad enough, but to have him go on and attempt to impeach the very witnesses on whom I most depended was extremely embarrassing. I met the situation upon the instant in the best way I could, which was to attempt to show by cross-examining Mr. Jenkins that he had promised immunity to Old Polk and his band, was attempting to deliver the goods; that he himself is afraid to go back to the agency under the terror that exists there unless he takes Everett Hatch back with him. Upon second thought I am deposed to believe that the explanation of Mr. Jenkins' conduct, seized upon in a desperate extremity is not very far from the truth; that at Salt Lake City when Polk, Posey, et al., were released and Everett Hatch brought to Denver, Mr. Jenkins presumed to improve upon the Department of Justice by assuring these Indians that the whole thing in Denver was to be simply a white wash, or expressed his belief in Hatch's innocence, and that the Polk renegades are looking to him to make good. Among other witnesses who were subpoenaed at the request of the defense was Old Polk, but he refused to come, and, presumably, is waiting to see what the outcome of this trial is to determine his future course.

During the course of the trial Mr. Jenkins openly aided the defense and sat at the table with the defendant and in consultation with him and his attorneys.

When Mr. Jenkins was subpoenaed to appear as a witness, I requested him to bring with him the complete correspondence of the Agency on this case.

I desired it for a particular purpose, viz., to get certain letters and petitions that went in from Bluff, Utah, signed by residents there, in order to use them in cross-examination of witnesses who were to go upon the stand and testify as to Hatch's good character. Mr. Jenkins brought me, upon his arrival in Denver, what purported to be the complete correspondence when I went over it. I found it was not the complete correspondence, because I had made a list of this correspondence when I was at the reservation in April. I immediately made formal request upon him to produce the missing correspondence, but have not yet received it. Had I had it, I might have made great headway against these character witnesses, although I cannot say definitely upon that point until I see the missing correspondence.

I enclose you herewith a transcript of the evidence of Mr. Jenkins, and your own judgment will dictate what course, if any, should be taken under the circumstances. I am particularly anxious to avoid anything that might appear to be a feeling of chagrin at the outcome, if it be unfavorable, or of being led to a spiteful attack upon Mr. Jenkins because of disappointment. This letter is hurriedly written at the end of a fatiguing trial and before the jury has returned its verdict. I have not wanted to do Mr. Jenkins any injustice and when I wrote you on May 6, I refrained from expressing as a conclusion the fears I then entertained, but subsequent events have more than justified my misgivings. Had Mr. Jenkins complied with the Commissioner's instructions of May 29, a trial which has cost the Government up wards of $5000 might have a different termination than it may now have.

Very respectfully,

Harry B. Tedrow
United States Attorney

During the trial in Denver, a medical examination of Tse-ne-gat revealed he had tuberculosis so he was moved from the federal wing of the Denver County Jail to St. Anthony's Hospital.

To Mr. Burris
United States Marshall
Denver, Colorado

Dear Sir:

In accordance with your request, I have to-day examined one Everett Hatch, a Ute Indian, and now in confinement at St. Anthony's Hospital, Denver, relative to the state of his health, particularly as regards pulmonary or cervical tuberculosis.

I found Mr. Hatch a rather good looking, well formed well nourished Indian, of medium height, apparently well muscled, with the typical dusky, copper hued skin of his race: hair in two long, black braids, face beardless.

Stripped to the waist, on inspection I noted many cicatricial, healed scars, both front and back of the chest; evidencing some former and quite severe attack of acne bulgaris; there were still present an occasional pustule to be noted. . . .

The examination of the lungs by percussion showed a marked change from the normal over the right; there is a considerable degree of dullness at the apex, clearing somewhat over the middle lobe, to again become intense over the lower lobe. The stethoscope revealed a number of muco-purulent rales, clearly heard at the apex of the right lung, but gradually disappearing toward the base; these sounds are also heard at the apex posteriorly.

At the base of the right lung the breath sounds are not clearly heard, and this may be in part due some thickening of the pleural wall, or to the tuberculous-invasion, inflammatory in character.

The left lung is involved but slightly, and while the breath sounds are not normal. . . .

Mr. Hatch coughs some, but mostly at night, according to Mr. Reed his guard. The latter informed me that the first night spent at St. Anthony's Mr. Hatch coughed most of the night, but the last few nights he has been much more free from the annoyance. The change from the city jail to the hospital has improved him already, and while I am of the opinion that the tuberculosis condition pre-existed his incarceration in the jail a good many months. . . . In as much as the place is well away from the city, and prac-tically in the country, Mr. Hatch can be out in the open practically all the time. . . .

I would further recommend, in the event of Mr. Hatch being detailed under your super-vision, the removal of the diseased tonsils, inasmuch as they are doubtless contributing factors in glandular involvement, it is not the exciting cause. If Mr. Hatch is returned to his reservation, and is under competent medical care there it is probable that he can by careful living over come the present extent of the lung involvement; however, he will need to be kept under fairly close observation, and more or less under constant treatment if he is to survive the malady. Statistically, from the racial stand point he is doomed to die in five years; but this is not necessary if he is given right care and attention.

St. Anthony's Hospital, Denver, Colorado.

Very respectfully yours,

Orville D. Wescott

Tse-ne-gat's parents had ridden to Durango to catch a train to join him at the last minute. When Old Polk reported that he was "Sick in belly, medicine man fixum," Etta (Tse-ne-gat's mother) left him there and traveled with her cousin to Denver.

The first night at the hospital, Etta wouldn't sleep on a bed and rolled her bed on the gravel driveway. After much pleading she was convinced to use a bed but would only sleep on top of the bedding rolled into her own blanket. She would not take a bath.

Tse-ne-gat was told he needed to stop smoking; he normally chained-smoked when he had them. His mother caught him while he was in the hospital and grabbed the cigarette from his mouth and said, "No smokum, you smokum you die, you son-bitch."

At his trial, Tse-ne-gat's mother was known as "Old Ma Polk." She wore her gray-streaked hair in a bob, which was called a Castle Clip; wore Navajo bracelets along with rings on most of her fingers; and had a blanket with a row of safety pins draped around her middle. In one hand, she had a brown sack filled with food and candy, and in the other, she waved a tiny American flag. During the trial, she squatted on the floor beside Tse-ne-gat's chair and smoked. While they were selecting a jury, she said, "Heap tired," and went to sleep.

SQUAW ATTENDS TRIAL OF SON

Brother Indian Testifies He Saw Tse-Ne-Gat Dragging Herder's Body.

Denver, Colo., July 7.—The introduction of evidence by which the United States government is seeking to convict Tse-Ne-Gat, a Piute Indian, of the murder of Juan Chacon, a sheepherder, in western Colorado in March, 1914, was begun in federal district court here today following the completion of the jury.

While the trial proceeded today, "Ma" Polk, mother of the defendant, crouched in her chair fumbling with trinkets about her neck and on her arms. Sisters at St. Anthony's hospital, where "Ma" Polk is quartered, stated that she had explained that they were charms that would prevent any ill from befalling her son.

Mrs. Nievecitas Chacon, widow of the herder, was in court.

A sturdy roan horse, money and a quantity of gaudy Navajo jewelry constituted the motive for the crime; District Attorney Tedrow declared in his opening statement. He declared it would be proven that Tse-Ne-Gat followed Chacon when the latter left a sheep camp in southwestern Colorado. Later, he declared, the defendant was seen dragging the herder's body, which he threw in a ravine. Tse-Ne-Gat, he said, it would be proven, later, appeared at Navajo Springs with a roan horse and spent money freely.

John Miller, a Piute Indian, testified that he and two others saw Tse-Ne-Gat dragging a body at the end of a lariat and saw him dump the body into a ravine. When discovered, he said, it was found that the body had been decapitated.

On cross-examination he said he had not reported the matter at first because he feared Tse-Ne-Gat and his father "Old Polk." Questioned further, he added that the Indian agent was away at the time.

Coroner G. M. Dufall of Montezuma county, testified that the body of Chacon was not mutilated when he received it.

When "Old Sam" began his story, the attention of spectators was directed to "Ma Old Polk," mother of Tse-Ne-Gat, who broke into a fit of uncontrollable laughter. A bailiff had been directed to ask her to remain quiet, when the interpreter began a translation of "Old Sam's" version of the feast. A wave of laughter then swept over the courtroom, in which Judge Lewis, himself, joined.

Tse-Ne-Gat, the witness said, told him that he had received money and the food at the agency at Navajo Springs.

Harry Tom, another Piute, testifying for the government today, corroborated previous testimony by John Miller and Little Tom, to the effect that they had seen the defendant dragging the body of the herder and later saw him throw it into a ravine. The witness declared further that he had been offered money to testify for the defense by Antonio Buck, a son of a Piute chief, but on cross-examination he swore positively that this was not true and that he had "made crooked talk" to the federal district attorney.

Old Ma Polk in later years.

Tse-ne-gat Charms Denver

When Tse-ne-gat was taken from southern Utah to Salt Lake and then to Denver, he was wearing some almost-worn-out high-heeled cowboy boots that hurt his feet while walking on the concrete sidewalks and city pavements. He asked if he could get a pair of moccasins. The hospital bought a pair that he soon found out were for tourists, so they didn't wear right. He then had word sent to his wife to make him a pair of moccasins out of deerskin and Ute beads.

Tse-ne-gat was allowed to make a flute from a willow branch and played to some of the female nurses; what they didn't know was the flute was only supposed to be played when a young Indian boy was courting a wife.

He got his first and probably only ride on a motorcycle from a Denver newspaper reporter. His comments on the ride were, "Chug horse go like hell, buck like hell, bump wind out of Tse-ne-gat." He also posed in the driver's seat of a number of cars.

Tse-ne-gat had four offers of marriage from white high society; one woman wrote that after seeing newspaper photos of him she fell in love with him and would pay for his expenses to Chicago to get married.

While in the hospital, he learned to play baseball. He also received offers of employment from a motion picture company and a circus if he was acquitted.

Tse-ne-gat in the driver's seat.

Meeting with Governor Mabey of Utah, 1921

Preparing to travel to the Natural Bridges with Governor Mabey to meet with Indians;
photo taken in front of Grayson Co-op, later known as Parley Redd Merc., 1921.

FACING, BELOW FAR LEFT
Ute Indians crossing Natural Bridge, 1921.

FACING, BELOW LEFT
Tse-ne-gat (standing) with Jess Posey in Hammond Canyon, 1921.

BELOW:
Governor Charles R. Mabey and Tse-ne-gat, 1921.

BELOW, RIGHT:
Tse-ne-gat (middle), Kumen Jones (with beard), and Governor Charles R. Mabey (right),
at Hammond Canyon, 1921.

BELOW: William Posey and Tse-ne-gat's band of Indians at Hammond Canyon, 1921

William Posey,
Kumen Jones
(with beard), and
Governor Charles
R. Mabey (right)
at Hammond
Canyon, 1921.

ABOVE: Jess Posey astride his horse; Tse-ne-gat stands to his left.

BELOW: Anson "Scotty" Cantsee (left), William Posey, Governor Charles R. Mabey, unidentified man (right) at Hammond Canyon, 1921.

After Tse-ne-gat's trial was over, he came back to his home pretty much the way he was before, except he was sick from all the rich food. Local whites felt he got away with murder and tried to steer clear of him.

In 1960, Eileen White—Ella Polk's daughter who was born in 1915, Chief Polk's granddaughter, and Tse-ne-gat's niece—was interviewed by author and journalist Forbes Parkhill concerning the incident:

"My grandfather was totally blind in later years. One time Polk said, 'One son [Tse-na-gat] was big and strong and had killed a Mexican sheepherder.'

"He told us that the Utes were not expecting the attack by the posse. They were, however, expecting trouble over another matter. Someone had killed a steer belonging to the white cattlemen and a Mexican sheepherder had told a lie on us by informing the cowboys that had seen the Indians slaughter the steer.

"The Utes captured the Mexican and tied him up with ropes and were holding him prisoner in a tepee on the morning of the attack on our camp. The camp consisted of one Hogan and several tepees. When the shooting started the Utes thought the cowboys were trying to liberate the captured Mexican. Not until later did they learn the real purpose of the posse.

"A group of squaws ran and hid in the rocks at the top of a bluff [in Bluff on the Lacy property]. An infant kept

Forbes Parkhill, an accomplished journalist, author, and historian of the West, had a very sympathetic attitude toward the plight of the American Indian. He interviewed Eileen White, Tse-ne-gat's niece, in 1960 (left column) and wrote Tse-ne-gat's obituary in 1922. Parkhill also wrote *The Last of the Indian Wars*, published in 1961.

crying and the mother, unable to quiet it, fearful that its wails would disclose their hiding place, threw the child over the rim of the bluff and killed it.

"When General Scott brought the Ute leaders back to Bluff they found that the posse men had built barricades of sandbags, and behind the barricades were many empty whisky bottles.

"That is what my grandfather told us."

Tse-ne-gat died on January 11, 1922, of consumption (tuberculosis). By then, national interest had subsided, all problems had been solved, the Indians were under control, and everyone could give full attention to World War I. This might have been somewhere near the truth if William Posey had been treated a little less royally. He now saw himself as the leader of the Indians, and his arrogance and his flagrant lawlessness gathered the young Indian hotheads around him and kept the settlers stirred up into annoyed impatience or towering rage all the time. Tension mounted until the final battle of 1923, when matters were permanently settled.

INDIAN WHO CAUSED 1912 UPRISING DEAD NEAR BLUFF

Tse-Ne-Gat, the young Piute Indian whose resistance of arrest in 1912 precipitated the Piute uprising in that year which was finally quelled by General Hugh L. Scott, chief of staff of the U. S. army, died several weeks ago in Allan canyon near Bluff, according to information that has reached the local forest office. The young buck had been suffering from tuberculosis for several years, and finally succumbed to the disease.

Tse-Ne-Gat was the son of Old Poke, one of the leaders of the Piute band which makes its headquarters in Allan canyon. In 1912 he killed a Mexican sheepherder, and when officers attempted to arrest him the entire band of Indians assumed a very hostile attitude and declared war on the white population of southern San Juan county. United States Marshal Aquilla Nebeker took charge of the situation and organized a posse to round up the recalcitrant Piutes. The Indians were overtaken west of Bluff and a fight ensued. One member of the posse was killed and another was wounded. After this fight, the Indians, under the leadership of Poke and Posey, escaped to the inaccessible country near Bluff and issued a defiance against the whites. The aid of the war department was asked, and General Scott, a veteran of many Indian wars and who had had much success in dealing with the redskins, was sent to round up the Piutes. He was accompanied by his aide and an orderly. Arriving at Bluff, he induced the leaders of the Piute band to come in for a pow-wow, and the fracas was amicably adjusted. Tse-Ne-Gat, Poke and Posey were taken to Salt Lake, where they were held for a time. Later, Tse-Ne-Gat was tried in the federal court at Denver on a charge of killing the Mexican sheepherder, and he was acquitted. During the trial a great deal of sympathy for the Indian developed among the people of Denver, and it was reported that the copper-hued Piute had several offers of marriage from leading "society" ladies of the Colorado metropolis.

Tse-Ne-Gat was released and returned to San Juan county, since which time he had been suffering from consumption. His death occurred in February, according to the information reaching the local forest office.

TSE-NE-GAT, PIUTE WHO CAUSED 1915 REBELLION, DIES

Renegade Was Tried for Murder Here; Women Flooded Cell With Love Notes, Red Ties and Pink Hose.

By Associated Press.

SALT LAKE CITY, Utah, April 9.—Tse-Ne-Gat, the Piute Indian who precipitated the Piute uprising in 1915 because of his resistance to arrest, and son of Old Poke, a Piute band leader, is dead, according to advices received by United States forest service officials here. The message of the Indian's death came from Bluff, Utah, near Allen canon, where Tse-Ne-Gat died. Tse-Ne-Gat was alleged to have killed a Mexican sheepherder in 1915, and when federal officials made an effort to arrest him he resisted, and the entire Piute band came to his defense and declared war on the whites of San Juan county. In a fight which ensued between the Indians and a posse, headed by United States Marshal Aquila Nebeker of Utah, one member of the posse was killed and another wounded. The Indians fled to an inaccessible region near Bluff, and successfully defied the white posse.

Fear of further trouble brought Gen. Hugh L. Scott to the scene with infantrymen. He soon succeeded in arranging a "pow-wow" and the Indians withdrew. Tse-Ne-Gat and his father were held and the youth was tried for murder in Denver and acquitted.

Tse-Ne-Gat Cost U. S. $30,000 in Twenty-eight Years.

Tse-Ne-Gat, alias Pa-Woo-Tsch, alias Everett Hatch, the notorious Piute, who is reported dead somewhere on the Utah desert, was the most costly Indian of his race. In his twenty-eight years he cost the United States government more than $20,000.

Approximately $12,000 of this sum went toward the capture of the renegade on a charge of murdering Juan Chacon, a Mexican sheepherder of

(Continued on Page 2, Column 2)

TSE-NE-GAT.

THE NEWS SUMMARY

13

POSEY STIRS THE POT

Rather than solving anything for either the Mormons or the Indians of San Juan, the 1915 episode made everything a good deal worse. Of the 160 Indians who were moved out of Utah onto the reservation in Colorado, most of them had returned in the next year or two, with William Posey not even spending one night on the Weeminuche lands.

By the 1920s, there were some eighty Ute Mountain Utes (Weeminuche) under Mancos Jim and Polk, and about half that many under Posey. However, the youths who grew up between 1914 and 1923 from all bands were more or less under Posey's spell of leadership. They admired his braggadocio, his dream of enticing the whites into the vast wilderness of the canyons and buttes between Grayson and Navajo Mountain, where he would spring a vast trap and wipe out all pursuit, leaving the whole country free again for the Indians. William Posey's son Jess may have thought his father crazy to consider himself exempt from white men's bullets, but the rest of the Indians were inclined to credit his claims. Posey seemed to be operating under his own law, that a smart Indian could rise to any level of elegance or command if he got the chance.

Posey had always owned good guns, the best he could get, and after the close of World War I, the 30.06 became popular and Posey soon armed himself with it. He traded up in his horses, too, and by the early 1920s, he had a fine black saddle mare that he rode everywhere. He was becoming a rather impressive figure, and it is no wonder the younger Indians, who were dissatisfied at the future of being pushed off their hunting grounds completely, viewed his projected campaign as their only hope.

Mancos Jim and his band lived in Allen Canyon and in Cottonwood Canyon, and Polk had more or less settled at Montezuma, but Posey and his followers lived along the San Juan below Bluff in the winter and on the Blue (Abajo) Mountains in the summer. They were always surrounded by cattle and other livestock owned by Mormons, and there was constant friction—complaints from the white stockmen, beef killed for food by the Indians who called this beef "slow elk," as well as other minor depredations of one kind or another. Horses were stolen, and the white owners reclaimed them or took them away from the new masters; cowboys were waylaid and beaten on the range. Some massacres were no doubt avoided by the judicious withdrawal of white men. On the whole, the situation was becoming very tense, and a showdown was close at hand.

The Mormons had come to San Juan partly to teach and civilize the Indians; they exercised more forbearance for that reason than any other group of people probably would have done. They extended a friendly hand to the Indians or hired them on their ranches or cattle drives (however, most of the time they were paid less than white workers doing the same job), welcomed them to the occasional rodeos, allowed the constant but affordable loss of beef to the starving families, helped them when they were sick, and buried their dead in the community cemetery. They were on pretty good terms with most of the Indians; it was only Posey and his outlaw pack who demanded constant watching. In the beginning they may have been too weak to prosecute a war, but by the 1920s a couple of generations of native sons had grown up, and there had been a substantial influx of Mormons from Mexico who were fleeing the scourge of Pancho Villa; these men, particularly, were far from overawed by the Paiutes.

OLD POLK (LEFT) AND OLD POSEY, the two chiefs of the renegade Piute Indians. The photograph was taken nine years ago by Mrs. H. P. Dalley of Salt Lake, whose life the two Indians once saved. Old Polk is said to have cut his hair to shoulder length in recent years.

In this clipping, Old Posey's son Jess (left) was misidentified as Old Polk. In locating new photos for the book, many people identified any male Indian as Posey to make it more interesting.

The situation had shifted while Posey was not looking. He had been shown the twentieth century in Salt Lake City, but he missed the message that his way of life was long past. When he incited the young fellows—Dutchy's Boy, Bishop's Big Boy, Sanup's Boy—to insolence and rebellion, the white man had settled so firmly into the land that it was far too late to drive them out. These youths, raised on the stories of vast and glorious adventures of the past, looked more upon the visionary wishes of the future than the cold hard facts of the present. Even when old habits held the Utes to their threadbare existence, it was more inertia on the part of the Mormons than a definite plan that kept them there.

Although at least one man a year was killed by the Utes between 1880 and 1920, not one of them was a Mormon; there seemed to be some strange immunity from savagery for these forbearing neighbors.

There were individual ruptures of the peace, where an Indian youth was dealt with more vigorously than was called for, resulting in kicked britches, beatings, and confiscated horses, but largely, their arrogance and sins went unpunished.

On May 25, 1921, Joe Bishop's Big Boy and Dutchy's Boy rode out amongst the cattle of the Mormons, killed a calf, ate all they wanted and threw the rest off a ledge. Killing a cow was not unusual; it had happened hundreds of times before. But for some reason, Polk resented the waste of the meat and reported the deed to the sheriff.

Three days later a posse in a Studebaker sedan and a Ford pickup approached the Indian camp. There were also four men on horseback in the forthcoming raid. The Indians saw they were in trouble. Dutchy's Boy fired at Allen Adams, one of the men on horseback, and there was a general burst of gunfire. Adams jumped off his horse to fight, and the horse jerked away from him and stampeded down through the camp, creating more confusion and noise. The Indians retreated to the river, swollen by spring flood, and the Boys jumped in and splashed across to a sandbar. Bishop's Big Boy ran on and escaped. John Rodgers and Gene Powell waded out and brought Dutchy's Boy back to shore. As they were standing around him, there came a shot from the hill above, and they looked up to see William Posey sitting on his black mare, his gun held ready for another shot. Indians, shooting as they ran, were coming from down the river, and the men gathered in Bluff to repel an invasion, while the Indians, feeling somewhat elated, rode toward the mountain.

Meeting three Grayson cattlemen, Bishop's Big Boy pistol-whipped Corey Perkins and threatened them all. "Whassamatta!" he demanded, "Mormonee 'fraid to fight. Allatime Talk-talk-talk, heapscairt. Ute no scairt."

Dutchy's Boy was taken to Grayson, where he was cared for until his wounds healed; he was indicted for grand larceny for the calf, and assault with a deadly weapon for his shot at Allen Adams. Ute leaders agreed to bring in Joe Bishop's Big Boy but nothing ever came of the farce of a trial that was held sometime later.

This aggravated an already tense situation, with Posey arrogant and taunting. When he was caught stealing a horse, he dragged it over a bank so quickly that he broke the animal's neck, killing it. Bishop Kumen Jones was manhandled in Bluff. On the range, caches of food were stolen, cattle were butchered by the dozen, horses were

William Posey
in later years.

led off, and meals were demanded by every wandering Ute from anyone he came across, whether on the range or at a ranch.

Mormon forbearance simply wore out. The uneasy truce that they had maintained for so many years had become too much to sustain any further; old hatreds, conflicts, insults, and threats were no longer the order of the day.

William Posey was elated, but whether it was mere love of violence, or restlessness, or hatred is moot. He dreamed of taking his followers in a body, with their families, goats, and horses, into the canyons, and when the white men came, victory would be his. He only dreamed. He didn't make any plans to carry out a campaign, and before he knew it, the explosion came.

14
THE FINAL BLOW

On January 10, 1923, Bishop's Big Boy, Dutchy's Boy, and Sanup's Boy killed a sheep from a herd on Mustang Mesa, east of Grayson, and robbed the camp, running the herder Disiderio Chacon off into the wilderness on foot. He was a relative of Juan Chacon, who had been killed in 1914, and he was in no mind to stay and argue with crazy hostile Indians. He made his way to Grayson, where he told his employer, Floyd Nielson, what had happened. Nielson swore out a complaint, but nothing was done and the affair died down.

In March, after the death of Dutchy's Boy from pneumonia, the other two had most likely forgotten the episode when a car pulled into the Indian camp south of Grayson. Sheriff William (Bill) Oliver and Old Joe Bishop gathered the boys up peaceably and hauled them off to Grayson. There was no jail, so the boys were turned over to John Rogers for safekeeping. He was building a house, and so he kept an eye on them in the

Joe Bishop.

daytime and bedded them down in a room of the house under his watchful eye at night. The first few nights, other men were deputized to watch over the boys with guns, and the two fathers came, fully armed, and watched over the deputies.

Mrs. Rogers fed them with her family. But one night, the boys ate scalloped potatoes, which they had never encountered before, and Bishop's Boy put on such a performance of internal agony that the boys were allowed to go back to the Indian camps with their fathers, under the promise that they would return for the trial on Tuesday, March 20.

The biggest hall in town was the basement of the school, so school was let out for the day and the trial was held there. Peter Allen was judge, and the boys came in with their fathers, Bishop's Big Boy limping as he leaned on a stout tree branch. They sat at one side, with William Posey next to him, and he kept talking to them in Ute, which the white men did not speak.

All of the Indians of Posey's band were in town, well mounted, with two extra horses tied along with Posey's black mare to the swings in front of the schoolhouse. Closest to the school was a

Standing: Mancos Jim (left), William Posey, Elfego Bacca, Joe Bishop's Boy (1), Posey's Boy, Dutchy, "Scottie" Cantsee, Joe Bishop's Boy (2), Joe Bishop's Boy (3); kneeling: Johnny Peterson (left), Johnny Cockeye Squaw, Charlie (interpreter), Jack Ute, Joe Bishop's Boy (4), Afain Boy, Johnny Cockeye.

PIUTE INDIANS FEAR JACK UTE, "MAGICIAN"

The Piute Indians of Southern San Juan county are in trouble again, but this time they are seeking the advice of the county attorney, as well as his aid, in giving them relief.

Last week Old Posey, accompanied by Scotty, another Piute, went to Monticello and asked the county attorney to relieve them of the presence of Jack Ute, a fellow tribesman, whom they accused of killing Indians he disliked by the aid of a sun glass. To make sure of permanent relief, they asked that Jack be hanged. When informed that so harsh a measure could not be put into effect, it was requested that Jack be removed to the Navajo reservation and be compelled to remain there forever.

The county attorney was informed that the women and children of the tribe are very much afraid of Jack Ute and that he has been the cause of the death of several Indians.

To strengthen their plea, Old Posey and Scotty said that bad Indians often caused the death of those whom they disliked by spreading coyote bait. When the victims walked over the stuff they died. The county attorney offered to take off his shoes and walk over coyote bait if the Indians would supply the bait.

Old Posey told the attorney that there is an Indian on the reservation who rolls a pebble around in his hand, gives it a flip into the air, and that the pebble takes a course like a bullet and unfailingly gets whatever Indian the pebble flipper desires to be rid of. According to the old timer, distance makes no difference whatever, as he said that the pebble would fly completely across the reservation if the intended victim happened to be that far away.

The county attorney tried to explain to the Indians the fallacy of their belief, but with little success.

The two Indians returned to Allan canyon hoping that in some manner they would be given assurance that their fears were truly unfounded.

chestnut sorrel horse named Tango that County Attorney Fred Keller had bought in Texas and had shipped into the country. Somehow, through trade or purchase, the Indians had gotten hold of him.

The Indians packed into the corners and along the sides of the courtroom, but the trial went along peaceably, and the boys were soon convicted of the sheep camp theft and burning a bridge along the road to Bluff.

It is a law that the sentence could not be imposed on the prisoner until the lapse of a short period of time, so the spectators and court opted to go home for lunch. Probably the boys would draw only a short sentence, a month or so of incarceration at most.

The white people streamed out of the basement of the schoolhouse, leaving mostly Indians and the officers of the court. The Indians were slower, but most of them had mounted up and were moving away when the break came. Bishop's Big Boy was walking with great difficulty, leaning on his heavy stick. Sheriff Oliver was planning to take the two to his house for dinner, but they were slow getting started. He finally got on his horse, and nudged the boy with the horse's shoulder, telling him to get going.

The boy threw away the stick, reached up and grabbed the horse's reins close to the bit, jerked them so that the horse reared, throwing Oliver off balance. Bishop's Big Boy jumped and grabbed the officer's gun, pointed it at him and fired, but it misfired. He tried again, but it still did not fire. Oliver raced toward home for another gun, and Joe Bishop's Big Boy mounted Tango and started running southeast of town, firing at Oliver as he went. The gun finally fired, hitting the officer's horse in the chest but wounding it only slightly.

Re-arming himself, Oliver returned to take the trail of the Indians. Before he

A composite of three photos: Sheriff William Oliver (left) and William Posey, in front of Grayson Elementary School, site of the Last Indian War, 1923.

left, he deputized some of the men, and they gathered up all of the Indians who were left in town—men and women and children—and put them in the basement of the schoolhouse. This took a little time during which the Indians warriors went to their camps in Westwater and got guns, came back, and cut ahead of the posse as they headed for Murphy's Point to ambush the white men.

In town, Old Joe Bishop offered to show the posse where the boys had gone, and was riding along saying, "I show you. I show you." But he was riding as slowly as he could, holding the posse back. Dave Black lost patience.

Posey's Gun

After World War I the Springfield Krag 30.06, which shot hard-nosed bullets much farther and with more penetrating power than the usual Winchester 25.35 and 30.30, became the prized passions of the gun public, and Posey's gun was foremost of these.

Posey's gun, courtesy of Alan Black;
Posey's gloves, courtesy of Lee Lewellen.

"You old son-of-gun, you get back to town or I'll lock you up, too," he told the old scoundrel. When Black had delivered Bishop to the schoolhouse, he headed back south again on the tracks of the Indians and following the posse.

About four or five miles down the long cedar- and pinyon-covered point, a family by the name of Murphy had taken up a ranch and built a house but found there was not enough water to live there, so they had moved back to town. The house was now vacant and the Indians forted up there.

Posey had started out with the Indians, but about the time they stopped at Murphy's he broke off and was racing around by himself, planning to go from group to group of the Indians and organize the return into the canyons. He was riding his black mare and carrying a better gun than most of the Indians could afford, a Krag 30.06.

When Oliver saw what was in store, he sent Craig Jackson, a boy who was staying with the Oliver family while going to school, back to town to ask for reinforcements. Bill Young saw Dave Black ushering Bishop back to the holding center and decided it was time to take a hand. He was a young man, just married, but it did look like the time had come to make a decisive stand, so he fell in with Dave Black when Black started out on the trail of the combatants.

John Rogers had been riding after cattle all morning, but when he came into town and found all the excitement, he told his brother Clarence to get him another horse out of the field, and after he had eaten, he would take a hand, also. Clarence knew the best horse they owned was Old Blue, a big blue-roan horse.

John didn't waste any time and came up to the posse at the Murphy house as they were planning how to proceed. The cabin was set in a thick grove of cedars on the south, east, and west; but on the north, where the posse was coming in, there was just big sagebrush, which offered little protection. The sheriff told John

LEFT:
Sheriff William Oliver.

ABOVE:
Joe Bishop's Big Boy (far right), watching Navajos and Paiutes play cards.

to take a man or two and go around the west side while one or two men would go around the east, and they would try to get down in the trees where they would be protected.

When Leland Redd and John Rogers got around toward the west side of the house, they saw fresh horse tracks running off toward Corral Canyon, going west. They signaled and took off, following the fresh tracks.

They started down the trail into Corral Canyon when a shot rang out, and Old Blue dropped with a broken back from the shot. John and Leland jumped off their horses and took to the rocks, but there was no further action. They decided later that this was Posey, scouting around by himself.

Clarence Rogers points to a bullet hole in the saddle belonging to his brother, John Rogers, along with the skull of the horse, Old Blue.

The Indians climbed out of Corral Canyon just in time to cut off a posse of a carload of men going to Bluff from Grayson. Edson Black had loaded four men into the back seat of his Ford, with a couple more in the front, and was driving south on the Bluff road just as the Indians emerged from the canyon. The Indians shot through the car, the bullet tearing through the back of the seat behind the four men.

Dave Black, the sheriff, and Bill Young had gone down into the trees by the canyon, and had just cut the Indians' trail when the shot that killed Old Blue rang out. They followed through, climbed out, and gathered around the car. It was night by this time, and the Indians went on to their camps while the posse returned to Grayson.

The next day the sheriff told a few men to go down toward Bluff, twelve miles south of Grayson, where there was an old abandoned ranch that belonged to Fred Lyman. The drought had forced him to move closer to town and he had left the buildings vacant. The Indians had already pulled out from there, and the posse moved on to Ruin Springs, south and west.

The sheriff had part of the posse stand guard that night because it was feared the Indians would send word to Old Polk, who was living over at Montezuma Creek. He might bring his band over with reinforcements, and there really would be trouble then. He dispatched John Rogers easterly toward Colorado to watch the trails and intercept anyone who might come in. John missed the action the next day because he was out the other way.

It turned out there was little need to worry; Polk was having no part of Posey's war. In fact, Posey was almost as much a nuisance to him as to the Mormonee, and he half hoped his old pest would get what was coming to him. He told someone that "if Posey get shot, pretty good all right." Besides, Polk's horses were spring-poor, too weak to carry riders to the scene of action.

The Indian trail went west again, and the posse followed. They got over to Butler Wash and as they were going along the white rim into the wash, they could see smoke over where the trail dropped over the Comb and knew it had to be the Indians. All of the Indians near Grayson had been rounded up and put in the schoolhouse basement; this was part of the Posey band that had been camped mostly in that area west of Grayson. From the smoke, it looked as if most of the band had gathered on top of the Comb, ready to fade into the canyons.

(Author's Note: Most of this material for 1923 has been taken from interviews with various people. The Rogers material comes from an interview with Clarence Rogers by Dr. Lacy, another source was Lynn Lyman, and Judge Fred Keller was interviewed by Michael Hurst on May 4, 1972.)

Piute Indians Again on War Path; Attack Southern Utah Community

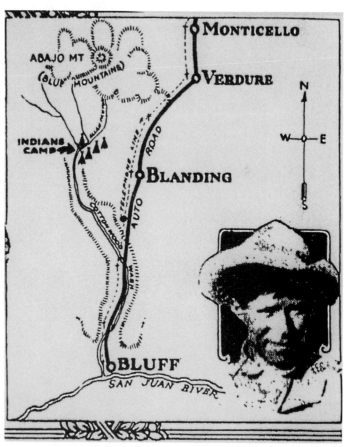

ABOVE: Joe Bishop's Boy.
LEFT: William Posey.

Posey's Trail,
1981 (notice the
ghost at the base
of the rock);
photo by Larry
R. Lyman.

15

ON THE TRAIL

The Indian trackers were easy to follow; the retreating group had gathered in extra horses, families (squaws, papooses, and old people), sheep, and goats. All left a broad trail.

When the posse saw the smoke, a council of war was declared and as they sat on their horses, it was decided to put Dave Black in charge. In Mexico, he had fought Pancho Villa and had helped capture the Apache Kid; he also had led the Mormon settlers north from Mexico to San Juan County a few years earlier.

When they got across Butler Wash where the trail started up the sloping ridge to get to the top of Comb Ridge, they left the horses tied in the deep wash in charge of two boys, Clisbee Nielson and Cecil Rogers. "We will go up this slope on foot to where we can see the trail off Comb on the other side, and see what is going on."

Dave was the type of man who moved fast, and Bill Young was one of the boys who kept up with the leader, so these two men moved out ahead of the posse. They topped out way ahead of anybody else. When they were almost where they could look down off Comb Ridge, they heard a shot ring out back toward the horses. "Bill, you stay here and watch this gap and I'll run down and see what the shooting is." There were several more shots fired as he ran down the ridge, over the brow of the hill, and on down to the posse.

In Grayson, the Indians were still being held in the basement of the schoolhouse, letting their livestock scatter. Jack Fly and another Indian were let out to gather the sheep and horses and take care of them. Instead of doing what they had been turned loose to do, the two saddled up, followed the tracks down into Butler Wash, and caught up with the posse just as the men were getting their horses tied up to climb toward the smoke of the Indian camp on Comb Ridge.

Jack Fly took a shot at Joe Smith, and Joe said later that he could feel the breeze of the bullet as it went past his ear. "I hated to see the poor devil die when I aimed at him, so I shut my eyes as I pulled the trigger," Joe added. Since this was March and the winds were cold, Jack Fly was wearing a blanket. The bullet went between his arm and body, through two or three folds of that blanket. That was too close for Jack Fly; he and the other Indian jumped off their horses into Butler Wash and took off south toward the

LEFT:
Posey's Trail, 1981; photo by Larry R. Lyman.

RIGHT:
William Posey.

San Juan and the Navajo reservation beyond; they had had all the Indian War they wanted. Amazingly, no one was wounded in this exchange.

Another man converging on the smoke on top of the Comb was William Posey. He had gone into town the evening before to see where his people were and discovered they were in custody. He then went to an abandoned camp, and the next morning started out to overtake the remnant of his band, going toward the smoke on Comb Reef. He was just a little ahead of Jack Fly.

As Dave Black neared the posse, he glanced across a little canyon and there was Posey, riding along, headed up the slope toward the Comb to get his followers. Bill Clisbee took a shot at him, and Barney Black, Coin and Glen's father, got off a shot; there were one or two others.

Posey was hanging down on the right side of his mare, running up the ridge as fast as he could make the little mare go, shooting under her neck as he used her for a shield. But his hind parts were high in the saddle. Dave Black drew down, and when he shot, they saw Posey wince and nearly fall off his horse. When he was found dead later, this shot through both sides of his buttocks had become infected and he had died from it. Nobody wanted to take credit for having killed a man, but among those involved, it was pretty generally agreed that Dave's bullet found its mark.

When Bill Young heard all the shooting, he figured the Indians were down below him, and he started down toward the action. Up on the ridge where he was, it was quite level for a short distance, a kind of sagebrush flat. Then it sloped off toward Butler Wash. Bill was running across that little flat near the break-off when he heard yelling and horses' hoofs. Over to his left, the two Indians boys who had started the whole uprising—Bishop's Big Boy and Sanup's Boy—were riding along the hill, Bishop's Big Boy still on Tango. They had their guns in their hands and they too had heard the firing below. When they saw Bill alone, they let out a yell and took after him, knowing they could overhaul him before he could make it to the edge of the canyon. Later Young said:

"I knew they would just ride up behind me and shoot me in the back and that would be the end of it. I knew I couldn't just keep running, but there didn't look like any good place to stop. There were a few stunted cedars on the slope, so I pulled into one of them, turned around and got my gun aimed across the branch of the tree, since I was so out of breath I couldn't hold it steady without a rest.

"The boys didn't know for sure where I had disappeared to, but one was coming on the right side of the tree and the other on the south. They were standing up in their stirrups with their rifles in their hands looking for me. I just waited until I could see that button on the boy's shirt, and pulled the trigger.

"Right quick I jumped to the other side of the tree and thrown down on the other fellow. He pulled his horse to a sliding halt and was fighting him to turn. I didn't want to kill him, I didn't want to kill anyone, so I held my fire and the Indian boy got his horse turned around and ran up over the little ridge out of sight. He called to his partner two or three times, but his partner didn't answer. I went on down and joined the posse."

Dave Black and the other leaders of the posse were worried. The Indians were supposed to be locked up; what kind of game was this when the enemy was let loose to attack from the rear. It was getting late in the afternoon, so they returned to town where they learned it was not really a rear action attack.

The posse was reorganized early the next morning (Friday) and left to take up the trail of the Indians. When they got over the slope of Butler Wash, one of them said, "Let's turn off the trail and go right over there just a little way and see if that Indian was killed." Dave didn't want to stop, but Floyd Adams and Cory Perkins stayed back with Chuck Clemmings. Floyd said later:

"I rode along there about to where I thought Bill Young shot Bishop's Big Boy, where the ridge broke off into the Butler, and sat on my horse looking down the slope. I couldn't see anything that looked like what I was looking for and had almost decided that Bill had missed his shot. Finally I lowered my gaze right under my horse and there the body was, practically under the horse's nose. I called Cory to come over and went and caught the posse in a short distance."

Later some fellows went out and buried the body, but the exact location of the grave has been lost.

There were two horse trails off Comb Ridge into Comb Wash, the old one that was not used anymore and the one that Dave Black had made a year or two before; the Indians chose the old way, which was traditionally familiar to them, taking their sheep, goats, horses, and families to Grayson (Blanding).

A group of men from Monticello with good rifles and fresh horses came out to lend a hand, but they missed the posse and the skirmish. They followed the tracks around from Ruin Spring to Cottonwood Canyon, up over Black Mesa, and down into Butler, finally coming on the battlefield but not really knowing what had happened. They knew about the older trail, however, and started up the ridge when they ran across the fresh track of a running horse. They followed it onto the ridge and then on up the trail to the top of Comb Ridge, and along the top where they could look off. From there they could see the horseman and later decided it must have been William Posey. He had met his people at the bottom of Comb Wash, and told them where to go. They had taken their goats and papooses and everything across Comb Wash to where Mill Creek Canyon comes in from a little mesa located close to a big mesa.

Posey's Trail, 1981; photo by Larry R. Lyman.

In his article "The Last Indian Uprising," Michael Hurst mentions the following situation:

Cowboys had always called this little mesa the Island. It was about half a mile wide with perpendicular cliffs all around, the perfect place for ambushing the posse. Posey told his people that he would join them later, but things went too fast for him. The Indians figured they had a real fortress, as they took their livestock up the one narrow crack in the cap rock, which they could hold against invasion and send the white men back to town like they had done for years. Times had changed; the white men had had enough and planned to pursue this to a decisive finish.

When the posse reached the foot of the Island, they dismounted and Dave gave word to go up on foot. When they reached the top, he looked down and saw William Posey on his little black mare go behind a tree in that saddle between the Island and the big Mesa. When the rest doubted that he could recognize Posey, Dave quickly climbed down the neck, untied the mare, and led her out.

Posey was hiding in the rocks close by as he watched Black lead the mare away. He knew of a little dripping spring under an overhang on the rocky ridge near his hiding place, and he dragged himself to this spring, keeping well hidden. (Hurst, "Last Indian Uprising.")

The Indians were just back of the rim, with their dinner all cooked and ready to eat. They had a stack of flapjacks and a pot of hot coffee just ready to start on when they looked up and saw the Mormonees climbing out on top and approaching. They knew William Posey had been badly wounded and that Bishop's

Boy had been killed, but not one shot the Indians had fired had found a mark. These men coming onto the mesa were not soldiers or cowboys; they were old friends of most of the Indians, and when they realized all these things, panic seized them. They didn't stop to fight or save any of their food. Grabbing their children and horses they ran to the far side of the mesa, sliding their horses over the rimrocks, jumping them over ledges fifteen and twenty feet high, with people scrambling down as best they could. Small children were dropped to waiting arms below. Except for a few horses, they escaped with nothing but their lives.

They started to work their way to the top of the next ridge, known as Baldy's Reservation, heading up little canyons and missing thick cedars until they finally climbed out on top. Over this mesa in Dry Wash was a big cave they were aiming for, but they found they couldn't get their horses up into the cave, so they left them. The last two or three miles across Baldy Mesa they tied white rags to the trees and to sticks shoved down into their moccasin tracks as signs that they wanted to surrender.

It was late afternoon, and the posse decided not to try to go back to Grayson for the night. Dave sent some of the men with all the horses to the Perkins ranch, where there was hay to feed them, and they planned to return the mounts the next morning.

John Rogers and Leonard Jones went around the head of the little canyon, where they knew they were right above the Indians, and some of the others went to the west side. But the main posse stayed put, a little reluctant to try to get over the cliff because a man would be completely unprotected while getting down that first fifty feet. In the discussion that followed, one of the fellows assured Dave Black that he could get a man to go over the cliff.

"Hey, Bill, come here," he shouted at Bill Griffith. "Dave says that you are afraid to go over this cliff."

Sheriff R. L. Newman.

"Well, he's a damn liar!" Bill retorted, and just piled over the cliff. Nobody shot at him, so some of the others went over then, and they gathered in the canyon below where they decided to make a big fire and stay there all night to keep the Indians pinned down.

During the evening a young Indian boy came warily into the fire-lit circle. He was told to go back and tell the others to leave their guns and come to the fire, one at a time.

After a few had come in and they were all standing around, R. L. Newman, a member of the posse who had lately come from Arizona where he had been a sheriff, noticed that one of the Indians was moving back into the shadows. Pretty soon the Indian thought he was far enough out to get away and broke into a run. Newman threw up his gun, pointed it, and pulled the trigger, but the Indian kept on going. "First time I ever missed a man in my life!" Newman complained, much disgusted with himself.

All of the Indians came down to surrender, and Dave Black sent a couple of men up to get the guns. The Indians had buried them in the sand of the cave, and it took a while to locate them.

As soon as it started to get light in the morning, Dave and the posse took the Indians and went down Dry Wash to where it comes into Comb Wash, which was quite a distance by foot. As soon as the horses came in, he sent a man into Grayson to get someone to bring a truck around by Bluff and up Comb Wash to pick up his prisoners.

Dave put John Rogers out on the hills and ridges on one side of the canyon as they herded the Indians down Comb Wash, and he took the other side. They were watching because Posey was still out, and for all they knew at the time, he was not even injured. The Indians wouldn't tell them anything. Also, they didn't know what had happened to Jack Fly and the Indian who escaped from the bonfire. A very small force in this broken country could set an ambush that would be disastrous.

Posey's Trail was marked in the late 1970s.

The rest of the posse had orders, too. There were just about the same number of white men in the posse as Indian men in the band, and the sheriff gave the men their orders. He put a man behind each Indian, and then they drove them down the wash, just like driving sheep. The orders were that if any Indian gave any trouble, or if William Posey or any-body attacked, "shoot the man in front of you and then do what you have to do after that." All was quiet, and after a march of a couple of miles, they met the truck.

The Indians, about thirty of them—men, women, and children—were loaded into the truck, which went back down Comb Wash to Bluff and then up to Grayson. The posse rode into Grayson; when the truck arrived, the white men helped unload the cargo into the basement of the schoolhouse where the Indians were being held.

By this time the word was out. Newspapers across the nation carried scare stories of the Indian uprising in eastern Utah. U.S. Marshall Ray J. Ward came down from Salt Lake City, and southern Ute Indian Agent E. E. McKean came over from Ignacio, since this was far too important an event to be handled by the sub-agency for the Weeminuche at Pacific Springs.

With this addition of about thirty Indians to the prisoners, the basement of the schoolhouse was too small for a holding tank. Besides, school had been let out, and parents were concerned about the break in the school year. Everyone got together and laid out a compound of a couple of acres in the middle of town, surrounded by a high fence. After a couple of hogans and several tents were added and pit toilets and water taps provided, the sixty-nine prisoners were removed to the stockade, heavily guarded by several men with high-powered rifles. Food was provided by the townspeople; while the Indians were under restraint, their living conditions were probably a little above what they were accustomed to.

16

THE STOCKADE

U.S. Marshall Ray J. Ward came down from Salt Lake City to take charge of affairs, but he found that everything was going along well under the authority of the sheriff and his deputies, which included most of the men of the town. The compound had been set up and was patrolled night and day by men with rifles; although Ward did not comment whether or not he considered holding the Indians in this manner to be exactly legal, he took considerable credit for the orderly state of affairs. He reported in a telegram to the Attorney General in Washington, D.C., that seven of the guilty were being held, with about seventy more in the compound.

The Mormons called a mass meeting, to which McKean was invited. Several men spoke, the gist of their remarks being that for several years there had been a great deal of annoyance from William Posey's band of Indians. Several cowboys had been attacked on the range by the Indians and beaten with quirts or ropes. On outlying ranches, Indians would come in and, finding the man of the house absent, force the woman to cook meals for them and provide them with food to take along. Often, Indians turned their horses into fields, and when the white men drove them out, the Indians put them back; this had been carried almost to a shooting conclusion several times.

During recent years some of the Indians, including William Posey, would commit crimes with a warrant issued for their arrest. They took to the hills, and the warrants were never served. They then decided that the Mormons were afraid of them and would not shoot them. After a few months, usually, the warrants were never mentioned again, and the Indians returned to the settlements with no fear of reprisal.

In fact, this case with Joe Bishop's Big Boy and Sanup's Boy had dragged on several months and probably would have ended with a light jail sentence for the two boys. But now that the Indians had made such an issue of it, the whole question would have to be settled. There was no doubt that Posey had been looking forward to some action; he had cached supplies on the top of Island Mesa for retreat. But no one, certainly none of the Indians, expected the Mormons to come out in such numbers and to show such determination. This changed everything; the Indians were confused and frightened.

The white men didn't want the Indians forced onto the reservation at Ute Mountain. They knew that

LEFT:
Ray J. Ward.

RIGHT:
Grayson
Elementary
School, site
of the 1923
Indian war.

the resident Indians would drive the newcomers away since there was limited range and water for their own sheep and horses. The Indians of William Posey's band wanted to stay where they were, and the white men believed that they did have rights there. However, until or unless Posey was brought in or accounted for, there was no way the leading edge would be relinquished by the Mormons.

McKean found the Mormon attitude strange: they believed that the Indians were from one of the Ten Lost Tribes of Israel, and were actually their brothers. Also, they had always believed it was cheaper to feed them than to fight them, a theory that had worked throughout Utah for years.

The red men seemed unable to accept the way of life of the white man, but their condition, especially these bronco Indians, called for considerable charity from the Mormons. The loss of cattle on the range had always been affordable; the Indians called this beef "slow elk" and they harvested it like it was their right. The Mormons knew it was either that or starve, so they looked the other way.

This looked as good a time as any to present the whole problem to the Indian Service. The men had written letters and complained about conditions, but nothing was ever done. One of the main solutions, the Mormons pointed out to McKean, was for the Indian Service to provide better care for these wards of the government—more clothing, more food, and some way to assure them of a place to live. The granting of allotments was again discussed, with the fact that Mancos Jim insisted on being allotted Allen Canyon, where his father and his father's fathers were buried, and where he planned to be buried, also. Allen Canyon was under the direction of the Forest Service, and it would have to be released before allotments to the Indians could be made there.

McKean was convinced that these men were humane and fair, but this time they meant business—the Indian matter would be settled so that the settlers could live with it. Immediately after the meeting, he set up a fund of $500 to feed the captives, and that drain was no longer a duty of the pioneers.

DEPARTMENT OF THE INTERIOR
UNITED STATES INDIAN SERVICE
Consolidated Ute Indian Agency
Ignacio, Colorado. April 9, 1923

The Honorable,
The Commissioner,

My Dear Mr. Commissioner:

I have the honor to submit the following report regarding the recent Indian trouble in and about Blanding, Utah. This report would have been submitted before but illness prevented me from doing so.

I left Ignacio March 21. I went by train and stage to Cortez [Colorado], where Mr. Reed, Principal of the Ute Mountain School, met me and we proceeded by automobile to Blanding, reaching there the afternoon of the 23rd. I found considerable excitement existing all through the country and pickets were posted around on the out-skirts of Blanding, to prevent, as was claimed, other renegade Indians coming to Blanding and affecting a release of prisoners held.

I found seventy-nine Indians, men, women and children being held as prisoners in the basement rooms of the public school. Those prisoners were guarded by several deputies all having Winchesters. It was necessary for the school authorities to dismiss the school in order to have the building to house the Indians. The basement was warmed and fairly well lighted and ventilated. The Indians were being well cared for.

About an hour after my arrival the citizens of the town called a mass meeting at which I was invited to be present together with several correspondents of the Associated Press. Immediately after the meeting was called to order the chairman invited me, as a representative of the Indian Office, to tell the people what I proposed to do and what relief the community was to receive from the Government. I advised them that I had just arrived at Blanding and before making any statements regarding the action of the Department it would be necessary for me to acquaint myself thoroughly with all phases of the present trouble and that more could be achieved if they would state their side of the case and their individual views regarding the present trouble. This they proceeded to do, several of the more influential men going into the past and present relation between the Mormons and the Indians.

Without taking up the conversation of each individual in this report I will simply state that they all agreed that these Indians had been a great source of trouble annoyance to them for a number of years. That upon several occasions two or three Indians had caught white men or boys out on the range and on their own ranches and whipped them with their quirts and ropes, and that they had continually turned their horses into the meadows and that when these ranch-ers would drive the ponies out the Indians would come and drive them back. These actions came very near resulting several times in serious shooting affrays.

They stated that the Indians had grown into the habit of coming to their homes when the men were away and compelling the women to prepare meals for them and often times to give them surplus food to take away with them on their rides. That of late years the Indians had become very insolent and over bearing in all of their relations with the white ranchers and stock men to the country.

Upon several occasions during recent years Indians have committed crimes and warrants have been issued for their arrest and they immediately took to the hills and avoided apprehension. The Indians had grown to believe that the Mormons were afraid of them and they were very positive that no Mormon would ever shoot one of their numbers.

The crime leading up to the present trouble was committed by two Indians, one known as Joe Bishop's Boy and the other as Sanup's Boy. Both are young Indians in their early twenties. These two Indians, during the month of last January, entered a sheep camp and drove the Mexican herder from the house and took possession.

They fed thus at the camp and upon leaving took some mutton, oats and other articles. The Mexican herder reported this matter to the sheriff at Blanding and a warrant was issued for the arrest of these two Indians. They could not be located and Posey and the rest of his band refused to give them up. After considerable talk to the Indians by the different authorities it was finally arranged that these boys should come to Blanding and give themselves up. This they did and were tried in the local justice court and found guilty.

It was the intention of the court to pass a very light sentence upon these Indians. He told that their sentence was to be ten days in jail. The trial terminated about 12 o'clock and as the laws of the state of Utah prescribe that six hours must elapse between the conviction and the sentence the boys were given over to the charge of the sheriff, who proceeded from the court house with them to his own house to give them dinner. After leaving the court house they refused to accompany him any further and in the scuffle that followed Joe Bishop's Boy grabbed the sheriffs six-shooter and tried to shoot him, snapping the gun three or four times which for some reason did not fire. Posey was in the front of the Court house, as were several other Indians. The boys then ran into the crowd of Indians and dared the sheriff to take them. Shortly after this they both mounted horses and rode away.

At this time I believe that several shots were exchanged between the Indians and some of the bystanders but no one was injured. The sheriff got a car immediately and with three or four other men pursued these Indians toward Bluff. When they were about eight miles outside of Blanding the Indians opened fire on the automobile, one shot passing through the rear of the car and missing one of the occupants by less than an inch, the sheriff's posse returned to Blanding and after consulting with the citizens it was determined that a larger posse should be formed to pursue these prisoners and bring them back. There were several Indians in Blanding at this time and these were held by the local authorities to prevent them joining with the others and increasing trouble.

During the pursuit of the Indians many shots were exchanged, three of the white men having horses shot from under them. Joe Bishop's Boy, the Indian who was killed, had been shooting at the pursuing officers and at the time he was shot was in the act of shooting at a white man. Joe Bishop's Boy one of the escaped prisoners was the only Indian killed or injured during the whole affair.

The Indians took refuge on a high, narrow plateau, which was very difficult to reach. They laid several traps to catch the posse but the sheriff's men seemed to be familiar with their methods and it was on this account that no white men were shot during this pursuit. The posse surrounded the plateau and after considerable difficulty made their way to the top and during the night of the second day of the pursuit the Indians surrendered to them and were brought back to Blanding. Posey, however, made his escape and up to the present has not been captured.

The Indians themselves say that Posey had planned this outbreak for the past two months and provisions and supplies which the Indians had on this table land, their strong hold would indicate the affair had been planned before hand. Never before had the settlers pursued the Indians beyond the boundaries of their own ranches, and it was due to the surprise on the part of the Indians as well as the over whelming number of white men that caused them to surrender without considerable blood shed.

Indian Children

Pacifying Papooses

Interestingly, the Indians had a unique way of making a pacifier for their babies: they tied a piece of fat to a leather strap about six inches long and then tied the other end to the baby's wrist. If the baby choked on the fat, the mother simply popped the piece of fat out of its throat.

Changing Diapers

In 1967, town barber Harvey John Kartchner spoke of a unique way the Indians had of changing diapers:

> "The Indians used to make a disposable diaper by taking the bark off the cedar tree and rub it together to get all the dirt out of it and to make it soft. They then put this inside of a leather diaper or flour sack. One day when I was there, one of the squaws was making fry bread and stopped to change the diaper, when finished she then proceeded to get at the dough again to continue to make more fry bread, never stopping to wash her hands."

Since he was the barber, they felt he could fill all medical needs should any arise.

Ute baby, 1920s.

Cutting Hair

Harvey John Kartchner also mentioned that he was the one who cut the hair of the Indian children who were being sent to the reservation to attend school. "I had to watch when I cut the children's hair as there were a lot of lice."

Many of the Indians have always realized that the Mormons were very reluctant to fight them. One of their doctrines, laid down by Brigham Young, was to feed the Indians instead of fight them. The Mormon also believes that the Indian race is one of the ten lost tribes of Israel. I state these two facts to show that the general public, which believes the Mormons are always attacking the Indians and are to blame for their uprising, are not familiar with the real Mormon character.

After these Indians had been held in the school house for several days a barb wire stockade was built near the main part of town with two large hogans in closed and several tents. The Indians were then moved from the school house to this stockade. This permitted the school to resume its work and was much more sanitary for the Indian prisoners.

During my visit with the Indians I spoke to them about their present trouble and I advised them that they should start sending their children to school. I told them that of course I could take forcibly all the children they had with them and put them in school, but I preferred to have the parents send them of their own free will, and I told them to talk the matter over among themselves and on the following day I would come to them again.

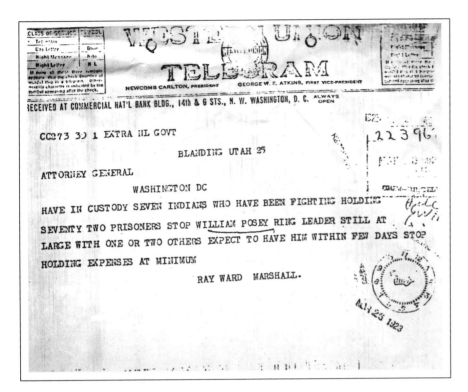

The next day they had picked out eighteen children whom they said they wished me to take and put in school. They retained the smaller children, and in some cases gave two or three children from a family and kept one. I hired an automobile and with the school car took them immediately to the Ute Mountain School; the children seemed delighted to go and during the journey were in the best of spirits.

During the last week of March the county Attorney secured sufficient evidence against seven of the Indians to have them committed for the trial by the United States Commissioner. These seven are being held to await the action of the local state court. The charges against them, for the most part, are aiding prisoners to escape, resisting officers, and firing upon officers. I have not been advised at present when their trial will take place but I will see to it that the court appoints an attorney to defend them.

It is not the desire of the Blanding people to inflict severe punishment upon any of these seven Indians. They do wish, however, to capture Posey and to sentence him as severely as the law will permit, as everyone regards him as the ringleader in all the Indian troubles in and about Blanding. Polk and his followers did not join in any way in the

Grayson Co-op, later known as Parley Redd Merc., was the informal gathering place for the Indian war in 1923.

present trouble. Polk remarked to several of the officers "if you fellows shoot Posey, pretty good all right." I am convinced however that one main reason that prevented Polk and his band from joining with them was the fact that their saddle horses were too poor to carry them to the scene of actions.

At the present time there are about sixty men women and children being held in the stockade at Blanding. This number includes the seven against whom charges have been filed. The people of Blanding have subscribed provisions and supplies to support these Indians until some favorable disposition can be made them. Their motives for this action are both business and humanitarian. Most of the Indians are without food or shelter, about one-half of their numbers are barefoot, and the whites reason that they can feed them cheaper where they are than to have them turned out and pray [sic] upon their stock.

I talked personally with nearly all the people of Blanding and I am convinced that had the two Indians yielded to arrest and taken the punishment due their offence that no trouble would have occurred. I am also convinced that the people of Blanding do not wish to persecute the Indians in any way, and that they would welcome any solution that the government might make in the present matter.

The whites realized that it would not be practical to send these Indians to the Ute Mountain reservation, since the Indians there object strongly to their presence, and would without doubt drive them away. It is my belief that these Indians should be given Individual Allotments of land and that this land should be located in the sections of the country in which they have always lived. I do not think it possible to secure a large area of land in Allen's Canyon because at the present time most of the soil throughout this canyon has been washed away. Old Mancos Jim seems to be about the only Indian who insists on living no where except in Allen's Canyon. The other Indians told me that whatever land is selected for them would be satisfactory to them.

After questioning Mancos Jim for a long time, I learned that his chief reason for wanting to remain in Allen's Canyon was that he believed upon the land which he claimed there is a gold mine. Whether this is true or not should be determined before definite action is taken towards abandoning the idea of placing the Indians in Allen's Canyon.

Allen's Canyon is not a suitable place for the Indians to live or run their stock during the winter season. The band that belongs to Posey have been living around Blanding and Bluff and Allen's Canyon. Polk's band lives along Montezuma Creek and Yellow Jacket. I do not think it possible for these two bands to live in harmony and it is for this reason that I would recommend individual allotments for all of these Indians instead of placing them upon a reservation un-allotted.

In Posey's band there are probably one hundred members including Utes, Piutes and a few Navajos, Polk's band numbers approximately eighty-five. In my former letter, I recommended the establishment of a Day School for these Indians. I believe that this would be a strong factor in their civilization. The Day School could be made the headquarters of the band and they would have a government employee to look after them and to assist them. Their allotments should be fenced and they should be required to live within their boundaries In this manner the Indian would be assured

ABOVE: Inside the Grayson Co-op: Ray Lyman (left), Morley Black, B. Frank Redd, Parley Redd, and Dora Bayles; written on the blackboard behind Dora: "Yes we have fresh meat, signed Oscar." Most of this crew was around during the last Indian war.

of his title to some land and the white man, realizing that the Indian had an allotment, would respect his rights and I believe, in most instances would assist him along lines of self-support.

The difficult matter in allotting these Indians would be to find land that will support them and their stock. There is very little water throughout the section in which they have been living, but I believe the water can be developed in sufficient quantities to supply their needs at least for several years to come.

I enclose herewith a sketch of the country occupied by Polk and Posey bands of Indians. I have sketched the outline of the body of land known as the Piute Indian Reservation but have been unable to learn the exact status of this land. I believe, however, that it would be as difficult to place these Indians on the land known as the Piute Reservation as it would be to put them at Ute Mountain. They have lived in their canyons so many years that they insist that these lands are their homes and I believe that their long occupancy has given them certain titles to these lands.

Looking east at Grayson Co-op, where Governor Mabey gets ready to meet the Indians at Natural Bridges, 1921.

I would recommend that an allotting agent be sent here at the earliest possible moment and that together with the Indians we decide upon the best location for them and that lands be given to them immediately.

I would call your attention to the fact that these sixty Indians are being held and supported by the people of Blanding who are expecting an early action on the part of the government. If it is consistent with the policy of the Office and funds are available, I would suggest $500.00 be immediately held for the present support of these Indians and relieve the citizens of Blanding of this burden.

I am ready and willing to undertake any work with these Indians that the Office may direct. I would respectfully request an early reply regarding any action contemplated by the Office in order that I may advise the Citizens of Blanding.

The large item in the minds of all the people of the Blanding section is the future disposition of the Indians.

They do not wish them banished from the country but they do insist that they should be confined to a certain area of land and have some government supervision and assistance. I believe that a working policy can be drafted for these Indians, that sheep and goats can be purchased for them under reimbursable regulations and that they can be prevailed upon to send their children to school and to accept many habits of civilization.

Very respectfully,

    E. E. McKean

    SUPERINTENDENT

The last Indian war took place in 1923 in San Juan County, Utah. Events leading to that final incident were disagreements between the Mormon settlers and the Paiute Indians. They didn't want to go to a reservation, so a small band of renegade Indians led by William Posey made life miserable for the settlers by plundering and killing. There was a final battle and William Posey was killed. The above photo is of the old Grayson Elementary School, where the battle started; below, the lonely bullpen where the Indians were kept stands empty. Photos of Posey's belt courtesy of Lee Lewellen.

In 1923, the last Indian uprising in San Juan, the Pahutes were rounded up and put in this stockade, until they

SALT LAKE CITY, WEDNESDAY MORNING, MARCH 28, 1923.   24 PAGES—FIVE CENTS

Indians Fire From Cliff on Posse in Camp at Adams Ranch Spring in Comb Wash

Scenes at Blanding during Indian controversy. No. 1 (Left to right)—United States Marshal J. Ray Ward, Old Posey's brother and Mancos Jim, the 108-year-old Piute, holding conference outside the guardhouse. No. 2—Street scene in Blanding. No. 3—Building the stockade in which the Indian prisoners will be retained. Many of the workmen are Navajo Indians, willingly aiding in the construction work. No. 4—Armed citizens guarding Indian prisoners in basement of schoolhouse.

SON ATTEMPTS TO SIGNAL OLD POSEY BY FIRE

Fleeing Redskin Believed to Have Gathered Recruits; Source Is Puzzle

Marshal Ward Shows Unusual Coolness While Bullets Are Flying

Living conditions in the stockade were marginal at best.

L EFT:
Location of
the original
stockade,
2004 photo.

Old Duchie (I believe) and four of his children. He tried to keep them combed-cleaner and better dressed than the usual, Ute child.

Lynn says Scottie

Anson Cantsee

Old Charlie
Ute on right.
Building is Bank

Old Dutchie
on left - Lyman
Lyman

DEPARTMENT OF JUSTICE
OFFICE OF
UNITED STATES MARSHAL
DISTRICT OF UTAH
SALT LAKE CITY

The Attorney General, May 1, 1923
Washington, D.C.

Dear Sir:-

The following is a report of the Indian trouble in San Juan County, Utah, from March 21st, 1923, to April 26th, 1923.

On March 21, 1923, word was received at this office that an Indian uprising was taking place at Blanding, Utah, and that a band of Indians under the leadership of Wm. Posey had defied the authority of the United States and State and after some fighting with authorities at Blanding had taken to the hills on the west. At the same time another report was received to the effect that the Piute tribe, located in Montezuma Canyon about thirty miles east of Blanding were very much excited and prepared to go on the war path, joining the Indians already out.

Feeling that the situation demanded quick action on the part of this office, I went as quick as possible to Blanding, Utah. On arriving, March 22nd, warrants were placed in my hand for Wm. Posey and seven other Indians, charged with insurrection against the United States Government.

My first act was to prevent the Piute Indians in Montezuma Canyon from securing their guns, most of which had been left in the hands of the trader who was holding them for security for goods purchased. I also instructed the trader to sell no ammunition to Indians. Finding that the Indians for whom I had warrants had gone to the hills with others, prepared to resist arrest, I organized a posse of twelve Deputy Marshals and went after them, taking with me three Indians to assist in locating the outlaws. At this time I found it necessary to round up and detain all Indians of Posey's tribe to keep them from giving information or assistance to the outlaws. This made it necessary to feed and guard them as well as to care for their live stock, consisting of horses and sheep.

For several days more Indians were captured, and confined with the others, at total of eighty-one. The posse worked from March 22nd until April 3rd., during which time it was necessary to use riding horses and pack animals, as the pursuit took to seventy-five miles west of Blanding, and all supplies were necessarily transported on pack animals, I found that it was impractical to pay the deputy Marshals per diem, as authorized, and expect them to provide their own subsistence, therefore, in lieu of per diem, I purchased all supplies used which was a considerable saving to the Government.

We succeeded in capturing all Indians for whom I held warrants, except Wm. Posey.

On April 3rd, I returned to Blanding and left three special Deputy Marshals on duty. I returned to Salt Lake to take care of the quarterly reports and accounts, it being the first of the quarter.

On April 19th, I returned to Blanding to again attempt to serve the warrant I had held for Wm. Posey. After considerable offers [in] a conference with the Indians there, three of them agreed to take me to Posey in the hills. I left with them and secured the body of Wm. Posey, finding him dead. With the assistance of the Indians he was buried, it being impractical to transport the body through the mountains.

While on the trail of the Indians I used the services of Jesse Posey, Indian Mike and Charlie Ute as trailers and also to persuade the Indians to surrender. For these services I paid them $5.00 per day, taking their receipt therefore, properly acknowledged before a Notary Public.

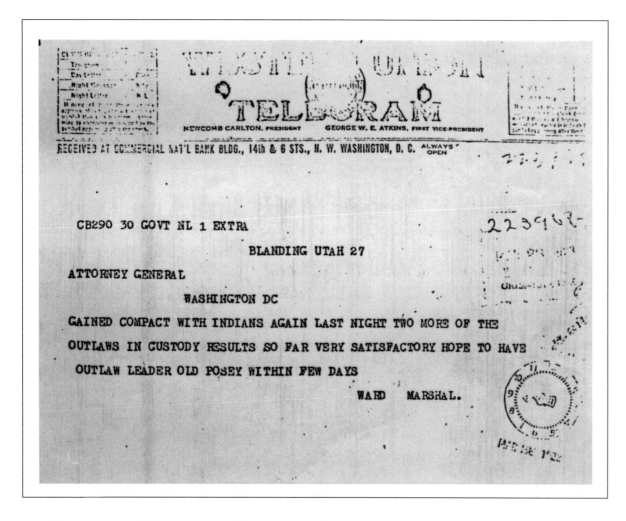

There was expended for subsistence in lieu of per diem for Deputy Marshals, the sum of $250.54.

There was expended for food for the Indians detained and their horses and sheep the sum of $255.60.

I ask for authorization of the above mentioned expense, it being a very unusual case and necessary in the interest of the government.

It was also necessary to deputize as Special Deputy Marshal the men who brought the supplies on pack animals and cared for the same, this making a total number of Special Deputy Marshals, more than authorized in your wire of April 23rd. These men were only used part time. Authorization for this expense is also requested.

I feel that the results obtained by the quick and decisive use of the posse of Special Deputy Marshals has forever ended the Indian troubles in that section of the State.

All Indians for whom warrants were issued were apprehended with the exception of the one found dead.

Respectfully yours,

J. Ray Ward
United States Marshal,
District of Utah

Being livestock men themselves, the captors released one or two members from each family to go out and take care of the sheep and horses from time to time. These Indians always returned, since there was food at the stockade and not in the camps.

THURSDAY MORNING, APRIL 5, 1923.

Old Posey Will Be Captured if It Takes Year, U.S. Marshal J. Ray Ward Says

Left to right—Posey's Big Boy, Frank J. Adams, rancher; Sam Rentz, white medicine man of the Navajos; Mike, one of the Indians who found Posey for General Scott; Charley Ute, charged with insurrection, and Marshal J. Ray Ward.

17
THE SEARCH FOR POSEY

Every night for about a month, there was a tiny flicker of light in the depths of the canyons. It was discussed, and most people thought it was William Posey, but there was no investigation; there was no knowing how many warriors he had with him out there, waiting in ambush.

Jess Posey was released and took food and blankets, which were never returned. It was thought he was taking them to Posey, and although the Indians were still not talking, it was thought that his father was wounded. Jess returned and asked that Ward be sent for; he wouldn't talk to McKean or any of his friends among the Mormons.

When Marshal Ward showed up on April 27, he was driving a big Packard car. He proposed to go to Bluff, down the river, and back up Comb Wash in the car and have Jess Posey meet him with horses after a shortcut out from Grayson. There was some doubt that a big car in the sand and rocks of Comb Wash could make it, but it just might be possible if he would get Lynn Lyman to drive it. Lynn was just a kid of about sixteen, but he was a mechanical

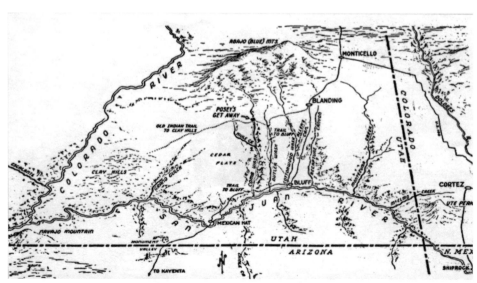

Posse members rounded
up the Indians and
marched them back to
the stockade in Grayson.

ABOVE:
Lynn Lyman took
the posse (left) on this
road to try to locate
William Posey.

BELOW:
Lynn Lyman and his
wife, Hazel, a few years
after the "Posey War."

genius. Ward was favorably inclined toward him because of his youth, telling someone that Lynn was just a kid and would not be able to find where he was going.

When the car came to where the horsemen were waiting, Ward got on a horse, leaving Lynn with the car. He was gone three or four hours, and came back and got in the car, sending the horses with Jess Posey, and retraced the morning's tracks back to Grayson. He called the leaders together and assured them that William Posey was dead; they didn't have to worry about him any more. "He is buried where no white man will ever find him. I don't want to answer any questions, because I am not going to tell you anything about it. But I assure you that he is dead and everything is taken care of. Things are under control." He jumped into the Packard and headed for Salt Lake City.

MARSHAL GIVES UP CHASE FOR POSEY

Officers Return to Salt Lake; Navajos and Scouts Still on Trail of Renegade.

United States Marshal J Ray Ward has abandoned his personal chase of Old Posey, although he states that his office will keep up its hunt for the renegade Piute until he is captured The marshal, accompanied by Deputy Marshal Ross and C A Sloan, reporter for the Salt Lake Tribune, passed through Moab yesterday on their return to Salt Lake from their spectacular trip into the wilderness south of Blanding, where they unsuccessfully stalked the redskin in his native haunts.

It is understood that the marshal has enlisted the aid of Navajos in running down Old Posey. The state and county have each offered a $100 reward for the capture of the Piute, and this money is said to look mighty attractive to the Navajos The marshal still has a number of local deputies in the field, among them Sam Rentz, who is familiar with the Indians and speaks Ute and Navajo fluently. It is probable that Old Posey may return from hiding after a few weeks, when he thinks the excitement has died down, and his capture then will be comparatively easy, it is believed.

Probably the most ridiculous of the many ridiculous press reports that have been published in the daily papers was one appearing under a Blanding date line Tuesday, giving the startling information that Old Posey had doubtless perished in a cloudburst the day before. It appears that the section in which the marshal and posse were located was visited by a heavy rain, with resultant floods in the canyons. The inspired "staff correspondent" immediately rushed through a column of "war stuff," giving the doleful particulars of Posey's probable demise in the flood To assume that a Piute Indian could be so foolish as to get himself drowned in a country every inch of which he knows by heart, is rather far fetched, to say the least

Just what to do with the captured Indians who are being held in an electrically-charged barb wire stockade at Blanding, is a problem that is troubling the Indian officials The seven or eight Indians who took part in the fight with the whites at the beginning of the trouble, will likely be prosecuted in the courts, but whether under a federal or a state charge has not been decided Marshal Ward will take the matter up with the state attorney general and the federal district attorney at Salt Lake City, and a decision will probably be reached The Indian agent from Ignacio, Colo., is opposed to taking the remaining Blanding Indians to the southern Ute reservation, for the reason that the Piutes and Utes are not friendly and it is not believed would live together in peace. In the meantime the Piutes, some seventy or eighty, including women and children, are being held in the stockand at Blanding, awaiting disposition of their fate. For a while the government defrayed the cost of their keep, but the Indian office is no longer doing this and the cost of feeding the Indians has devolved upon the people of Blanding. This situation cannot continue long, as the expense is too heavy for the community to meet for any length of time

Men who would have to be on the range soon to care for their stock were not satisfied with this explanation. They were concerned about going there without knowing for sure that Posey was out of the picture. They said, "How do we know he buried Posey? He didn't know Posey; he could have buried anybody."

Several of the younger men gathered up Lynn Lyman for a guide and went to find out the truth of the matter. Joe Smith, Marion Hunt, Bill Washburn, and a couple more rode out to where the Marshal and Jess Posey had mounted up. The tracks led up onto the Island and down into the saddle and up that side hill. It wasn't far up that side hill to where Posey was buried. It was rocky, and the ground was hard and dry; they tried several places with no result. Finally they looked over to where Marshal Ward had had a fire, and not seeing any reason why he would need a fire, they scraped the ashes away; the grave lay beneath.

For some reason they had neglected to bring a shovel. After investigating under the ashes, they started digging with their hands. When they got down about a foot deep or a little more, a fellow took off his Levi jacket and got down in the hole to put the dirt in it and hand it up to somebody to empty. He dug more and got rid of it the same way. It had gotten dark by then, and they were working by the light of a fire they had started.

One of the fellows went around the big rock and found that there was a deep crack in the rock on the lower side into which they could throw the dirt and get rid of it faster. They dug up Posey, unrolled the new government blanket that covered him, verified that it was Posey, and ascertained that he had died from a wound through both buttocks, which had infected from lack of care and killed him. They rolled him back up again and buried him, using what dirt they had left.

Walking back down the hill to their horses, they mounted and rode back into Comb Wash, where they spent the rest of the night at the Perkins ranch. With time to think things over, they got worried about digging up a man's grave, one that had been buried by a U.S. Marshal even, and no telling what would happen

FOREST RANGER FIRST TO FIND POSEY'S BODY

Forest Ranger Marion Hunt of Bluff, and not United States Marshal J Ray Ward, was the first white man to see Old Posey's body after the Piute chieftan had died from wounds received in the recent battle with the whites at Blanding.

In making one of his regular reports to the forest office at Moab, Ranger Hunt has this to say about finding the body of Posey:

"While on a trip to the head of Comb wash on range examination, I accidentally found the dead body of General Posey Uta. He had a large bullet hole through his left hip and a large bruise over his right eye, and had apparently been dead for several days."

The body was not concealed in an inaccessible cave, as first reports had it, but was lying in a clump of junipers in the open, according to Ranger Hunt.

to them as body snatchers or worse. They agreed among themselves that when they got to town they wouldn't tell anyone they had found Posey. If anybody asked them, they would say no, they didn't find anything.

This worked with most people, but Leland H. Redd was stake president, and a very shrewd and forceful man. He took one of the young men involved off to one side and talked to him straight and firm as he often did to young culprits. Shaking his finger in front of this lad's face, he said: "Young Man! You're lying to me. You're lying to me. I want you to tell me the truth!" This worked and the story was soon on the street.

In a day or two, after getting directions from the first group, Ancel Redd, Morley Black, Omni Porter, and Leland Redd found the graves of Posey and Sanup's Boy, dug up the bodies, and took pictures.

RIGHT:
Lemuel H. Redd.

FAR RIGHT:
Leland Redd Jr.,
with the body of
William Posey.

Photo by Brooks, Utah Arch. Exped.
LEMUEL H. REDD, PRESIDENT OF
SAN JUAN STAKE
President Redd for many years has been
a prominent figure in San Juan affairs.

Agent McKean went out with a group and took pictures for the government. Today, either everyone has forgotten which one of the big rocks on the side hill is the right one, or Posey no longer lies on that side hill. After a great deal of illicit digging, the body wasn't found. It was rumored that in the early 1960s, his skull was dug up and is in the Midwest on a mantelpiece.

A letter from E. E. McKean to J. Ray Ward, dated May 9, 1923, states the following:

The local Justice of the Peace as well as all the citizens of Blanding, were not satisfied with the reported death and burial of Posey. The Justice, therefore, appointed a jury to hold an autopsy on the case. This was done and I arrived at the grave in company with Mr. Siminton, allotting agent, Bishop Redd and his brother before Posey was reburied. I am now in a position to report officially the death of Posey. A copy of this letter to the Commissioner today will act as such report.

In those days, the little spring back in a shallow cave where Posey got his water, and the camp on the hill where he painfully dragged up wood to make a signal fire every night, which was never answered, told the plain story. He prodded and padded the ground with a stick around in a circle through the endless cold days and freezing nights while he packed his painful wound with pitch gum and hoped for rescue. Jess was too late with blankets and food to do any more than reduce the misery of his last hours. William Posey died an outcast.

(All photos of the search for Posey are from the H. E. Blake Collection; Mr. Blake was a former editor of the *San Juan Record*.)

Morley Black (left),
Leland Redd, Jr.,
Omni Porter, and
Ancel Redd, with the
body of William Posey.

18

THE PAIUTES' TREATY

The final treaty turned out to have three participants: the Indians, the white settlers, and the Indian Service. With William Posey accounted for and the rest of the Indians considerably subdued by their incarceration, there was no point in continuing the stockade. About the first of May (none of the reports gave an exact date), the Indians were called to the gate of the stockade. McKean was there to enroll them and to represent the government, and the Mormons laid down the rules for future conduct of their red neighbors. From then on, they were to abide by the law; no more were they to enjoy "slow elk," or to raid gardens or orchards, or to intimidate lone women on isolated ranches, or to catch the cowboys in small groups and whip them with quirts, ropes, or guns. They could settle down on their allotments, or where they had lived before, and use the range as other permittees did, abiding by the same rules and regulations.

The Indians agreed to this. Joe Bishop said, "You come to arrest me, I hold up my hands." And he held up his arms, wrists together for handcuffs. However, he had more to say about the state of affairs. "Blupp City Mormons fight little bit yesterday, little bit today, go home, give Indians biscuits, friends. Mexican Mormons fight like hell. Dave Black fight like somabitch, fight yesterday, today, tomorrow—heap plenty fight!"

For the Indian Service, Agent McKean enrolled all of William Posey's and Mancos Jim's band, and he promised that they would be more liberally allotted rations as well as other services to which the Southern Utes were entitled. He said it would take a little time, and it did, but a couple of years later the allotments in severalty had been assigned in Allen Canyon (which included Cottonwood Canyon) and on White Mesa. Edwin Z. Black was hired to oversee the Indians of that area, to help them with their livestock, to plant gardens and crops, as well as to distribute food and clothing to them.

The Aftermath

ABOVE:
Anson "Scottie" Cantsee.

RIGHT:
Charlie Ketchum (left) and
Anson Cantsee on the front
porch of Parley Redd Merc.

ABOVE:
Mancos George in front of Grayson Elementary, and in a field in Allen Canyon; these photos were taken in the late 1930s.

FACING, ABOVE:
Sanup in Grayson, Utah, at Washburn's house (3rd West 1st South).

FACING, BELOW:
Jack Fly wearing Posey's beaded gloves, photo by Charles Alma Jones, Grayson, Utah, 1938; courtesy of Lee Lewellen.

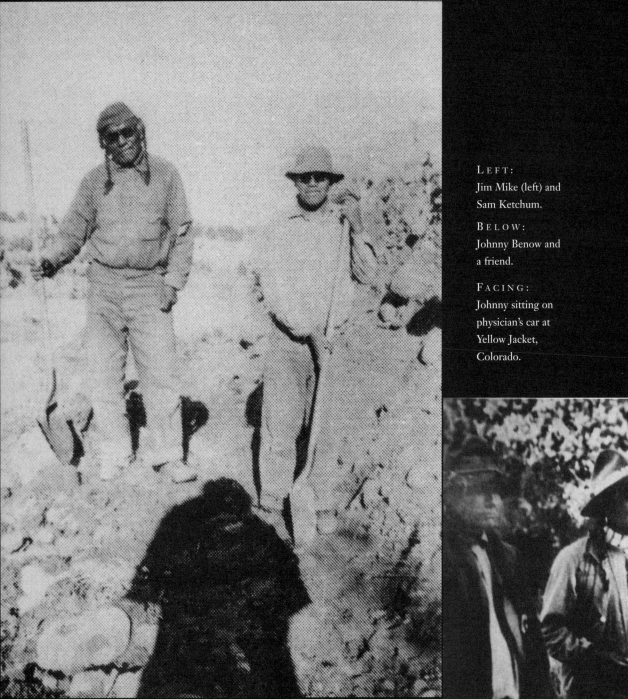

LEFT:
Jim Mike (left) and
Sam Ketchum.

BELOW:
Johnny Benow and
a friend.

FACING:
Johnny sitting on
physician's car at
Yellow Jacket,
Colorado.

In an interview conducted with Mrs. Zelma Black Acton in 1980 by Gregory Thompson and Floyd O'Neil for the University of Utah American West Center, she recalled some of her life as a child while her father was overseer for the Indians. The family lived in the summer in Allen Canyon, where they raised a huge garden that was shared with the Indians, who worked in it to learn how to grow gardens. Supplies were brought in at first by freight outfits, but later by truck, and ration day was a big event. The squaws would gamble their soap, coffee, bacon, flour, canned peaches, and tomatoes away, and some of them would return home empty-handed. Her father forbade gambling with rations, but the squaws loved to gamble, and they used baskets, beadwork, and other personal property as stakes.

Sometimes bolts of cloth were sent instead of clothing, and Mrs. Black helped the squaws make these into garments for their families, using her treadle sewing machine. She also tended their sick and helped them whenever she could.

The Blacks set up a boardinghouse in Grayson for schoolchildren who could attend public school. The Indian children have always attended school in Grayson, staying at home if the camp was close enough to reach by school bus.

The agency at Pacific Springs was expanded to handle this added load, and was moved to Towaoc, Colorado, which means "good place to live." Edwin Z. Black was also moved there to help the Indians with their livestock and permits; he lived there many years.

In another interview in 1981, Clarence Rogers stated the following:

"This Indian fight of 1923, the last real Indian War in the United States, was one of the best things that ever happened to these Indians. Before, they were a smart-aleck group, several of them liked to show off and be smart, but after 1923, they were completely conquered, and without William Posey to keep them stirred up, they really settled down. They have been cooperative, have worked well ever since and sent their children to school. Of course, some of them have done a little petty larceny and things like that along, but nothing to amount to anything.

"I think the two things that settled the dispute with them was that we conquered them thoroughly and then tried to treat them fairly afterward. None of us wanted to kill any of them, least of all Posey, but it had to be done.

"Old Posey's son Jess was one of the finest men I have ever known. He was the one that found his father and tried to take care of him. Then he went back with Marshal Ward and buried him. He wasn't a troublemaker and he had a little herd of horses and some sheep and goats, the best sheep and horses among the Utes, unless it was Jim Clark, who had fine animals, too. Jess was never mad at people for this Indian War, just took it in his stride and later on we became good friends. I bought sheep from him for many years.

"Jess had two wives, they were sisters, daughters of Mancos Jim, and were very hard workers, good workers. They made the finest buckskin of anybody in the tribe. Their work was just a little bit better—their buckskin was just softer, and the baskets they made to sell at the store were a little better than most. They lived in Allen Canyon."

Mary Posey, Ned Posey (Mary's son), and Anson Posey had allotments in Allen Canyon, but Jess did not. Nobody can remember Anson, and it is believed that he went back to Weeminuche Reservation and lived; Jess probably lived on his allotment.

Posey, the play

D r. Steve Lacy wrote the play *Posey* and produced it in 1981, from which the following photographs were taken.

ABOVE:

Cast rehearses in front of the Grayson Co-op.

BELOW:

Mormonees share an evening with their Indian friends.

ABOVE:
Terry Perkins portrays Posey.

RIGHT:
Trevor McCloud Curb shows his courage as Hard Tarter.

Posey, the play

LEFT:
Eric J. Osborn
(kneeling), Terry
Perkins, and Jeri
Kaye; Posey acciden-
tally kills Toorah.

BELOW:
Posey burns
Toorah's body as
Albert R. Lyman
looks on.

LEFT: Bob Greenwell (left), Meyers Cantsee, Chester Cantsee, and interpreter Marie Ketchem.

BELOW LEFT: Alan Black (left) shows Posey's pistol to cameraman Bob Greenwell.

BELOW RIGHT: Bob Greenwell (left), Meyers Cantsee, and Chester Cantsee.

FACING: Lynn Lyman (left), cameraman Bob Greenwell, reporter Richard Bingham, and Clarence Rogers are part of the filming process overlooking the Island.

Posey Wars, the film

A reenacted special presentation by Dr. Steve Lacy and KSL TV titled *Posey Wars* aired on Prime Time Access in 1985. The following images were photographed in and around Blanding (Grayson), Utah.

Posey Wars, the film

ABOVE: At one location of Posey's Trail, Stan Bronson sings his song "Posey."

BELOW: Lynn Lyman (left) and Clarence Rogers search for Posey's grave.

In 1983, Pearl Baker commented to Lynn Lyman that this was a unique way to settle Indian disagreements: the Indians were not gathered up and moved to a strange or often hostile place, but were allowed to stay where they had lived for generations. The invading whites had also established an acceptable way of life; it appeared that for some reason the two cultures lived together and retained their own ways, but there was little friction. Mr. Lyman agreed,

That's right, and I can tell you the reason. The Bluff Mission was called to settle San Juan County, and to civilize the Indians. It took a lot of sacrifice and hanging on to make this country a fine place to live—and it is that. As for the Indians: they are gradually learning a better way to live; they send their children to public school, and often send them to college.

It has taken over one hundred and twenty years, but the Mormonees never lost sight of their calling and their goals no matter what William Posey did, the descendants of the Hole-in the-Rock migration can proudly say that the Bluff Mission was a success.

BIBLIOGRAPHY

A

Aberle, David Friend, and Orner C. Steward. *Navajo and Ute Payotism: A Chronological and Distributional Study.* Boulder: University of Colorado Press, 1957.

"The American General Who Hypnotizes Piutes, Moro and Mexican Bandits into Good Behavior." *Current Opinion* (May 1915): 322–24.

Anderson, Joseph F. "Pioneers and Pioneering in Southeastern Utah." *Improvement Era* 18 (1915): 710–16, 870–74.

Hans Aspass Papers. Western Historical Collection, Norlin Library, University of Colorado in Boulder.

B

Baldwin, Gordon C. "The Pottery of the Southern Paiute." *American Antiquity* 16 (July 1930): 50–56

———. "Basket Making Among the Utes." *Indians at Work* 3 (April 15, 1936): 42.

Beck, D. Eldon. "Mormon Trails to Bluff" (series). *The Utah* 4, 5 (1940–41).

Billings. Alfred N. "Journal of the Travels of the Elk Mountain Missionaries to the Elk Mountains" (A47). Salt Lake City: Utah State Historical Society, May 21, 1855–October 31, 1955.

Bryner, Ellen (Redd). *Settlement and Growth of San Juan County.* N.p., n.d.

C

Cannon, John Q. "When the Utes Invaded Utah." *Improvement Era* 32 (1928): 41–46.

Casillas, Rex. "Annotated Bibliography of San Juan County, Utah" (A2429). Salt Lake City: Utah State Historical Society, 1977.

Christensen, C. L. "San Juan County, Utah: How an Indian War was Averted." *Improvement Era* 31 (1927–28): 776.

Conetah, Fred A. *History of the Northern Ute People.* Salt Lake City: University of Utah, 1982.

Conrotto, Eugene L. "America's Last Indian War." *Desert Magazine* 24 (1961).

Correll, J. Lee. "Navajo Frontiers in Utah and Troublous Times in Monument Valley." *Utah Historical Quarterly* 39 (spring 1971): 145–61.

Covey, Claude C. Letter to Commissioner of Indian Affairs, November 24, 1914.

Crampton, C. Gregory. *Standing Up Country.* Salt Lake City: University of Utah: Alfred K. Knopf, 1965.

Creer, Leland Hargrave. "Spanish American Slave Trade in the Great Basin, 1800–1853." *New Mexico Historical Review* 24 (July 1949): 171–83.

Cummins, D. H. "Society and Economic History of Southwestern Colorado, 1860–1948." PhD dissertation, University of Texas, 1952.

D

Daniels, Helen Sloan, comp. *The Ute Indians of Southwest Colorado.* Durango, Colorado: Durango Public Library Museum Project, 1941.

Dean, James Clawson. *San Juan Pioneers and Hole-in-the-Rock.* Salt Lake City: LDS Institute of Religion, 1954.

Deets, Emerson. "Paradox Valley—An Historical Interpretation of Its Structure and Changes." *Colorado Magazine* 11 (1934): 186–98.

Delaney, Robert W. *The Southern Ute People.* Phoenix: Indian Tribal Series, c. 1974.

Denver Post, Denver, Colorado, 1914–15, 1921–1923.

Denver Republican, Files, Denver, Colorado, 1894.

Denver Times, Files, Denver, Colorado, 1915.

Deseret Evening News, Salt Lake City, 1915, 1921, 1923.

"Diary of Platte Lyman." Special Collections, Brigham Young University, Provo, Utah.

Dolores Star, Dolores, Colorado, 1915, 1923.

Doris Duke Oral History Collection. Special Collections, Marriott Library, University of Utah, Salt Lake City, Utah.

Durango Herald, Durango, Colorado, 1915, 1923.

Dutton, Berthia Pauline. *The Rancheria: Ute and Southern Paiute Peoples.* Englewood Cliffs, New Jersey: Prentice Hall, 1976.

E

Emmitt, Robert. *The Last War Trail: The Utes and the Settlement of Colorado.* Norman: University of Oklahoma Press, 1954.

Euler, Robert C. "Southern Paiute Ethnohistory." *Anthropoligical Papers* 78. Salt Lake City: University of Utah, 1966.

F

Fay, George Emory. *Land Cession in Utah and Colorado.* Greeley: University of Northern Colorado Museum of Anthropology, 1970.

Fort Lewis College. Durango, Colorado. Center of Southwest Studies Microfilm Collection, Fort Lewis. Records, National Archives, OH. Military Records, Fort Lewis Collection, New York Times Oral History Project, Southeastern Utah Oral History Project, 1972.

G

Gillmor, Frances, and Luisa Wade Wetherill. *Traders to the Navajos: The Story of the Wetherills of Kayenta*, 2nd ed. Albuquerque: University of New Mexico Press, 1953.

Gregory, Herbert E. "Scientific Explorations in Southern Utah." *American Journal of Science* 243 (October 1945): 527.

Gottfredson, Peter. *History of Indian Depredations in Utah.* Salt Lake City: Skelton Publishing Company, 1919.

Grand Valley Times, Moab, Utah, Feb–July 1915, Feb–May 1923.

H

Hafen, Leroy R., and Ann W. Hafen. *Colorado: A History of Progress.* Denver: The Old West Publishing Company, 1919.

Hall, Frank. *History of the State of Colorado.* Chicago: The Blakely Printing Company, 1890.

Handbook of American Indians North of Mexico. Bureau of American Ethnology, Bulletin #30. Washington, D.C.: GPO, 1910.

Harrington, John P. "Origin of the Names for the Utes and Paiutes." *American Anthropologist* 13 (1911): 173–74.

Heyman, Max L. *Prudent Soldier: A Biography of Major General E. R. S Canby, 1817–1873.* Glendale, California: The Arthur H. Clark Company, 1959.

House Resolution #6792. *Congressional Record* 36.

Hughes, Johnson Donald. *American Indians in Colorado.* Boulder, Colorado: Pruett Publishing Co., 1977.

Hurst, George A. "The Life of George Arthur Hurst" (A1804). Salt Lake City: Utah State Historical Society, n.d.

Hurst, Michael Terry. "Bluff City, An Historical Sketch." San Juan High School Library.

———. "Posey." Unpublished manuscript, 1972.

———. "The Last Indian Uprising," *The Sundance News,* March 1973.

I

Indian Rights Association. *The Case of the Southern Utes* (pamphlet). Reprinted from *Harper's Weekly,* April 2. Philadelphia: Indian Rights Association, 1892.

———. The . . . Annual Report of the Executive Committee . . . for the Year Ending December . . . Philadelphia: Office of the Indian Rights Association, 1884–.

———. *The Ute Indians: Why People in Colorado Want Them to be Removed* (pamphlet). Philadelphia: Indian Rights Association, 1890.

J

Jacknick, Sidney. *Early Days on the Western Slope of Colorado.* New Mexico: Rio Grande Press, n.d.

Jefferson, James, et al. *The Southern Utes, A Tribal History.* Ignacio, Colorado: Southern Ute Tribe, 1872.

Jensen, Bryant L. "An Historical Study of Bluff City, Utah, from 1878 to 1926." Master's thesis (history), Brigham Young University, 1966.

Jones, A. A. Letter to First Assistant Secretary to the Attorney General of the United States, 1915.

Jones, Kumen. "First Settlement of San Juan County." *Utah Historical Quarterly* 2 (1929): 8–11.

———. "The San Juan Mission to the Indians" (A24). Salt Lake City: Utah State Historical Society, n.d.

Jorgenson, Joseph G. *The Sun Dance Religion: Power for the Powerless.* Chicago and London: The University of Chicago Press, 1972.

Journal History of the Church, 1853–. Salt Lake City: Historical Department of The Church of Jesus Christ of Latter-day Saints.

Judd, Neil M. *Explorations in San Juan County, Utah.* Smithsonian Institution, Miscellaneous Collections. Washington, D.C.: GPO, n.d.

———. *Men Met Along the Trail.* Norman: University of Oklahoma Press, 1968.

K

Kane, Francis Fisher, and Frank M. Riter. *A Further Report to the Indian Rights Association on the Proposed Removal of the Southern Utes.* Philadelphia: Press of William F. Fell and Co., 1892.

Kelly, Charles. "Chief Hoskanini," *Utah Historical Quarterly* (July 1953).

———. "The Poke and Posey Wars." *Desert Magazine* 28 (1965): 18–19.

Kildare, Maurice. "Murder at Rincon." *Frontier Times* (May 1971): 26–.

Kinney, J. P. *A Continent Lost, A Civilization Won.* Octagon Books, 1975.

Kluckhorn, Clyde, and Dorothea Leighton. *Children of the People.* Cambridge: Harvard University Press, 1947.

Kneale, A. H. *Indian Agent.* Caldwell, Idaho: Printers Ltd., 1950.

L

Leup, Francis E. *The Latest Phase of the Southern Ute Question, A Report.* Philadelphia: Office of Indian Rights Association, 1895.

Literary Digest, March 6, 1915.

Lyman, Albert R. *The Edge of the Cedars: The Story of Walter C. Lyman and the San Juan Mission.* New York: Carlton Press, 1966.

———. "The Fort on the Firing Line" (serial). *Improvement Era* 41–53 (1948–1950).

———. *History of Blanding, 1905–1955.* Published privately, n.d.

———. "History of San Juan County, 1879–1917" (A42-3). Salt Lake City: Utah State Historical Society, 1969.

———. *Indians and Outlaws: Settling of the San Juan Frontier.* Salt Lake City: Bookcraft, 1962.

———. "The Outlaw of Navajo Mountain" (serial). *Improvement Era* 39–41 (1936–1938).

———. *The Outlaw of Navajo Mountain.* Salt Lake City: Deseret Book Co., 1963.

———. "Pahute Biscuits." *Utah Historical Quarterly* 3 (1930): 118–20.

———. "A Relic of Gadianton: Old Posey as I Knew Him." *Improvement Era* 26 (1922–23): 791–.

———. "The Settlement of Bluff, San Juan County." *Improvement Era* 59 (1949): 86–.

———. *Trail of the Ancients.* Trail of the Ancients Association: Blanding, Utah, 1972.

M

Mayfield, Clara. *The History of the Southern Ute Indian.* New York: Carlton Press, 1972.

McGue, D. B. "John Taylor, Slave Born Colorado Pioneer." *Colorado Magazine* 18 (1941): 161–68.

Mikkelsen, Robert S. "The Indian War Nobody Knows." *True West* (November–December 1960): 16–19.

Miller, David E. *Hole in the Rock.* University of Utah Press, 1959.

Montezuma Journal, Cortez, Colorado, 1915, 1923.

Montrose Press, Montrose Colorado, March 3, 1915.

N

Nankivel, Major John H. "Colorado's Last Indian War." *Colorado Magazine* 10 (1933): 222–34.

———. "On the Weed-Grown War Path." *Literary Digest* 50 (March 6, 1915): 461.

Nebeker, Aquila. Letter to Attorney General, December 7, 1914.

———. Night letter to Attorney General, March 1, 1915.

New York Times, New York, New York, 1915, 1923.

Nuwuvi: A Southern Paiute History. Reno, Nevada: Intertribal Council of Nevada, 1976.

O

O'Neil, Floyd A., and Kathryn L. MacKay. "A History of the Uintah Ouray Ute Lands." *Occasional Paper* 10. Salt Lake City: University of Utah American West Center, 1978.

Ogden Standard Examiner, Ogden, Utah, 1915, 1923.

Opler, Marvin K. "Southern Utes of Colorado." In *Acculturation in Seven American Indian Tribes.* Edited by Ralph Linton. New York: Harper and Son, n.d., 119–206.

Otes, D. *The Dawes Act and the Allotment of Indian Land.* Norman: University of Oklahoma, n.d.

P

Painter, C. C. *Protest of the Indian Rights Association Against the Proposed Removal of the Southern Ute Indians.* Philadelphia: Indian Rights Association, 1890.

———. *Removal of the Southern Utes.* Philadelphia: Indian Rights Association, 1890.

Palmer, John Franklin. "Mormon Settlement in the San Juan Basin of Colorado and New Mexico." Master's thesis (history), Brigham Young University, 1967.

Palmer, William R. "Indian Names in Utah Geography." *Utah Historical Quarterly* 1 (1938): 5–26.

———. "The Right Way to Deal with Indians." *The Outlook* (March 31, 1915): 747–48.

———. "Utah Indians, Past and Present." *Utah Historical Quarterly* 1 (1928): 35–52.

Parkhill, Forbes. *The Last of the Indian Wars.* New York: Collier Books, 1961.

Perkins, Cornelia Adams, et a1 (Daughters of Utah Pioneers). *Saga of San Juan.* Blanding, Utah: Mercury Publishing Co., 1954.

Peterson, Charles. *Look to the Mountains: Southeastern Utah and the LaSal National Forest.* Provo, Utah: Brigham Young University Press, 1975.

R

Redd, Amasa Jay, ed. *Lemule Hardison Redd, Jr., 1856–1923, Pioneer–Leader–Builder.* Privately published, 1967.

Redd, Laura. *The Utah Redds and their Progenitors.* Privately published, 1973.

Rockie, W. A. "Old Posey." *The Pacific Northwesterner* 6 (winter 1962): 30–32.

Rockwell, Wilson. *The Utes, A Forgotten People.* Denver: Sage Books, 1956.

Rogers, Fred B. *Soldiers of the Overland, Being Some Account of the Services of General Patrick Edward Conner and his Volunteers in the Old West.* San Francisco: Grabben Press, 1938.

Rogers, John D. "Piute Posey and the Last Indian Uprising" (A1552). Unpublished. Location: the original is in Salt Lake City with the Utah State Historical Society; a copy was donated by the Rogers family to Footprints From The Past Museum, Salt Lake City.

Ruffner, Lt. E. H. *Reconnaisance in the Ute Country.* House Executive Doc. 43/1 Serial 1610: 1–101. Washington, D.C.: A.P.O., 1873.

Russell, James. "Conditions and Customs of Present-Day Utes in Colorado." *Colorado Magazine* 6 (1929): 104–12.

S

Salt Lake Herald, Salt Lake City, Utah, 1915, 1921, 1923.

Salt Lake Telegram, Salt Lake City, Utah, 1915, 1921, 1923.

Salt Lake Tribune, Salt Lake City, Utah, 1915, 1921, 1921.

San Juan (County, Utah) Indian Seminaries, Schedules, and Comments Misc. . . . San Juan County, Utah, 1970. Historical Department of The Church of Jesus Christ of Latter-day Saints, Salt Lake City, Utah.

Scher, Zeke. "The Man Who Discovered Rainbow Bridge." *Empire Magazine* (December 9, 1973): 14.

Scott, General Hugh L. Papers, 1919–1933. Bureau of American Ethnology Anthropological Archives, Smithsonian Institution, Washington, D.C.

———. Papers, n.d. Library of Congress, Washington, D.C.

———. *Some Memories of a Soldier.* The Century Co., 1928.

Seymour, Flora Warren. *Indian Agents of the Old Frontier.* Appleton Century Co., 1941.

Shepardson, Mary. *The Navajo Mountain Community, Social Organization and Kinship Terminology.* Berkeley: University of California Press, 1970.

Silvey, Frank. "Early History and Settlement of San Juan County, Utah." Writers' Project Administration (Al006-3) (4 versions). Salt Lake City: Utah State Historical Society, 1937.

———. "Monticello, Utah, Pioneer Answers to Questionaire" (Al006-1) (several interviews). Writer's Project Administration. Salt Lake City: Utah State Historical Society, 1937.

———. "Written for Historical Records Survey of San Juan County, Utah" (several manuscripts). Writer's Project Administration. Salt Lake City: Utah State Historical Society, 1937.

———. "When San Juan County Was Given to the Southern Ute Indians." Unpublished manuscript, 1944.

Sniffen, M. K. *The Meaning of the Ute War.* Philadelphia: Indian Rights Association, 1915.

Snow, Apostle. Letter to President John Taylor, November 6, 1879.

Stacher, Samuel F. "Indians of the Ute Mountain Reservation, 1906–1909." *Colorado Magazine* 36 (1949): 52–61.

Steward, Julian Haynes. *Basin-Plateau Aboriginal Sociopolitical Groups.* Bulletin #120. Washington, D.C.: Bureau of Ethnology, 1938.

———. *Notes on Hillers' Photographs of the Paiute and Ute Indians Taken on the Powell Expedition of 1873.* Smithsonian Miscellaneous Collections 9, no. 18. Washington, D.C.: B. P. O., 1939.

Stewart, Orner C. "Culture Element Distributions: XVIII Ute Southern Paiutes." *Anthropological Records* 6. Berkeley and Los Angeles: University of California, 1942.

———. *Ethnohistorical Bibliography of the Ute Indians.* University of Colorado Series in Anthropology 18. Boulder: University of Colorado Press, 1971.

Sutton, Imre. *Indian Land Tenure.* Clearwater Publishing Co., 1975.

T

Tanner, Faun McConkie. *The Far Country.* Salt Lake City: Olympia Press, 1972.

Tedrow, Harry B. Letter to Attorney General, Washington, D.C., April 9, 1915.

Thompson, Gregory Coyne. *Southern Ute Lands, 1848–1899; The Creation of a Reservation.* Occasional Paper No. 1. Durango, Colorado: Fort Lewis College, Center of Southwest Studies, 1972.

Todd, Sam. Letter to Glen Hanks, March 2, 1925, from Kline, Colorado.

Todd, Sam, to Glen Hanks. "A Pioneer Experience," March 2, 1925, Utah State Historical Society.

Tyler, S. Lyman. "Before Escalante: An Early History of the Yuta Indians and the Area North of New Mexico." PhD dissertation (history), University of Utah, 1951.

———. *The Ute People: A Bibliographical Checklist.* Provo, Utah: Institute of American Indian Studies, Brigham Young University, 1964.

U

"U.S. Indian Affairs Office: Posey War." Salt Lake City: Utah State Historical Society (BB 1&2). (Photographic copies of National Archives and Denver Federal Records Center Ute and Consolidated Ute Documents, R.G. 75).

Utah: A Guide to the State (WPA American Guide Series). Salt Lake City: Hastings House, 1941.

Ute Indians I and II. New York and London: Garland Pub. Inc., 1974.

W

Walker, Dan B. "Cowboys, Indians and Cavalry: A Cattleman's Account of the Fights of 1884." *Utah Historical Quarterly* 34 (summer 1966): 255–62.

Warner, Ted J., ed. *The Dominguez-Escalante Journal.* Provo, Utah: Brigham Young University Press, 1977.

Warren, (first name not given). Letter to U.S. Attorney General, February 19, 1915.

Welsh, Herbert. Letter to the Public-at-Large. Philadelphia: Indian Rights Association, 1890.

Y

Young, Lloyd L. "The 1923 Indian Trouble in Blanding, San Juan County, Utah" (A2022). Salt Lake City: Utah State Historical Society, n.d.

INDEX

ACKNOWLEDGMENTS

My special thanks go to the following individuals and organizations:

Posey, the play by Dr. Steve Lacy

Eric J. Osborn, Peggy Rock, Amy Wakins, Jeri Kaye, Terry Perkins, Elroy Lehi, Susan Slade, Barbara Carlson, Julie Tate, Larry R. Lyman, Carlene Baker, Pete Jackson, Norman Billsie, Linda Lameman, Elouise Denny, James W. Lacy, Janet Begay, Colleen Treton, Jeff Atene, Jolin Hosler Redd, Burdette Shumway.

Posey Wars, the Prime Time Access Special by Dr. Steve Lacy and KSL TV

Richard Bingham (reporter), Bob Greenwell (cameraman).

Guests

Clarence Rogers, Stan Bronson, Lynn Lyman, Chester Cantsee, Meyers Cantsee, Alan Black.

Research

Faye Lynette Adams, Melinie Austin, Jim Beckstead, Anthony M. Best, Sherian Black, Effie Brockmier, Lynn Burton, Coy Clawson, Trevor McCloud Curb, Mike Cook, Jesse Michael Dornan, Bill Fossat, Dee Anne Gilgen, Viola Green, Jacob Hardy, Todd Scott Hinkins, Roy Hudson, Lea Hurst, Mike Hurst, Barbara Kuipers, Emma Kuykendall, Claude & Thelma Lacy, Mike B. Lacy, David A. Lacy, Michael Langston, J. Bracken Lee, Lee Lewellen, Albert R. Lyman, Larry R. Lyman, Lucie Lumis, Macen Mace, Edith McKendricks, Jessie Mae Redd McDonald, Robert S. McPherson, Lynette Montoya, John T. Orme, Diane Orr, Cindy Oster, Jarrod West Pickett, Velma Pilling, Vione Pilling, Bob Politz, Van Porter, Ron Prettyman, Bonnie Purcell, Jolin Hosler Redd, Gordon Redd, Vint Redd, Jasone Rose, Chad Smith, Quen Lyman Smith, Joe Smith, Eric Robinson, Helen Shumway, Laverne Tate, Sam Taylor, Fae Thomas, Dr. Greg C. Thompson, Dee & Cathrine Warner, Denise Warren, Janet Wilcox, Ruth Blake Wilcox, Tony Wojack, Cathy York.

Organizations

Footprints From The Past Museum (Utah's Greatest Little Museum), University of Nevada–Reno Special Collections Library, San Juan Historical Society, Utah State Historical Society, Dan O'Laurie Museum, *Moab Times Independent.*

Smith's Photo Lab

DeAnn Bullock, Judy Lang, Missy McArthur, Rachael Burnett, Rochelle Cauldwell, Scott Patterson and Color Graphics.

Gibbs Smith, Publisher

Gibbs Smith; Editorial—Suzanne Taylor, Madge Baird, Linda Nimori, Melissa Dymock, Sarah Rigley, Renee Wald; Production—Marty Lee; Marketing—Alison Einerson.

If you gain anything from this book,
I hope it is this:

"If you were born in America, you are a Native American."

Help stop racism.

ABOUT THE AUTHORS

Dr. Steve Lacy

A former high school drama teacher who has a doctorate in dramatic arts, Dr. Lacy is remembered best from his TV shows on KTVX, where he did 339 shows called *Centennial Photo*. He has been nominated for two Emmys for his productions *Old Fights, Good Times, The J. Bracken Lee Story*, which aired on KUTV, winning best documentary for 1989, and *The Governors of Utah*, which aired on KTVX in 1993. He has also done a number of specials for the old Prime Time Access show on KSL. Dr. Lacy is the author of nine books, including *The Lynching of Robert Marshall, Whatever Happened to Denise Sullivan*, and *Last of the Bandit Riders Revisited*. He resides in Salt Lake City, where he is curator of the Footprints From The Past Museum, Inc..

Pearl Baker

Pearl Baker, who died in 1992, wrote *The Wild Bunch at Robbers Roost, Recollections at Robber's Roost, Rim Flying Canyons with Jim Hurst*, and *Trail on the Water*. She was raised on a ranch that included the Robber's Roost area in southeastern Utah, moving in two years after she was born; she grew up in the cattle business and ran the Robber's Roost Ranch for many years. She was a well-known historian of southeastern Utah and taught a class on Instant English at Green River High School. She and Dr. Lacy have worked on this publication since 1978.